Retirement Income

Retirement Income

Risks and Strategies

Mark J. Warshawsky

The MIT Press
Cambridge, Massachusetts
London, England

MIT Press books may be purchased at special quantity discounts for business or sales promotional use. For information, please email special_sales@mitpress.mit.edu or write to Special Sales Department, The MIT Press, 55 Hayward Street, Cambridge, MA 02142.

This book was set in Palatino by Toppan Best-set Premedia Limited. Printed and bound in the United States of America.

Library of Congress Cataloging-in-Publication Data

Warshawsky, Mark.
Retirement income : risks and strategies / Mark J. Warshawsky.
    p.   cm.
Includes bibliographical references and index.
ISBN 978-0-262-01693-3 (hbk. : alk. paper) 1. Pensions—United States. 2. Retirement income—United States. 3. Portfolio management—United States. I. Title.
HD7105.45.U6W37   2012
331.25'20973—dc23

2011024368

10 9 8 7 6 5 4 3 2 1

Contents

Acknowledgments

I have worked on the subject of retirement distributions and annuities for most of my professional career. In this line of research, I have often had the honor and privilege of working with others. The coauthored work collected in this book represents no exception. Gaobo Pang and Tomeka Hill are my smart and talented colleagues at Towers Watson, where we are all fortunate to be together in a quiet and productive environment of the Corporate Research and Innovation center in Arlington, Virginia. The center, which is primarily concerned with practical applications and knowledge, encourages independent, deep, and rigorous inquiry using various methodologies. Jeffrey Brown of the University of Illinois, Brenda Spillman of the Urban Institute, Christopher Murtaugh of the Visiting Nurse Service of New York, and Jason Brown and David Brazell of the U.S. Treasury Department have been my research colleagues over the years; they are all highly capable and careful scholars with great integrity. Thanks to Susan Farris of Towers Watson, who assembled the final manuscript for the publisher expertly and quickly. My thanks also go to John Covell, editor at the MIT Press, and two anonymous reviewers, for their helpful comments and advice.

I dedicate this book to my parents, Arthur and Dorothy Warshawsky: may they live and be well for many more years. They have shown me the virtues of hard work, prudence, persistence, sensible risk taking, independence, and quiet dignity.

Despite all the help and assistance I have received, any errors that remain in this book are my responsibility. None of the views expressed here should necessarily be taken to represent the views of Towers Watson. Because of their exploratory and broad nature, the views expressed here should also not be considered tax or investment advice.

1   Introduction and Overview

The Current Context

Past cohorts of workers in the United States retiring in the 1980s and 1990s had many comprehensive benefits and insurance protections in place. In particular, nearly all had a Social Security retirement benefit that is fairly generous, especially to lower-income workers and single-earner couples, and that can begin as early as age 62. Many older workers had accrued some defined benefit (DB) pensions, especially if they worked in the government sector or for a large corporation; indeed, in the government sector or in some union plans, many workers could retire at ages ranging from 50 to 60 with full benefits. Many of these same people also had a retiree health plan whose premiums were being paid, in whole or in part, by a former employer, providing health insurance coverage for an early retirement and to supplement Medicare coverage after age 65. This is in addition to near-universal coverage by Medicare, the generosity of whose health insurance benefits for retirees was enhanced in 2006 by the inclusion of fairly comprehensive benefits for prescription drugs and generously subsidized Medicare Advantage plans. Lower-income and low-asset retirees could also qualify for Medicaid, which pays for Medicare premiums and copays and deductibles, as well as home health care and nursing home care if needed.

Most, at least in the middle- and upper-income groups, also came into retirement with accumulated financial assets held in tax-favored 401(k) and other individual defined contribution (DC) retirement accounts and other savings vehicles. These individual accounts held growing asset holdings that were the result of employer and worker contributions and sometimes large investment earnings. And significant holdings of rising home equity extended down into lower deciles of the income distribution.

Although there were undoubtedly gaps, this state of affairs probably represented the high point of retirement assets and a support structure and safety net for older workers approaching retirement in the United States. Now as the large baby boom generation is entering its retirement years, it is clear that they will not be as generously equipped and supported. Consider this generation's leading edge, born in 1946, which came to the modal retirement age, 62, in 2008. Already for many years, most workers in the private sector, even those employed by large corporations, have had their accruals under traditional DB plans stopped. Similarly most of these workers approaching retirement now will no longer have any paid-up retiree health coverage outside of Medicare. At the same time, health care costs increased rapidly during most of the first decade of the 2000s and continue to outpace general inflation and wage increases. This raises the burden of health insurance premiums, deductibles, and copays on both current workers and retirees, as well as limits the salary increases (and hence future retirement plan benefits and employer plan contributions) of current workers, as employers divert fixed compensation funds to pay for increasingly expensive health care benefits.

Current government workers approaching retirement have thus far been largely unaffected by these private sector trends. But the recent deep recession and stock market decline has severely affected state and local government finances and the funding of employee pension plans so that cuts to government employee pension and active and retiree health benefits are beginning to be made that will affect future cohorts of workers. More severe and widespread cuts and increased employee contributions are surely in store in this area.

Social Security and Medicare are still untouched, despite years of attempted reform efforts motivated by enormous long-range and now even short-range projected fiscal deficits for the programs. But the overall highly negative fiscal position of the federal government now and projected for near- and intermediate-term years is beginning to force the realization that these programs too must be put on a sustainable foundation, which will entail some combination of benefit cuts and tax increases. In fact, reform has been put off for so long and overall fiscal conditions are so bad that it is no longer certain that the natural political aversion to cutting benefits of current beneficiaries can continue to hold.

The recent deep recession was proceeded and accompanied by severe declines in stock market and housing values. Shrunken equity values significantly reduced 401(k) and IRA account balances, particularly for many older workers and retirees. Lower housing values, net of mortgages, directly reduced the net worth of retired households and those approaching retirement who may have been planning to scale down soon or to use their housing equity later to finance nursing home care should the need arise. Although, as of spring 2010, there has been some recovery from the lows of early 2009, the prerecession high levels of 2006 and 2007 still represent a faint memory for the stock market and, especially, real estate values.

The net impact of the recently passed health care reform legislation on retirement and retirees is unclear. There is a general redistribution from young to old and from rich to poor through subsidies for health insurance, expanded Medicaid eligibility, and more comprehensive Medicare prescription drug benefits, but there are also higher taxes and cuts in Medicare reimbursements to providers and subsidies to Medicare Advantage plans. So the net effect on household work and retirement decisions and financing is uncertain and various. Moreover, the long-term political, constitutional, and fiscal viability of the legislation is controversial, thereby clouding any definitive judgment of outcomes on the parts of workers close to retirement and retirees themselves and of forecasting analysts.

Some of the secular decline in retirement resources and freeing up of institutional structures can be made whole through longer working years. Increased participation in the labor force at older ages indeed makes good sense anyway, even with a comprehensive safety net, as life expectancies have lengthened significantly, extending the retirement period that must be financed. Continuing to work gives a salary, and usually health benefits and increased retirement plan benefits and accumulations, in addition to purposeful activity and social interaction. It also postpones the need to claim Social Security retirement benefits, thereby also increasing its inflation-indexed life annuity benefit through retirement delay credits and perhaps higher and more earnings credits. But not every older worker is able to stretch out his or her working career at will, either because of poor health or bad opportunity. For example, in 2008 and 2009, claims for Social Security retirement benefits increased significantly above earlier projections, with massive increases in unemployment and underemployment, even as labor force participation rates at older ages have been increasing steadily over the years. Even older workers planning on extended careers need to consider the possibility of suddenly crimped circumstances or the gradual loss of ability and interest.

This more sober environment will influence many late-middle-age people—those who recently retired, as well as older workers still in the labor force. No longer can they count on the elaborate structure of retirement security that supported and protected their parents and even older brothers and sisters. No longer can they automatically assume a generous cushion that allowed ample discretionary spending and bequests to children and other heirs, as well as the ability to take risks, say with investments and personal contingencies. Rather, many older workers and retirees will now have to take out their sharp pencils to maximize their retirement income and reduce their risk exposures. At the same time, some of the changes in the retirement security structure reflect more than a reduction in resources available; some also reflect different attitudes of a new generation that has consistently desired more flexibility, opportunity, and self-expression—in a word, control. These changes in attitude must be taken as given facts and constraints on our suggestions for new approaches to improving retirement income security for the cohorts now approaching retirement.

This book is about strategies, products, and public policies that will help retiring middle-class workers and retired middle-class households to maximize their incomes and reduce their risks. Although it employs a scholarly style, and indeed is a collection of recently published and updated work from various professional journals and conference volumes, as well as a new chapter and other new material, the topics considered here are not abstract theory or highly technical methodology. Rather, the book is applied economics; it is about practical and possible ideas, based on the results of empirical investigations and analyses, that ultimately can be used in household decision making and private product and public policy design. I have been the author or a coauthor of the collected work in this book, which has been written over the past several years. Hence the book represents a largely consistent, if evolving, viewpoint. At the same time, the several methodologies, approaches, and writing styles on display also clearly show off the varied considerable talents and deep understanding of the learned other coauthors. Finally, this book represents further developments and thinking on the specific subject of life annuities—a topic covered about a decade ago in another collection in which I was a coauthor.[1]

The remainder of this chapter summarizes briefly the balance of the chapters in this book. The second section gives a description of two insurance vehicles that can be used to hedge two of the major financial risks facing retired households: life annuities and long-term care insurance, for the extra costs arising from the realization of longevity and disability risks, respectively. This section also summarizes chapter 2 on recent trends in life annuity pricing and product design. The third section, summarizing chapter 3, reviews some of the research on the economic case for and against the use of life annuities during retirement; it also gives a more detailed contextual and institutional description of recent developments in employer-sponsored retirement plans as they affect the means available to assist retirees in the distribution phase of their plan participation.

The fourth section, summarizing chapter 4, considers survey evidence on older worker and retiree attitudes toward life annuities and lump-sum distributions, painting a more nuanced picture than the common wisdom that retiring workers always choose lump sums. The fifth section, covering chapters 5 through 7, moves to the next, more practical, and specific, stage: Given these facts about products and preferences, what should retirees do with their assets as they embark on a potentially long road ahead to protect against risks and create a comfortable retirement? Asset allocation and distribution strategies and new insurance product designs are considered in the context of uncertainty about asset returns and the personal contingencies of longevity and health care expenses. The modeling results give some good strategic directions for households and design of possible new products.

In the sixth section of this chapter, summarizing chapters 8 and 9, the innovation of the life care annuity is reviewed, that is, the potential product design and available tax characteristics of an integrated product of the immediate life annuity and long-term-care insurance. This product is intended to improve risk-hedging opportunities for households by lowering prices, increasing access, and addressing attitudinal blocks. The seventh section focuses again on life annuities, encapsulating chapter 10, which considers the public policy environment for retirement plans and distribution strategies, both current and possible future paths. The eighth section concludes the chapter and, in essence, the book, drawing practical lessons from all the data and analysis for the prudent and enlightened retired household and the legal and regulatory framework in which it lives now and into the future. An appendix is added at the end, explaining the meaning of some technical terms used throughout this book.

Relevant Insurance Vehicles

Two insurance vehicles or products are particularly important to understand in some detail as background to many of the chapters in this book: the life annuity and long-term care insurance.

A life annuity is an insurance vehicle that pays out a periodic (usually monthly) amount for as long as the insured is alive, in exchange for an accumulated amount from the insured, sometimes paid as a single premium. It may be available from an employer's retirement plan or from an insurance company. If the annuity is immediate, the delay between the premium paid by the insured and the first annuity payment by the plan or insurer is short—generally a month. If the annuity is deferred, the delay between premium and annuity payments is longer, often years; the date of the first annuity payout can be established as a set number of years in the future, or it may be discretionary at the choice of the insured. Generally, deferred annuities issued by insurance companies have a cash value; that is, if the insured dies before the beginning of the life annuity payout phase, then his or her beneficiaries get the cash value of the policy. Alternatively, the insured can cash out the policy before payments must begin (by tax law, before age ninety-five). By contrast, in some DB pension plans that pay only in life annuity form, if the participant dies and does not have a spouse, there is no further benefit.

Life annuities can differ on several dimensions. One relates to the number of lives insured. Single life annuities pay until the insured individual dies. Joint-and-survivor annuities pay until the last of the insured group (generally a married couple) dies, although when the first of the group dies, often the payment is reduced—say, to three-fourths or half of the initial level—for the remaining member. Another dimension relates to period-certain or refund guarantees that provide continued payments to a named beneficiary of the insured if the insured dies before a set period expires or a minimum amount of payments are made. For both joint-and-survivor and guaranteed payment forms of life annuities, the extra expected benefits are costly and therefore are reflected in an increased premium charged or reduced level of periodic payments made, compared to single and straight life annuities, respectively.

The type of payout can come in different forms. The most common for both pension plans and commercial insurance products is a fixed payout, constant in nominal terms for the lifetime of the insured. Graded annuities increase at a predetermined percentage rate. Inflation-indexed annuities have payments that rise with the rate of inflation, generally some type of consumer price index, sometimes capped at certain rates of increase from above and zero from below. Pension plans provided by governments to their employees generally give inflation-indexed annuities, but these are rare in private sector plans. Of course, for the same level of initial payouts, a graded or an inflation-indexed life annuity is more costly than a fixed life annuity.

Variable immediate annuities have payouts linked to an underlying investment portfolio of funds and will rise and fall with that portfolio's value. Generally the insured chooses the composition of the investments in a variable annuity, although in a few pension plans, that decision is made by the plan sponsor. Note that the variable immediate life annuity should not be confused with a deferred variable annuity policy commonly sold by insurers. The former is a vehicle or product whose payouts, while variable, cease with the death of the insured. By contrast, the latter is a tax-favored individual accumulation product with a cash value, invested in one or several mutual funds of the policyholder's choice from a menu offered. It may or may not eventually be converted to a payout annuity, at the policyholder's discretion, generally on nominal terms fixed in the contract or at market rates.

The older the insured is, the less expensive is the life annuity or the higher the payout, everything else being equal, because the expected period of benefit payments is shorter. Indeed, age is one major distinguishing characteristic that influences the cost of the life annuity, but, where allowed by law, the gender and, rarely, the health of the insured can also be reflected in the annuity price or promised payout because of the expected influence of these characteristics on mortality rates in consistent directions.

The primary appeal of a life annuity is that it offers the opportunity to insure against the risk of outliving assets by exchanging these assets for a lifelong stream of guaranteed income. In the pure form instrument of an immediate straight life annuity, that is, with no guaranteed periods, the policyholder pays a single premium to an insurer in exchange for the promise that the insurer will pay a series of periodic payments for the lifetime of the insured (or the joint lifetimes of those who are insured), regardless of the longevity outcomes of the individuals insured, but not beyond. Such an annuity transfers the uncertainty of the individual's or couple's life span with respect to that single premium amount to the insurer, which reduces its own uncertainty by pooling many annuitant policyholders with similar longevity expectations (always by age, where allowed by law, by gender, and, rarely, by health) together.

Abstracting from any unique issuer costs of the life annuity, the return on investment, contingent on survival, to a life annuity should be higher than a bond portfolio of similar risk, because the investments of the dying policyholders are, in essence, redistributed to those who remain alive—the so-called mortality premium. Indeed, as the issuance age increases, the return, again contingent on survival, from the life annuity also increases as the investments of the larger numbers of dying policyholders (because expected mortality increases with age) are, in essence, redistributed to those who remain alive. Owing to its nature, however, when a straight life annuity is used, the ability to bequeath assets is eliminated, and advance access to future payments is not available or is strictly limited. Stated more bluntly, the return to a straight life annuity at the death of the insureds is −100 percent. But if there is no interest in leaving a bequest, this postdeath return is of no concern to the insured, and liquidity needs may be addressed, at least partially, by other insurance coverage and other assets.

Chapter 2 further describes the provisions and characteristics of life annuities as insurance products currently sold in the U.S. market. Focusing on the immediate life annuity, the chapter looks at trends in, and the volatility over time of, simulated and actual market quotes daily of monthly fixed payouts from single-premium annuities issued for $100,000 to older single men, single women, and couples. The simulation model is based on U.S. Treasury yields and annuitant mortality rates. Treasury yields are used because an annuity from a large, regulated insurance company may be thought to have credit risk character similar to that of the federal government. Annuitant, as opposed to general population, mortality rates are used because voluntary purchasers of life annuities select against the insurer; that is, those with long expected longevity are more likely to buy the product, while those with average or, especially, short expected longevity will avoid it. This phenomenon is called adverse selection of mortality risks and will be present, at least to some extent, in any situation, whether in the commercial market or even in retirement plans, where annuitization is not mandated but at least some use life annuities.

Looking at the simulations of market conditions from 1983 through 2009, three conclusions may be drawn. First, monthly payouts declined over time, for example, from over $1,000 to less than $500 for annuities newly issued to 65-year-old couples, as bond yields declined and mortality rates fell. Second, single men at age 65 receive consistently about 5 percent more than single women do owing to the higher expected mortality of men. Third, there is considerable short-term timing risk in terms of purchase—year-over-year differences of 20 percent or more in fixed lifetime payouts are common, for example, from December 2008 to December 2009. These inferences from simulation evidence are confirmed by Internet price quotes of a couple of commercially available products.

The chapter continues to explain that variable immediate annuities do not suffer from the large volatility of fluctuating initial fixed lifetime payouts. This is because at the time of annuitization, the insured selects an assumed investment return (AIR). The AIR, together with the insurer's mortality guarantee, determines how many annuity units the insured gets for the premium. For the same AIR, every insured starts out with the same initial payment for the same premium paid. But the subsequent payments to the insured, conditional on survival, are equal to the number of annuity units multiplied by the value of each unit, and therefore they evolve with the net investment performance of the underlying investment funds chosen by the insured, relative to the AIR. The payment stream will rise if the net investment return is higher than the AIR. The insured can choose a higher AIR to receive larger payments in the early years of retirement, but she risks more income volatility later in life and smaller payments if investment performance is poor. Stated another way, the volatility of the returns on the underlying portfolio is translated into a constantly changing payout. In addition there is a large annual "insurance charge" for variable annuity product.

Another hedging product is the inflation-indexed life annuity. Here too the fixed real lifetime payment guaranteed will fluctuate with conditions in the market for Treasury inflation-protected securities at time of purchase, but payouts subsequently will increase with consumer price inflation (although often with a cap of 5 or 10 percent) and do not decline with deflation. The evidence shown from a simulation model and from market prices of annuities indicates that terms are almost as fair as for nominal annuities, on average over time, but conditions were quite unstable during the recent global financial crisis, and it may be premature to draw firm conclusions. Past evidence from the U.K. market shows some generally poorer pricing, that is, a larger load, for inflation-indexed than nominal products, perhaps owing to a more limited investment portfolio available to insurers to back inflation-indexed products.[2] To pay for the cost of indexing, the initial and some subsequent payments from an inflation-indexed annuity will pay less than the nominal fixed annuity purchased for the same premium. Timing risk arising from market changes yields on Treasury securities is nearly as significant with inflation-indexed as with nominal fixed annuities.

Other new annuity product features described in chapter 2 are intended to improve the liquidity of life annuities, allowing the distribution of some cash value during retirement or to reflect market investment performance on the upside (this latter guaranteed minimum withdrawal benefit product will be explained in more detail below). But these enhancements come at the cost of extra charges and complexity.

While life annuities have been around for hundreds of years, going back to Roman times, long-term care insurance is a relatively new insurance product, going back about thirty-five years.[3] Almost all long-term care insurance policies now cover the incurred expenses of nursing home and assisted living stays and home-health-care visits up to certain maximum amounts specified; a few will make payment on determination of disability regardless of receipt of care. Indeed, payments from the insurer to the insured are universally triggered by disability, defined in federal law as an inability to perform at least two of the six main activities of daily living, such as bathing, eating, and so on without standby assistance, or if cognitively impaired to the extent that the insured needs constant supervision.

Most long-term care insurance policies are issued to an individual or couple, even if they are sometimes distributed through an employer. That is, even employer-sponsored policies are fully portable, unlike group disability or health insurance, where if the employee leaves the company, the coverage terminates. Policies are issue-age-rated, that is, the premium increases with the age of issuance, but once a policy is purchased, the stated premium is the rate for the remainder of the life of the insured, barring any general rate increase for an entire class of policyholders. In particular, the insurance is guaranteed renewable; it cannot be canceled or rates increased if the individual who is insured develops poor health.

For policies distributed through brokers or agents to individuals, the initial underwriting of applicants is strict, so that people with significant health problems will be denied coverage, have coverage delayed, or be charged much higher premiums. Often the age or work status of the applicant determines the level of scrutiny, with workers and younger applicants getting a shorter review by the underwriting department of the insurer. A common issue age is the early 60s for individually purchased policies and the mid-40s for employer-sponsored policies. Premiums are usually paid periodically; if premiums are not paid, the policy is considered lapsed and insurance coverage canceled after a short period. Also, most policies contain the provision that premiums are waived when an insured starts to receive benefits.

At the time of issuance, the insured chooses certain parameters in the policy—the benefit period, the elimination period, and the daily maximum. The benefit period, or payout horizon, is often three or five years or a lifetime. The elimination period is often ninety days, that is, the disability has to have been recognized for ninety days before expenses can be considered incurred for insurance reimbursement. The daily maximum should be chosen to reflect the cost of care in the geographical region in which the insured resides. Currently nursing home care in large coastal urban areas costs about $300 a day but is much less in rural areas or in the South and Midwest. Sometimes the daily maximum chosen is allowed to be lower for home-health-care benefits than for nursing home benefits, to reflect likely relative costs of care, as well as to lower the overall premium charged.

Most policies have benefits paid on a pool-of-money basis: the benefit period in days is multiplied by the daily maximum to produce the total resources that the policy will pay, subject to the daily caps. For example, if the policy has a four-year benefit period and a daily maximum of $150 a day for home-health-care visits but the visits are costing only $100 a day or the visits occur every other day, the pool of money will last much longer than the benefit period chosen. The longer the benefit period, the shorter the elimination period, and the higher the daily maximum, the higher the premium charged for the policy. It is also thought that there is some moral hazard when the lifetime benefit period is chosen, because there is then little incentive to economize on care below the daily maximums, and therefore insurers may charge more for this choice, even beyond the pure effect of a slightly longer expected average benefit period.

Spousal discounts are common in policies currently sold. That is, discounts as high as 50 percent are given if both members of the couple are insured. This reflects the experience that members of a couple tend to care for each other, postponing the need for nursing home care. Premiums on long-term care insurance do not reflect gender (despite the allowance of law to do so for commercial, as opposed to employer-provided, products), even though women are more likely to claim benefits for longer periods. Therefore, policies sold to couples, almost universally mixed gender in this older population, are less costly to the insurer per insured than policies sold to singles, who are more commonly women, and insurers can provide discounts in the premiums charged to covered couples.

Federal law mandates that all policies offer the insured a policy rider for a 5 percent compound inflation for the daily benefit maximum and a rider for a shortened benefit period nonforfeiture benefit.[4] Both riders will increase the cost of the policy and are reflected in the total premium. The former rider is widely selected because the period between purchase and claim may extend many years, while the cost of care inexorably escalates; the latter rider is rarely chosen because few insureds believe that they will allow their policy to lapse. Other riders commonly offered include a 3 percent annual increase and a guaranteed purchase option. In the latter case, the insured is given the option, as long as she does not decline too many times, to purchase additional insurance every two or three years without evidence of insurability, at a premium appropriate to the policyholder's new attained age.

Nearly all long-term care insurance policies currently sold are tax qualified. This means that if the policy has certain basic provisions, premiums paid are deductible health expenses provided the insured policyholder is an itemizer on his or her federal taxes and total health expenditures exceed 7.5 percent (10 percent after the health care reform law kicks in) of adjusted gross income. Benefits paid from these policies are not included in taxable income, although then any reimbursed expenses are not deductible.

Because of the long time horizons of long-term care insurance policies—premiums are usually collected for many years before claims are made—the underlying assumptions used in pricing about investment returns for the insurer and the lapse rates of policyholders are critical. Indeed, in the early years of the product on the market, insurers assumed high investment returns and lapse rates and accordingly priced the policies cheaply. When experience indicated otherwise, premium rates had to be raised on most classes of policyholders, an unfortunate process for both insurers and policyholders. More recently, insurers have requested from regulators across-the-board premium rate increases owing to claims higher than expected, along with lower lapses and interest rates.

Available evidence indicates that a relatively small percentage of the retired population currently has long-term care insurance—less than 10 percent. Most sales are done commercially to individuals or couples; the employer market is quite small. Several analysts ascribe a significant part of the explanation of the lack of private insurance coverage to the crowd-out effects of Medicaid coverage of long-term care services, at least for the bottom half of the income distribution.[5] Another significant part can be attributed to issuance exclusions owing to the conservative underwriting of insurers, as about a quarter (perhaps as many as a third) of the population approaching retirement has health and lifestyle conditions that prevent coverage under current underwriting criteria.[6] The recent recession has reduced new purchases of policies, and the number of insurers writing policies has declined over time.

Some Research about the Annuity Puzzle

Over the past thirty years or so, many economists have pursued a line of research that essentially asked, "Why doesn't every retiree convert his or her entire stock of wealth into a straight life annuity?" The underlying presumption of the question is the so-called life cycle hypothesis, whereby the main motivation explaining the savings behavior of household is the need to finance retirement and not, for example, for bequests. Given this rationale for saving, combined with the considerable uncertainty about the length of life arising from mortality risk, all retired households should hold their entire financial and real asset portfolio in life annuities. As reviewed in chapter 3, past research, using a model of lifetime utility maximization, measures the gains in individual welfare from using actuarially fair life annuities. For example, the utility gain from obtaining access to an actuarially fair inflation-indexed life annuity for a 65-year-old male with quite modest risk aversion would be equivalent to his getting a 50.2 percent increase in wealth. Higher, but still plausible, levels of risk aversion would increase that annuity-equivalent wealth to 100 percent!

The full use of fixed life annuities also has the virtue of simplicity to the household in terms of investment strategy, where responsibility and risk fall entirely on the insurer, who guarantees the payment flows (which include investment and mortality returns). The distribution strategy is also quite simple: a fixed income flow from an annuity frees the retired household from having to manage the size of withdrawals from its pool of savings. It also blocks the opportunity to entertain rash temptations for large, imprudent expenditures. It is also likely that simplicity is more highly valued and becomes more appropriate as the retired household ages and its cognitive abilities decline.

Clearly this analysis suggests an enormous level of demand for life annuities. Casual observation, confirmed by more formal empirical evidence, is, however, seemingly inconsistent with the analysis: commercial sales of immediate life annuities are quite modest. A substantial literature has developed to explain this puzzle. One strand notes that Social Security and some DB pension plans automatically provide life annuity coverage; particularly for lower-income retired households, these amounts may be sufficient, and even for higher-income households, this coverage reduces the demand for other life annuity assets. A second strand finds that life annuities are not priced on an actuarially fair basis for the average person in the population because of adverse selection, as noted above. The empirical finding in the literature is that this effect produces about a 10 percent reduction in annuity payouts.[7] This "expense" deters some relatively healthy individuals from purchasing the life annuity and, moreover, is consistent with a significant share (perhaps as much as a third) of the older population's avoiding life annuities because their health is poor at the point of retirement. A third explanation invokes the desire for bequests and other similar transfers outside the retired household. This "family consciousness" is somewhat related to, but still different from, mortality risk sharing between spouses, whereby model results show that the annuity equivalent wealth produced by utility models for couples is significantly below that of individuals.

Still another explanation is concern about the solvency risks of the insurers that are issuing the life annuities, although state guarantee funds pay up to certain limits in a bankruptcy situation.[8] Also, because interest rates are quite volatile, the prices charged for fixed annuities are also volatile. This is a type of risk—timing risk—that may deter investors from the purchase of life annuities unless it is hedged in the retirement asset portfolio or managed through, for example, gradual purchases, that is ladders, of smaller immediate life annuities.

Two other explanations for the annuity puzzle are summarized in chapter 3, written in the early 2000s, that subsequent research and developments have qualified somewhat. The first notes that the absence of inflation coverage would diminish the expected utility value of annuitization owing to a lack of hedging for inflation risk; the subsequent development of the inflation-indexed life annuity, documented in chapter 2, removes that as an adequate explanation for the lack of demand. The second explanation is health uncertainty during retirement, that is, a liquidity constraint could arise if significant uninsured health and disability expenditures, especially for long-term care, occur. Because of this risk, some analysts suggest that retirees would therefore want to avoid irreversible annuitization in the absence of full health and disability insurance. Subsequent research, discussed in chapter 6, however, demonstrates that the existence of this risk actually increases the demand for annuities, albeit later in life, when the mortality credit, and therefore rate of return on life annuities, increases, which helps pay for the expected costs of disability, which also rise with age. Moreover, long-term care insurance covers this risk well, and as I explain later in this chapter in the summaries of chapters 8 and 9, the creation of a life care annuity would do an even better and more widespread job of hedging the expenses associated with disability risk.

Still even the accumulation of all these explanations does not fully solve the annuity puzzle. For example, the existence of risk-sharing opportunity in couples, combined with the cost of adverse selection, can explain why couples do not buy joint-and-survivor annuities, but it does not explain why widows and widowers later in life do not purchase individual life annuities. Similarly the existence of Social Security and DB plans explains why lower-income households and those with large pensions would avoid life annuities, but not middle-income healthy households with just defined contribution plan coverage. So the final explanations in chapter 3 turn away from the traditional rational actor models of classical economics to behavioral and institutional explanations found in some more recent economic theories.

Retirees may simply not understand the advantages of annuitization, in the context of a sometimes heated investment culture and confusion about the nature of various types of risk and return. Also, retirement plans in the private sector, which are increasingly DC in type, but even including DB plans, have moved away from automatic and, for DC plans, even any possible, life annuity distribution. Owing to the inertia of plan participants, this movement by itself could already be having implications for the demand for life annuities, as it is difficult, both practically and behaviorally, for individuals to enter the commercial market for life annuities on their own. For sponsors of DB plans, which are mandated by law to offer an annuity choice, the avoidance of annuitization by plan participants shortens the effective duration of the plan, a desirable outcome to the sponsor because the riskiness of the plan in terms of the volatility of required contributions is thereby lowered.

For sponsors of DC plans, adding a life annuity option, which is not required by law, increases administrative and fiduciary burdens. Empirical evidence shows relatively low offer rates of annuities by DC plans and low pickup rates of life annuities by DC plan participants or those DB plan participants given a lump-sum distribution choice. If the behavioral and institutional aspects of the annuity puzzle are dominant, it could reasonably suggest more activist policies on the part of the plan sponsor (e.g., more and better education of workers) and of federal regulators and legislators to remove barriers, provide encouragement, and perhaps even to mandate disclosure, income illustrations, and the offering of options.

Survey Evidence on Participant Attitudes and Choices toward Annuities

Different theories, observed behavior, and institutions provide many possible reasons that together seem to offer a comprehensive explanation for the general lack of voluntary annuitization today. But these are mostly inferences and theories and not direct evidence. It would be good, therefore, to get further evidence on plan participant attitudes and choices through direct survey questions. Survey evidence is, unfortunately, not perfect because there are no real consequences to respondents for incomplete or "lazy" or confused answers. Moreover, the skill and fairness of the designer of the survey instrument are essential to the usefulness of the results. Nonetheless, we do not expect misrepresentations from respondents. The statistics presented in chapter 4 are based on responses to a survey carefully designed and administered by a major benefits consulting firm. Therefore, such evidence should also be considered as we develop our suggestions for strategy and policy.

In 2007, Watson Wyatt Worldwide conducted a survey of a large, nationally representative sample of older workers and retirees, asking about their payout and risk preferences and their payout expectations, as well as about their socioeconomic and health characteristics. The first tables in chapter 4 report that while the vast majority of older workers and recent retirees with coverage by a DB plan expected to receive at least some of their retirement plan benefits as an annuity, only about 10 percent with only a DC plan have similar expectations. To elicit preferences, the survey posed hypothetical questions about the choice between a larger annuity payout and a smaller annuity payout plus a lump sum of a certain dollar value, which is the approximate actuarial equivalent of the smaller annuity. A follow-up question changed the dollar amount offered. A majority of both older workers and recent retirees preferred the smaller annuity plus the lump sum, but the answer changed if the size of the lump sum changed. Most want a lump sum if it is big enough. The majority want a full annuity if the lump sum is too small. Only 27 percent say they would choose the full annuity regardless of the lump-sum amount, and less than 40 percent say they would always opt for the combination of a smaller annuity and a lump sum.

Looking at cross-tabulations of the data related to preferences and personal characteristics, older workers who are female, are unmarried, have lower education levels and lower earnings, and are more risk averse are more likely to prefer full annuitization. These results generally also hold for recent retirees. When comparing self-reported health status and expected longevity to the expectation of receiving at least some annuity payout from their retirement plan, both older workers and retirees indicated that poor health and shorter life expectancy lower significantly the expectation of receipt of retirement benefits in the form of any annuity. This presumably reflects that all DC plan participants and many DB plan participants have a choice in how their retirement plan benefits are distributed to them. Ordered logistic regressions in the chapter appendix indicate that the preference for full annuitization increases when the older worker or retiree has DB as well as DC plan coverage and is risk averse, and it falls when the retiree wants to give an inheritance. The preference for lump sums decreases with longer expected lifetimes and lower income and wealth. Still, the regressions leave most of the variance in preferences unexplained, especially among retirees.

Several conclusions may be drawn from this survey evidence. Mandatory annuitization, even on a partial basis, will be harmful and disliked by many plan participants. There is a strong desire for at least some liquidity and continued ownership of assets. At the same time, there is a latent widespread market and demand for life annuities if they can be offered conveniently and economically, for example, through the retirement plan. This is especially true for certain types of older workers and retirees: women, unmarried, lower paid, in good health, and risk averse. All of these types are a growing presence in the labor force.

Evaluating Distribution Strategies in Retirement

Given the competing desires for income and wealth, security and flexibility, and current needs and future desires, it is appropriate to compare carefully various distribution strategies and products to evaluate their properties and likely outcomes. Chapter 5 compares six strategies for the same initial account balance at retirement age of 65 for an individual worker:

1. Systematic withdrawals (as a constant percentage distributed) from a portfolio of mutual funds invested in a mix of equities and bonds

2. Purchase with the entire account balance of a straight immediate fixed life annuity

3. Purchase with the entire account balance of a straight immediate variable life annuity, with underlying allocations to a mix of equity and bond funds

4. Purchase with the entire account balance of a deferred variable annuity with a guaranteed minimum withdrawal benefit (GMWB) rider, with investments in an underlying mix of equity and bond funds

5. A mix of systematic withdrawals from mutual funds and a one-time purchase of a fixed annuity, split at retirement at 70 percent mutual funds and 30 percent fixed annuity

6. A mix of systematic withdrawals from mutual funds and laddered purchases of fixed annuities, gradually moving to complete annuitization by age 75

As briefly noted in chapter 2, the new innovation of the GMWB rider protects the investor against market declines and offers the possibility of market improvements in the fixed-percentage (generally 5 percent) withdrawal amounts. While the minimum income flow is guaranteed by the insurer, the account balance is not and indeed may go down, even to zero. Also, there is an additional charge for the GMWB rider on top of the investment and variable annuity charges, thereby reducing the income flows and account balances compared to other strategies. As long as there is an account balance, this product provides liquidity to the investor, and there is also no timing risk.

In chapter 5's stochastic analysis, the asset mix, where relevant, is set to a 50/50 balance between equity and bonds, except where there is also a fixed annuity included and then the annuity is considered as a bond for asset allocation purposes. For example, the fifth strategy therefore has a 50/20/30 equity/bond/annuity mix. Systematic withdrawals, where relevant, are set at 5 percent of the account. Various fee charges are considered, estimated from market information; annuity pricing is modeled as well. The details of the stochastic process of investment returns, bond yields, inflation, and mortality realizations are explained in the chapter. The possibilities of catastrophic losses and insurer bankruptcy are not yet considered, as they will be in chapter 7.

In terms of the probability distribution of real wealth balances, the first strategy produces the highest levels in almost all scenarios. Liquidity is excellent, with no insurer insolvency risk and little timing risk. But real income flows are low. The fourth and fifth strategies are quite similar, producing the next highest levels of real wealth balances, although the fifth strategy does better in tougher investment and inflation environments. The second and third strategies produce no real wealth, by definition. In terms of real income, these strategies produce the highest levels, especially noticeable at younger ages in retirement. The main advantage of the third strategy is that it eliminates timing risk. For the same AIR, every investor starts out with the same initial payment for the same initial account balance. There is some upside potential but also considerable risk for a 50/50 portfolio that income will fall short. The sixth strategy produces the highest levels of real income at later ages and in tough investment and inflation environments. The fourth strategy, despite its guarantees, is not noticeably superior to the first strategy in terms of income levels across the scenarios because of the force of extra charges and inflation erosion, while the fifth strategy is slightly stronger overall. A more aggressive investment allocation (70/30) in the fourth strategy, as might be sensible given the GMWB guarantee, does improve its ranking somewhat. Lower charges obviously raise wealth and income across all strategies and scenarios, but it particularly favors the relative rankings of the third and fourth strategies.

While there is no obvious winner among the six strategies, and clearly the choice will depend on the risk and bequest preferences of the retired worker and actual product charges, there is some indication that the fifth and sixth strategies may serve well as the basis for income and wealth management for the average retired household. The simulation results show some nice characteristics for these combinations. The fifth strategy produces quite a bit of liquidity, with account balances nearly as high as those produced by the fourth strategy. It also gives a higher average real income flow, with some upside potential, than some of the other strategies. The sixth strategy, by definition, provides liquidity for only the first ten years of retirement. Its income characteristics, however, are the best of all the strategies modeled. In particular, mean real income flows are the highest, and the risk of shortfalls is the lowest. There is substantial upside potential, and the downside is protected. The timing risk of annuitization is hedged by the gradual laddering of purchases of annuities. Postponing annuitization increases income flows because of the positive impact of the mortality credit, given fixed proportional loads on life annuities. Both combination strategies have some insurer insolvency risk and higher fees and the cost of adverse selection but, by definition, less than in the pure annuitization solutions. Because these combination strategies have not yet been automated in the marketplace, they are currently complex for a household to pursue.

Chapter 6 looks at the issue of investment/annuity/distribution strategy in a more formal model of utility maximization, with additional consideration for uncertain uninsured health care spending, especially for long-term care services. The model in that chapter also considers the joint household decision for investment in bonds, equities, and life annuities, as well as the consumption decision over the retirement period. The retired households modeled have differential exposure, by income deciles, to mortality and uninsured health spending, in addition to facing common stochastic capital market returns. Coverage by Social Security and traditional DB plans (preexisting annuities) also differs by income deciles. Households are modeled alternatively as not having or having a bequest motive.

With flexible choices among equities, bonds, and annuities, households would optimally annuitize their retirement wealth sometime during retirement—fully or partially depending on their bequest motive. The superiority of annuities in hedging against longevity risk is attributable to their eventually higher returns than the reference returns on conventional assets, because of the substantial mortality credit in life annuities issued at older ages, even with product and adverse selection loads. In the absence of fuller insurance coverage, this superiority also applies to hedging against uncertain health expenses because both annuity returns and health expenses are life contingent and rise with age. As the health spending risks induce a portfolio shift toward safer assets, annuities are more efficient and eventually dominate bonds. This higher degree of annuitization also provides a greater leverage for more equity holdings in the portfolio, everything else being equal, without increasing the overall investment risk exposure.

For example, consider an average middle-income (fifth decile) retired household with a bequest motive or some liquidity needs. In the optimum, it initially holds an asset portfolio invested about 35 percent in equities and the rest in bonds, and draws down slowly on it, until it turns about 72 years old. Then the household begins to annuitize and simultaneously increases the share of its remaining financial asset portfolio to equities. At age 80, it has annuitized about half of its asset portfolio and increases the equity share of the remaining portfolio to about 70 percent. Thereafter, the household slowly reduces the equity share, but that share does not reach the pre-age-72 level until it turns 100. The portfolio size itself is rather stable in the mid-80s because continued annuity purchases offset asset growth, but the portfolio then starts to grow, as consumption is contained and further annuity purchases are financed from income flows. These patterns are actually similar across income deciles, except that the lower-income decile results do not show much of an uptick in the equity share of the portfolio with age. The central insight here is that the life annuity, purchased in stages later in life, can serve as a hedge against investment risks and against uninsured health and long-term care spending risks, which increase in probability and amount with age, in absence of specific or complete insurance coverage.

In chapter 7, we return to the somewhat simpler model of chapter 5, focusing on the fifth and sixth strategies. Several improvements and embellishments, however, are made to the model. First, it is updated with data through 2009. Second, the possibilities of catastrophic disasters, not present in the U.S. data from 1962 to 2009, are added to the model, based on horrible historical global experiences from the past century. This affects the means and probability distributions of asset returns, inflation, and interest rates, as well as allows for government and insurer bankruptcies. Investment in equities becomes relatively less attractive, but the choices among other strategies do not change as much. Finally, an intuitive risk-minimization approach is taken to model the preferences of the retiree between income security and real balance protection. In particular, we assign weights, summing to one, to the separate risks of income and portfolio balance shortfalls of certain sizes. Strategies are evaluated and selected as good based on minimizing the weighted shortfall risks for individuals and couples.

If one posits preferences that are dominated by concerns about income security risks (and only secondarily about real account balances), then a good strategy for an individual retiree at age 65 is to start with moving 10 or 15 percent of the retirement portfolio to an immediate life annuity initially and then to gradually convert the rest of the remaining portfolio to immediate life annuities over the next twenty years. Withdrawals from the unannuitized portfolio should be 5 percent per year. The equity share of the asset portfolio, while mainly determined by the risk aversion of the retiree, should increase with the degree of annuitization. Similar strategies are good for couples, although they may start with a lower fraction of wealth in immediate annuities and extend the arc of annuitization to twenty-five to thirty years; this result reflects the internal risk-sharing characteristics of a couple with independent mortality probabilities.

Integrated Life Annuity Product with Long-Term Care Insurance

The existence of uncertain uninsured health spending, primarily on long-term care needs, has an important influence on the optimal distribution strategy. Currently long-term care insurance is not widely used, in part because it is not available to a significant portion of the population in relatively poor health as they approach retirement, the natural time for households to consider this issue. In order to address this problem, as well as to improve the pricing of life annuities by reducing the significance of adverse selection there, I have developed the life care annuity (LCA). Chapter 8 is the seminal publication on this topic, explaining the motivation, design, and empirical evidence for this product idea.

The LCA is an integrated insurance product consisting of a life annuity and long-term care insurance (LTCI). In return for the payment of one or more premiums the LCA gives a stream of fixed (in nominal, increasing, or inflation-indexed terms) periodic income payments for the lifetime of the named annuitant. (In return for higher premium charges, income payments would continue for the lifetime of a named co-annuitant survivor, usually a spouse.) In addition, the LCA pays an extra stream (referred to as a "pop-up") of fixed payments (again, nominal, increasing, or inflation indexed) if the annuitant (or the co-annuitant, or both) is cognitively impaired or is unable to perform, without substantial human assistance, at least two of the six recognized ADLs, such as walking or eating. These are the same triggers used in LTCI policies that are qualified under current tax law.

Because this second, pop-up, segment of the LCA is intended to function as comprehensive LTCI, it is important that the level of the additional layer of payments to the disabled annuitant be sufficient to cover the extra expenses incurred for home health care or nursing home care as soon as possible after the care needs begin and for as long as they continue. For that reason, the inclusion of yet another, third, layer of pop-up disability payments in the LCA may be advisable for when the disability is very severe (e.g., four ADLs) or if it lasts a particularly long time (e.g., two years), that is, when the extent of needed care will tend to be greater and hence costs will be even higher. Moreover, the costs of these types of care have been increasing rapidly over time, often in excess of the rate of general inflation, and therefore inflation-indexing or automatic increases of the level of disability payments would seem particularly advantageous for these segments.

What is the motivation for the integration of life annuity and LTCI? After all, these insurance products are available and have been marketed for decades as separate instruments. The integration is intended to address inefficiencies in the separate markets for those products. Empirical research has shown that the costs of immediate life annuities increase by up to 10 percent because of adverse selection by mortality risk classes in voluntary choice situations, that is, individuals with lower life expectancies avoid life annuity purchase. The research also showed, in simulation analyses using a life cycle framework and reasonable estimates of risk aversion, that a large improvement in utility could be achieved by the annuitization of assets at fair actuarial value in retirement. But this improvement in welfare is, at least in part, blocked by market inefficiencies. Especially for couples, deviation from fair value (i.e., loads arising from adverse selection and marketing costs) dissuades annuity purchases.

On the LTCI side, empirical research has shown that insurance company underwriting practices eliminate from 25 to 33 percent of the retirement age population (ages 65 to 75) from purchasing individual LTCI policies because, through issuer underwriting, individuals in impaired health or unhealthy lifestyles cannot purchase this insurance. Other research has demonstrated, using simulation analysis, substantial willingness to pay for actuarially fair private LTCI coverage for individuals. So, here too, market inefficiencies compromise otherwise large welfare gains available from insurance markets. Moreover, these insights are not academic; many of these empirical research findings about annuities and LTCI are confirmed by observations in the insurance industry, such as high rejection rates on LTCI policy applications at older ages, discussions among actuarial professionals and financial advisors of "expensive" annuity pricing, and so on.

But there is a market solution to these problems. Chapter 8 shows a positive correlation between impaired health and unhealthy lifestyle and mortality probabilities. This empirical finding leads to a proposal for an integrated insurance product, combining the life annuity and LTCI into one that addresses the market inefficiencies. The proposal itself is an application of economic theory—a practical attempt to produce a self-sustaining pooling equilibrium that is superior, by lowering prices and increasing available insurance coverage, to the separating equilibrium currently in existence, that is, where insurance coverage is restricted. The LCA works so as to blend the low mortality and disability risks of annuity buyers who would like cheaper life annuities with the high mortality and disability risks of those desiring, but denied access to, LTCI coverage, combining these population pools of risk classes. Because the risk classes are pooled through the LCA product, average mortality is higher (and the annuity segment cheaper) while the liberalized underwriting lets those with higher disability risk get coverage of LTC risks in that segment of the LCA.

Using a unique data set of population disability and morality experience, the premium at age 65 is calculated for a unisex individual for a basic integrated product—it is about 4 percent lower than for the two products sold separately. Only about 2 percent of the age 65 population would be rejected by the looser underwriting standards of the integrated product—essentially those already in LTCI claim status. Finally, some evidence is produced for the assertion that a self-sustaining and stable pooling equilibrium is likely. In particular, those who are rejected by current LTCI underwriting but would be eligible for the LCA are made better off in simple value terms. That is, the ratio of actuarially fair premiums for the relevant risk groups (major illness, stroke, poor lifestyle) relative to those for the expanded purchase pool is above one for the LTCI coverage. The pooling property of this positive effect on value should be enhanced when the expected utility ("insurance") value of LTCI coverage is considered, to say nothing of the insurance value of having a life annuity. Moreover, sensitivity analysis demonstrated that the likely "wood work" effect of insurance coverage on disability claims, as well as inflation indexing of the LTCI segment, increases value to those currently rejected by LTCI underwriting, and therefore further supports the maintained hypothesis that the integrated product will be cheaper and more desired in a self-sustaining pooling equilibrium.

The current troubles of the LTCI market would also be addressed by the LCA. It is hard to price LTCI policies, sold to young insureds, because it is impossible for the insurer to hedge very long-term disability and interest rate trends and changes. Moreover, lapse rates have come in consistently lower than expected and are hard to forecast. Therefore, it makes more sense for insurers to give up on any lapsation and shorten the duration of the product. The LCA achieves all these objectives nicely, while also having the product advantages to the insureds just described.

One can envision various possibilities for an LCA in qualified retirement plans. It could be the normal accruing benefit of a traditional DB pension plan, with the LTCI segment denominated as some proportion of the final benefit, so that for an average-wage full-career employee, the level of disability payments accrued would be sufficient to cover nearly all expected LTC needs. Alternatively, an LCA could be added as an alternative choice to the DB pension plan's distribution options, just as various joint-and-survivor payout options are currently available, at cost. In particular, if the plan sponsor would like to respond positively to a demand from participants for lump-sum distributions or already has a lump-sum distribution choice, but is concerned about the impact of adverse mortality selection on its plan annuity offering, providing a LCA could be an effective response. Moreover, provision through a retirement plan may be a more popular way for employers to offer LTCI coverage to workers than through group LTCI plans, which have not taken root in the marketplace.

Similarly, if the sponsor of a DC plan offered a life annuity distribution option, the LCA could be added to the menu of choices. More broadly, it is important to consider IRAs as a home for the LCA, which opens a very large market. Various laws and regulations, however, pose insurmountable hurdles to the LCA in qualified retirement plans, and its tax treatment under current law is anyways adverse. Chapter 9 describes these challenges in a qualified plan arising from minimum distribution, joint-and-survivor, and incidental benefit rules preventing or disadvantaging the inclusion of the LCA in a qualified retirement plan or IRA. Unisex pricing for employer-provided benefits would also be a disadvantage to the pricing logic of a LCA.

Chapter 9 also explains and illustrates the tax treatments of various insurance products purchased with after-tax money: a separate life annuity, LTCI, and the LCA, before and after the introduction in the Pension Protection Act of 2006 (PPA) of somewhat favorable tax treatment of the LCA beginning in 2010. In particular, the PPA provides that any charges against the value of an annuity contract for coverage under a qualified LTCI contract will not be includable in the taxable income of the insured. On the other hand, such premium charges will not be treated as medical expenses for purposes of the itemized medical care deduction, and the investment in the annuity contract will be reduced by the amount of the charge. The premium charge, however, continues to be tax exempt even if the investment in the contract is zero. In this latter circumstance, the PPA provision gives an exclusion from taxable income for the full amount of the LTCI premiums.

The net effect of various tax treatments of the LCA compared to the tax treatments of separately purchased life annuity and LTCI is illustrated. Under various reasonable assumptions, the favorable tax treatment of the LCA lowers the cost of coverage by about 4 percent for moderate-income individuals and by more than 8 percent for high-income individuals over their expected lifetimes.

Public Policy Environment

Retirement plans and insurance products are regulated heavily and taxed uniquely. Therefore, the public policy environment can be expected to have an important influence on the distribution strategies of employer sponsors of retirement plans and of retired households. Chapter 10 has two main sections: the first describes recent and proposed regulation and legislation in this area, particularly affecting the use of annuities in retirement plans, and the second gives five proposals to encourage annuitization.

Pension plans that offer lump-sum options to participants are generally subject to specific requirements in the law on how those lump sums must be calculated, converting from the annuity form, in terms of interest rates and mortality tables. From 1994 through 2007, the law gave a favorable interest rate in this calculation, thereby inflating the lump sum; this may have had some impact on increasing rates of lump-sum selections. In PPA, however, this bias was rectified, and we are now in a transition phase, whereby lump-sum distributions will be reduced, everything else being equal. PPA also added another option required to be offered on annuity distributions, as a joint-and-survivor annuity, increasing the payment to survivors (often widows). PPA also removed a stringent fiduciary requirement from the Department of Labor on DC plans offering annuities, mandating the "safest available" annuity. Plan sponsors however, are still unhappy with what they believe are the diffuse and uncertain fiduciary exposures remaining.

Another possible impediment to innovative design of distribution strategies including annuities are the minimum distribution requirements. These requirements, although loosened somewhat by regulation in 2004, are still quite mechanical and therefore might not allow certain strategies, like the life care annuity, or our preferred combined retirement income and wealth management strategy, that otherwise would fit the spirit of the requirement: that the retirement account should be paid out over the lifetime of the worker and his or her spouse.

Recent legislative and think-tank proposals have been put forward to encourage annuitization, in particular, required disclosures of the account value converted to annuity form, and default-delayed annuitization or recalculated withdrawal programs. The second section of chapter 10 puts forward and evaluates some additional proposals: mandate a minimum level of annuitization; make annuitization the default option for DC plan distributions; mandate primary DC plans to offer life annuities at retirement; encourage, through favorable taxation, the choice of life annuities as a distribution from all retirement plans; and create a government-sponsored agency to offer or a clearinghouse to market unsubsidized life annuities to retirement plan participants.

Conclusion

There is considerable reason and scope to improve and widen access to life annuities and long-term care insurance vehicles as part of retirement plans and planning. The current economy and likely further future rationalization of government programs and employer-sponsored retirement plans and resources, and the consequent movement away from traditional payout structures, reflect both budget realities and workers' preferences. Therefore, new structures and products must be created and offered widely to replace what has been lost and provide what will inevitably be needed. At the same time, these products must recognize the need and desire of many retirees for flexibility and liquidity while also addressing the welfare improvement for most retirees from coverage for the extra costs arising from longevity and disability risks. The extensive stochastic simulation, empirical, and theoretical work presented here indicates that these distribution strategies and mechanisms should include systematic withdrawals from a mix of bond and equity funds, and income from immediate life annuities, with increasing purchases of life annuities with age. The life care annuity could provide both life annuity and long-term care insurance coverage on a favorable underwriting, pricing, and tax basis, currently outside of qualified retirement plans.

A default selection of a structured payout option, preferably including a life annuity, for all retirement plan types is necessary and appropriate. Confusion and unsupported investment optimism by plan participants seem to be among the main reasons for an aversion to life annuities. Moreover, the poor pricing of life annuities can be reduced if adverse selection is also reduced, which will occur if utilization rates increase. Indeed, the main reason that sponsors of DC plans do not now offer life annuities from their plans is their belief that plan participants do not want them and therefore strong external encouragement is warranted.[9] But the exact requirements, to be set by regulation, for the default selection of a structured payout option need to remain flexible and inclusive, as plan sponsors and the market develop new solutions, strategies, and products. Simply requiring the purchase with almost all of the DC account of a straight life annuity no later than a certain age, as has always been mandated in the United Kingdom but is now under reconsideration, is too restrictive and would harm workers who are approaching retirement in poor health and expose them unnecessarily to interest rate risk.

Although use of a life annuity is likely to be part of a good strategy, there are many other reasonable combinations, as well as new products, such as variable annuities with minimum withdrawal benefits, annuity ladders, or systematic withdrawals from the investment portfolio. From the point of view of public policymakers, the important thing, as a minimum default standard, is to set up a structured payout option to cover the expected life expectancy of the plan participant and his or her spouse (plus a few extra years as a conservative margin) as the setting for the plan to distribute assets to retiring workers. In this way, workers, regardless of the type of plan by which they are covered, including a DC plan, will learn that retirement plans are meant to support spending in retirement and not just accumulation of lump sums.

How might the preferred strategy indicated in chapters 5, 6, and 7 be operationalized? One possibility is a series of products, essentially reverse target-date funds, that would be dynamic packages of mutual funds and immediate fixed life annuities that would produce income streams to retired plan participants. Each package would be designed to be appropriate to specific households with various retirement and current ages and marital status, for example, a married couple aged 65 to 70 who retired at age 60, or a single person aged 75 to 80 who retired at age 65, and so on. Another possibility, more customized, is a software package that elicits risk, liquidity, and bequest preferences and, based on these preferences as well as the demographics of the household, designs a specific strategy that is then implemented automatically. Even further along this spectrum, one can imagine the assistance of a financial advisor. These implementations might take place as part of the retirement plan or as part of an IRA rollover scheme, and would also consider the relative expense loads of the investment and annuity component products.

What could be the tax treatment of the life annuity payments and LTCI benefits in those qualified retirement plans? PPA provides an exclusion from taxable income for pension distributions that are used to pay for qualified health insurance premiums up to a maximum of $3,000 annually. This exclusion, however, is available only to retired or disabled public safety officers, although it may be used for health insurance or LTCI. This is equivalent to above-the-line deductibility of LTCI premiums, and it is, by far, the most generous tax treatment available. This provision should be used as a model for taxing the LTCI segment of an LCA for a more widely defined set of retirees and qualified retirement plans, that is, including the private sector and all three retirement plan types—DB, DC, and IRA.

Under current law and regulations, taxable distributions from qualified retirement plans and IRAs must begin in the year following when the participant turns age 70 1/2, unless the participant is still working and is covered by the retirement plan. The law and regulations specify the details of the level of minimum distributions that meet this requirement under a variety of circumstances. The public policy purpose of the requirements is to ensure that qualified plans and IRAs serve primarily as vehicles for providing income to workers and spouses during retirement, and not as tax-avoidance schemes or estate planning devices. Legislation and IRS regulatory activity in the early 2000s lightened the burden of these requirements and simplified them somewhat. Nevertheless, there is still scope for further improvements to update and simplify, even while keeping the current structure.[10] The allowance for use of an LCA and dynamic combined income and wealth management strategies should also be included under revised minimum distribution requirements.

Appendix: Glossary of Technical Terms by Topic

Retirement Plans

A *defined benefit pension plan* determines retirement benefit payments to workers according to a fixed formula that is usually based on salary, years of service, and perhaps age. The benefit payments are guaranteed to workers by the employer and often are supported by a fund of investment assets accumulated through contributions and investment earnings.

A *traditional plan* is a defined benefit plan: the benefit formula specifies that annual benefit payments for the life of the worker are based on a fixed percentage of average earnings (during the last few years of the worker's service or over the entire career) multiplied by the number of years of service. Actuarial adjustments are often made if payments start on a date other than the normal retirement age specified in the plan.

A *hybrid plan* is a defined benefit plan where the benefit formula specifies an individual account for each worker that will accumulate, notionally, as a balance over the worker's career, which is generally paid out as a lump sum on the conclusion of service.

In a *cash balance* hybrid plan, the plan sponsor specifies a pay credit (e.g., 6 percent of pay) and a rate of interest on the accumulated balance (e.g., the current yield on the thirty-year Treasury bond).

In a *pension equity* hybrid plan, workers are credited in their accounts a fixed or age- or service-weighted percentage accrual for each year of service applied to their final average earnings.

A *defined contribution retirement plan* determines the value of the individual account balance on the basis of actual contributions to the account and investment earnings thereon. Generally any employer contributions are made as a percentage of the worker's pay, often matched to employee contributions. It is also common for the plan to give employees a choice of investment options.

A particular type of defined contribution plan, the *money purchase plan*, has a fixed employer contribution and must offer a life annuity as the default payment mechanism.

Another type of defined contribution plan, the *401(k) plan*, is a deferred compensation option established by an employer that allows employees to contribute a portion of their earnings to a retirement account on a pretax basis. Most employers make matching contributions to the account.

Frozen retirement plans are closed to new employees and often also limit or stop future benefit accruals for some or all active plan participants.

An *individual retirement account (IRA)* is a retirement savings plan set up by an individual worker or a small employer for its workers. Contributions are limited by maximum dollar amounts set in federal tax law.

All of these plans are subject to the *minimum distribution requirements*, that is, some specified percentage amount, related to age and marital status, must be taken from the plan and distributed to retired workers and become subject to income taxes. More broadly, in most cases, an employer-sponsored retirement plan is a *qualified plan*, which means it meets numerous requirements set in the Internal Revenue Code and regulations in order to receive certain tax benefits. Long-term care insurance, even that individually issued and not employer sponsored, is qualified if it meets certain requirements and, as a result, tax benefits can be claimed.

The *Pension Protection Act of 2006 (PPA)* was major legislation that improved the funding and security requirements of defined benefit plans, removed legal uncertainties from hybrid plans, and eased the way for the introduction of automatic enrollment and contribution escalation in defined contribution plans.

A *retiree health plan* provides coverage to a retiree beyond what is mandated by health insurance continuation (COBRA) laws. Premiums may be paid in whole or in part by the retired worker or the former employer, and coverage may extend just to eligibility for Medicare (age 65 or disability) or beyond as a supplemental plan.

A *401(h) account* is a separate fund within an employer's defined benefit pension plan that can be used (within limitations) to pay for the medical expenses of retired employees and their beneficiaries.

Medicare Advantage plans are health plan options under Medicare where the beneficiary gets all Medicare-covered health care benefits through the plan, including hospital, home health, physician, and, if chosen, prescription drugs. Called Part C plans, they often provide extra benefits such as vision and dental and lower copays than Medicare fee-for-service. The beneficiary may pay a premium for the MA plan, in addition to the Part B (physician insurance) premium.

Economic Theory and Methodology

Utility function is a mathematical formulation for quantifying the satisfaction of wants and needs achieved through consumption, status, or ownership or the worsening of individual welfare through the exertions and risks of consumption, work or investing.

Risk aversion is when a consumer or investor values a certain income or wealth holding more than an equal amount that involves risk or uncertainty.

Constant relative risk aversion (CRRA) is a particular mathematical formulation of a utility function (power form) showing risk aversion such that, no matter the level of income or wealth being analyzed, consumers and investors with the same coefficient of risk aversion will make the same choices in trade-off situations, and choices in one time period do not affect choices in another time period. A lower value of RRA means more risk tolerance.

Elasticity of intertemporal substitution (EIS) measures the degree of substitutability of consumption across time. A lower value means that the consumer is more concerned about consumption smoothing from year to year because fluctuations are painful.

The *life cycle hypothesis* explains how households decide to split their income between spending and saving and how much they borrow over the adult lifetimes of the households. In particular, it rationalizes the observation that income fluctuates more than consumption does and posits that all financial and real assets should be spent by the end of life. If there is a *bequest motive*, however, then households want to leave inheritances for their progenies, and therefore not all assets are consumed by the end of life.

Real wealth balances are financial assets held by a household, adjusted by the consumer price index to normalize the consumption opportunity represented by those balances.

Liquidity is the ability of an individual or business to quickly convert assets into cash without incurring a considerable loss.

Equilibrium is the state that exists when opposing forces (such as buyers and sellers) exactly offset each other and there is no inherent tendency for change. An equilibrium, while stable, may not be optimal socially. In models of insurance buying and selling, with asymmetric information, there may be a *separating equilibrium*, where one group is constrained from buying all the insurance coverage it wants, at any price. By contrast, in these models, a *pooling equilibrium* is generally better, where all groups are quoted the same price and terms of coverage.

A *vector autoregression (VAR)* is an econometric model that estimates the evolution and interdependence between multiple time series. All the variables in a VAR are treated symmetrically by including for each variable an equation explaining its evolution, based on its own lags and the lags of all the other variables in the model. A VAR is a relatively theory-free way to estimate economic relationships.

An *ordered logistic regression* is a regression model for ordinal (1,2,3, . . .) dependent variables. An example of a multiple ordered response is an opinion survey with responses ranging from "strongly agree" to "strongly disagree." A logistic regression is used to estimate the probability of occurrence of an event or result by fitting data to a logistic curve.

Monte Carlo simulation is a technique used to approximate the probability of certain outcomes by running multiple trial runs, called simulations, using random variables.

Variance is a measure of variability based on squared deviations of individual observations from the mean value of the empirical probability distribution. Its square root is the *standard deviation*.

Insurance and Financial Planning

A *life annuity* is an agreement by an insurer or pension plan to make periodic payments that continue during the survival of the annuitant(s). If there are no further benefits after the death of the annuitant, it is a *straight life annuity*. If payments are made for either the life of the annuitant or a guaranteed period, it is a *life annuity with period certain*, or if at least until a guaranteed amount has been paid, it is a *life annuity with refund*. A *joint-and-survivor annuity* is a series of payments for the life of the insured and an annuity (not necessarily for the same payment level) for the life of a named beneficiary, generally a spouse. The *life care annuity* combines lifetime income payments with increased payments if the insured is disabled with an inability to perform at least two activities of daily living (ADLs) or is cognitively impaired.

An *immediate annuity* begins its payments immediately or within a year. A *deferred annuity*, by contrast, serves mainly as an asset accumulation vehicle, with or without automatic conversion into an income payment stream after several years.

A *fixed annuity* provides a guaranteed minimum interest rate, sometimes with the potential for crediting higher interest rates if conditions allow. By contrast, a *variable annuity* allows the owner or participant to allocate the account among several investment funds, so that the account value, and eventually the income payment flow, will vary with market conditions.

Single-premium annuities are bought into once, generally with a significant amount of money. By contrast, *multiple-premium* annuities require more than one premium payment, and *flexible-premium* annuities allow several or few investments in the policy, at any time.

Adverse selection is the tendency of individuals who believe they have a greater-than-average likelihood of loss to seek insurance protection to a greater extent than do those who believe they have an average or a less-than-average likelihood of loss.

Underwriting is the process of identifying and classifying the degree of risk represented by a proposed insured.

Activities of daily living (ADLs) are everyday functions—specifically, bathing, continence, dressing, eating, toileting, and transferring—that individuals usually do without assistance.

Long-term care (LTC) refers to a variety of services used by the elderly, the disabled, and persons with chronic health or mental impairment issues who need assistance with the ADLs. It can be provided at home, in the community, in an assisted living facility, or in a nursing home.

The *elimination period* is a type of deductible. It is the length of time the insured must pay for long-term care services before the insurance policy begins to make payments.

The *benefit period* is the length of time that a long-term care insurance policy will pay the daily benefit that the policy owner chooses.

Inflation indexation provides for increases in benefit levels according to a specified cost-of-living index.

Systematic withdrawal is a method of withdrawing funds from an investment account in specified amounts or percentages for a specified payment frequency (often monthly).

Adjusted gross income (AGI) is the total annual income such as wages and dividends minus certain federal income tax deductions such as contributions to a 401(k) account.

Aggressive portfolio is an investment fund allocated almost entirely to equities.

Asset allocation is an investment strategy that splits up a portfolio's assets to different asset classes and types, according to the investor's goals, risk tolerance, and, sometimes, investment horizons.

A *baby boomer* is an individual born between 1946 and 1964.

Exclusion ratio is the portion of the return on a payment from an after-tax annuity that is not taxed because it represents a return of the initial investment.

Life expectancy is the length of time a person of a given age (and often a given demographic group) is expected to live.

Notes

1. See Brown, Mitchell, Poterba, and Warshawsky (2001).

2. See Brown, Mitchell, and Poterba (2001).

3. Some of the material here about long-term care insurance is based on an excellent description of its historical development and current features in a discussion in the Society of Actuaries (2005), especially the remarks of Dawn Helwig, a prominent actuary in the field.

4. Nonforfeiture means the benefit is provided even if the policy lapses.

5. See Brown and Finkelstein (2008).

6. See Murtaugh, Kemper, and Spillman (1995).

7. See Mitchell, Poterba, Warshawsky, and Brown (1999).

8. Insurers are not allowed, however, to advertise this state protection, as banks do with FDIC insurance.

9. See Watson Wyatt Worldwide (2009, figure 7).

10. See Warshawsky (2001) for analysis of more detailed proposed provisions.

References

Brown, Jeffrey R., and Amy Finkelstein. 2008. The Interaction of Public and Private Insurance: Medicaid and the Long-Term Care Insurance Market. *American Economic Review* 98 (3): 1083–1102.

Brown, Jeffrey R., Olivia Mitchell, and James M. Poterba. 2001. The Role of Real Annuities and Indexed Bonds in an Individual Accounts Retirement Program. In *Risk Aspects of Investment-Based Social Security Reform*, ed. John Y. Campbell and Martin Feldstein. Chicago: University of Chicago Press.

Brown, Jeffrey R., Olivia S. Mitchell, James M. Poterba, and Mark J. Warshawsky. 2001. *The Role of Annuity Markets in Financing Retirement*. Cambridge, MA: MIT Press.

Mitchell, Olivia, James Poterba, Mark Warshawsky, and Jeffrey R. Brown. 1999. New Evidence on the Money's Worth of Individual Annuities. *American Economic Review* 89 (5): 1299–1318.

Murtaugh, Christopher, Peter Kemper, and Brenda Spillman. 1995. Risky Business: Long-Term Care Insurance Underwriting. *Inquiry* 32 (3): 271–284.

Society of Actuaries. 2005. The Basics of Long-Term-Care Insurance. *Record* 31 (1): 1–29.

Warshawsky, Mark. 2001. Further Reform of Minimum Distribution Requirements for Retirement Plans. *Tax Notes* 91 (2): 297–306.

Watson Wyatt Worldwide. 2009. *Managing Defined Contribution Plans in the Current Environment.* Arlington, VA: Watson Wyatt Worldwide.

2   Recent Developments in Life Annuity Markets and Products

Introduction

The change in the nature of predominant retirement plans in the United States, in particular, the movement from traditional defined benefit (DB) pension plans to individual account plans like 401(k) and hybrid plans, is well known. The former generally pay out benefits as a life annuity, while the latter pay out benefits as a lump sum. But plan sponsors, financial advisors, and public policymakers are just beginning to consider how to assist plan participants in the distribution phase as more and more workers retire with individual accounts as their sole formal source of retirement support outside of Social Security.

According to the U.S. Bureau of Labor Statistics (BLS), the share of private industry full-time workers covered by DB plans remained at around 23 percent over the 1999–2009 period (and was 87 percent for state and local government workers in 2007). Other data from various sources, however, indicate that an increasing number of these private sector workers are in frozen plans. For example, the BLS reports that in March 2009, 20 percent of full-time workers covered by a DB plan were in a frozen plan. More familiarly, the percentage of all private industry full-time workers participating in defined contribution (DC) plans increased from 42 percent in 1999 to 51 percent in 2009. Moreover, according to data reported by the Employee Benefit Security Administration of the Department of Labor, in 2007 (latest data available), almost 25 percent of active participants in DB plans were in cash

This chapter is based on, and updates, the article of the same title that was published in *Benefits Quarterly* 23 (2) (Second Quarter 2007): 46–57. This article is used with permission and originally appeared in the Second Quarter 2007 issue of *Benefits Quarterly*, © 2007 International Society of Certified Employee Benefit Specialists Inc.

balance plans, which are based on individual accounts and usually pay out benefits as a lump sum.

Overall, there seems to be an increased demand by employees for portability and participation in investment performance, liquidity, and choice. Yet we also know from other sources that workers, especially older ones, appreciate security and guidance. Hence, it is a fair inference to draw from these trends that there will (or should) be an increased need for formal individual distribution mechanisms from retirement accounts, which currently do not generally give much assistance or structure in that phase. This is in contrast to traditional DB plans, which are designed to, and typically do, pay retirement benefits in the form of a life annuity.[1]

The other major, indeed nearly universal, source of lifetime inflation-indexed retirement income, Social Security, is in need of reform. It is running a long-run financial imbalance at 3.4 percent of covered payroll as of 2009. According to some analysts, advance-funding the program is an appropriate and intergenerationally fair policy, given the prospect of the retirement of the large baby boom generation. Many people are uncomfortable, however, with the accumulation of large government-owned trust funds, especially invested in private securities. Hence, many reform proposals include personal individual accounts, either as carve-outs from the DB formula of Social Security or as add-ons—either compulsory or voluntary, sometimes with incentives given. Therefore, here too there would be a need for some formal individual distribution mechanisms to provide for the retirement income security needs of households.[2]

The traditional immediate life annuity product, which pays a stream of payments for the life (or lives) of the insured in exchange for a single or stream of premiums, could serve either entirely or partially as such a distribution mechanism. It has the highly desirable advantage, documented in many places and ways, of ensuring that the insured cannot outlive his or her assets. Stated in another manner, the life annuity should produce a higher stream of income than available from other unpooled assets of similar return and risk characteristics. There are documented cost issues with this product that reduce this advantage; in particular, individual immediate annuities are subject to adverse selection, that is, the tendency of individuals with higher-than-average mortality expectations, owing, say, to poor health, to avoid their purchase.[3] Nevertheless it is becoming increasingly clear that a life annuity needs to be included in at least part of the retirement planning strategic choices of households with individual accounts.

This chapter reviews recent developments in markets for traditional life annuities and describes some new products. In particular, it looks at trends in, and the volatility over time of, daily simulated and actual market quotes of fixed lifetime monthly payments from single-premium immediate annuities (SPIAs) issued for $100,000. It then explains how another traditional immediate annuity product—the variable immediate annuity—works, making the initial payout fixed across time of issuance, but introducing subsequent volatility in the stream of lifetime payouts. The chapter then considers and explains briefly some new life annuity products and features that make the life annuity more flexible or comprehensive: inflation-indexed, enhanced liquidity, individual "defined benefit," and lifelong distribution products. The chapter also contains a brief summary of an idea for a new integrated annuity product with long-term care insurance that has been proposed elsewhere. It concludes with a brief analysis of the possible implications of these trends in markets and products for retirement plan design, policy, and strategy.

Single-Premium Nominal Immediate Life Annuities

Research has shown that one of the most effective ways to reduce the risk of outliving one's retirement assets is by converting at least some of those assets at some older age to a fixed life annuity.[4] To do so, a DC plan participant could use her account balance to buy an SPIA in the commercial marketplace. But the open-market cost of annuities is volatile, making such purchases subject to considerable timing risk, as I show below. In addition, as interest rates have declined over the past two decades in the United States, the purchasing power of a set account balance has similarly declined.[5] And, unlike in employer-sponsored pension plans where, since a 1983 Supreme Court decision, equal payout benefits for otherwise exactly situated men and women workers are mandated, women must pay more than men do for life annuities in the commercial market.

The analysis uses a pricing simulation model for SPIAs based on the projected mortality of purchasers of individual annuities, by gender, and the ever-changing term structure of interest rates on Treasury securities.[6] The cost of adverse selection is reflected through the use of annuitant mortality rates. Research indicates that this model at least approximates the practices of many single-premium immediate annuity issuers, as indeed it must in a competitive commercial market for insurance products and financial instruments.[7] The advantage of using the simulation model is that historical information is thereby estimated in the absence of actual price quotes. Moreover, because the actual market quotes I present are from single companies, and other research shows that different insurance companies use different pricing strategies in their businesses, simulation results may be more robust.

The basic SPIA product is quite simple. A single premium paid to a life insurance company purchases a guarantee of a fixed stream of nominal payments for the life (or lives) of the insured (insureds). In its pure form of a straight immediate annuity, there is no investment value. Common options available, however, include a guaranteed period, joint-and-survivor features of various forms, cash refund, and, for a few issuers, a fixed rate of increase in future payments.

Figure 2.1 shows the fixed monthly lifetime payout from the model-simulated SPIAs hypothetically available to 65-year-old men, women, and couples for a single premium of $100,000 issued on any day from January 3, 1983, through December 31, 2009.[8] More specifically, simulated fixed lifetime monthly payments (in nominal terms) changing daily with the issue date are shown for SPIAs (with guaranteed periods of 10 years for individuals and 20 years for couples) bought for $100,000, every business day from the beginning of 1983 to the end of 2009.

Reading figure 2.1, three important features can be readily discerned:

1. Monthly payouts from SPIAs are simulated to have declined over time. For example, at the end of May 1984, a $100,000 premium bought a monthly payout of $1,134 for a couple. By the end of June 2003, however, as interest rates fell to secular lows, the same $100,000 bought only $503 in fixed monthly lifetime benefits. At the end of June 2006, $100,000 bought a somewhat higher monthly payment of $573, as long-term rates rose a bit, even as the Federal Reserve raised short-term rates significantly. Thereafter, monthly fixed payment guarantees continued around $520 to $550 until the dramatic events of the recent global financial crisis. By December 30, 2008, the fixed monthly lifetime payment on newly issued SPIAs had dropped to only $417 before recovering throughout 2009 to the $500 level. The short-term big dip was the result of the flight to quality by investors and the resulting

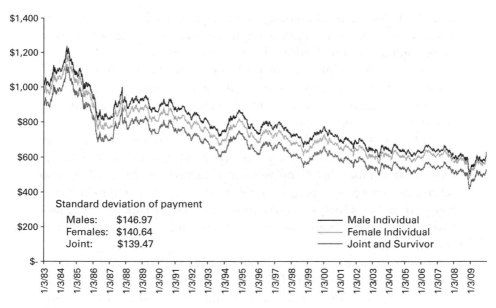

Figure 2.1
Monthly fixed lifetime payment per $100,000 single-premium nominal immediate life annuity, daily simulations: 1/3/83 to 12/31/09. *Source:* Towers Watson

extremely low Treasury bond yields. The long secular decline in payment levels owes to the general decline in yields, as well as the slowly but steadily increasing longevity of older people.

2. Monthly payouts to women are lower than those to men for the same premium because of women's longer life expectancy. For example, in May 2006, a male retiree would receive $667 monthly versus $637 for a woman for a newly issued $100,000 SPIA.

3. Buying a SPIA carries considerable short-term timing risk or scope for regret. For example, from the end of June 1984 to the end of June 1985, the monthly lifetime payments a couple could buy for $100,000 declined from $1,119 to $893—a difference in annual income owing to purchases one year apart of $2,712.

Figure 2.1 also shows a formal measure of the volatility of SPIA fixed lifetime payouts over this time period. The standard deviation, which measures the dispersion of a series of numbers around the mean, in the same unit of measurement as those numbers, was calculated to measure timing risk. For the joint-and-survivor SPIA, for example, the standard deviation is $139, meaning that across this time period, changes of that magnitude for the fixed lifetime monthly payment from an issued life annuity from the mean monthly payment over the whole period were fairly common and well within the range of experience.

Perhaps a more intuitive way of conveying volatility is by subtracting the monthly payouts from SPIAs purchased in a particular day from the payouts from SPIAs purchased one year earlier and calculating the percentage change. For example, assume that Jane bought a SPIA for herself and her husband with $100,000 from her 401(k) account at age 65. Mary, one year older, who worked in the office next to Jane's for many years and earned the same salary, also retired at age 65 and bought a SPIA for herself and her husband just year earlier. (This is a fairly direct way of measuring regret and frustration arising from timing risk.) This measure of volatility is shown in figure 2.2.

Looking at figure 2.2, we see considerable volatility (and scope for regret). By waiting one year, from the end of March 1985 to the end of March 1986, Jane lost 27.4 percent in monthly fixed lifetime income compared with her former colleague. Comparing the last day of May 2006 to the last day of May 2005, by contrast, Jane beat Mary by 10.9

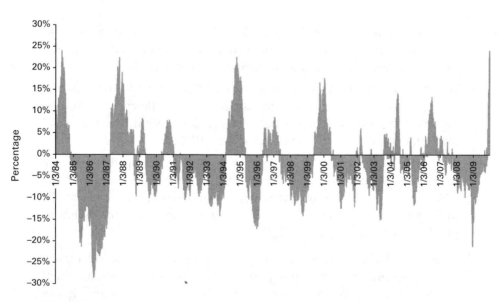

Figure 2.2
One-year difference in monthly fixed lifetime payments from single-premium nominal immediate joint-and-survivor life annuity, daily simulations, 1/3/84 to 12/31/09. *Source:* Towers Watson

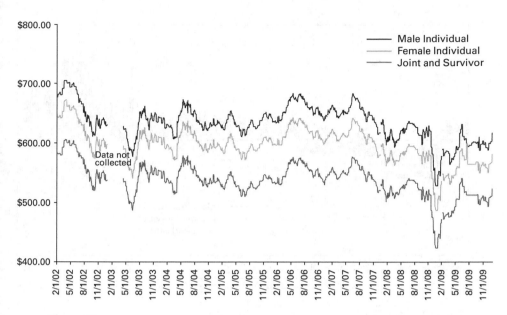

Figure 2.3
Monthly fixed lifetime payments per $100,000 premium, single-premium nominal imme-
diate life annuity, daily Internet quotes, AAA-rated life insurance company, 2/1/02 to
12/31/09. *Source*: Towers Watson

percent, as the Fed's policy of rate increases finally affected long-term
interest rates somewhat. Quite recently, Jane would have 24 percent
more income for life than Mary if they retired one year apart on the
same dates (December 30) in 2009 and 2008, respectively.

Figure 2.3 shows the fixed monthly payments quoted daily for
newly issued life annuities since February 2002 over the Internet by
a highly rated life insurance company for $100,000 SPIAs with the
same product characteristics as those simulated above. We see similar
volatility and overall trends as in the simulations shown in figure 2.1
over a comparable time period, in particular the drop in the depth
of the financial crises, illustrating directly that our simulation model
seems to be a broadly realistic view of the commercial individual
SPIA market.

Figure 2.4 shows one measure comparing the simulation model to
actual SPIA quotes—the ratio of the actual payments quoted to payments simulated. In the literature on this topic, this ratio is often called
money's worth. A ratio of one is interpreted as a fair deal because
it shows a reasonable reflection of the product's cost of production

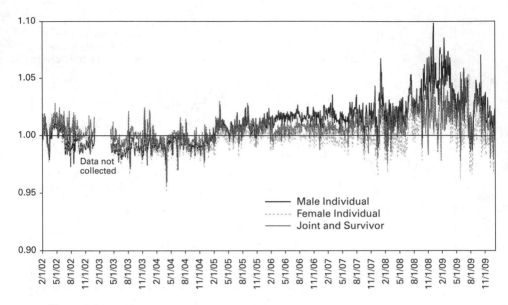

Figure 2.4
Daily money's worth ratios, single-premium nominal immediate life annuity (actual payment/simulated payment), 2/1/02 to 12/31/09. *Source:* Towers Watson

and risk properties, at least in the view of the underlying simulation model's assumptions. Any marketing and administrative costs, buildup of reserves, and company profit margins are likely covered by the ability of the insurance company to invest at rates more favorable than the rates on Treasury securities we assume in our simulation. The money's worth indeed averaged just above one for this time period and for this particular issuing insurance company, indicating a fair deal, although adverse selection still adds to the cost when considered from the vantage of the general population, rather than life annuity purchasers. During the extremely volatile market conditions of late fall 2008 and early 2009, however, this particular issuer allowed its quotes on certain days to increase relative to deemed fair value, so that although absolute payments were dropping to all-time lows, relative values were increasing to all-time highs. Among possible explanations for this behavior are pricing inertia on the part of the issuer, the simplicity of the simulation model missing important characteristics, or a view by the issuer that the extreme market conditions then occurring were temporary. By the end of 2009, more typical pricing relationships were returning.

Variable Immediate Life Annuities

Another traditional immediate annuity product is the variable immediate life annuity. It has been marketed since the early 1950s, although outside of a particular large DC pension system, sales volume is small. The variable annuity functions like a SPIA, with similar features and options, but its income payments are not fixed over the lifetime of the annuitant. Rather, payments vary (as frequently as monthly or as slowly as annually) over the lifetime of the annuitant, with the investment performance of the underlying asset portfolio selected by the annuitant.

Initial income from the variable annuity is determined by an assumed investment return (AIR), selected by the annuitant, generally between 3.5 and 5.0 percent. For example, for one insurance company, the following are initial monthly lifetime payments quoted to a 65-year-old man on February 24, 2010: $668.94 variable for a 5 percent AIR, $583.50 variable for a 3.5 percent AIR, compared to $626.58 fixed for a SPIA. The lower the AIR, the more likely and more significantly future payments will increase. The higher the AIR, the larger the initial payment. For the same AIR, though, the initial payment will not change over time given the same premium. Obviously variable annuity payments will be more volatile over the lifetime of the annuitant than a fixed annuity; the degree of volatility and expected return will depend on the specific asset portfolio selected. It is possible to change these asset allocations at any time, even during the payout phase, typically only with mutual fund-like restrictions on frequent trading and market timing.

In addition to a state premium tax and annual charges for the investment account (like mutual fund charges), the average industry charge for mortality and guarantee expenses, that is, "insurance charges," for variable life annuities is 1.22 percent.

New Life Annuity Products and Features

Recently there have been a number of innovations in annuity products. Some of these innovations are incremental changes in product design, while others represent complex financial engineering arrangements.

Inflation-Indexed Annuities

A straightforward product development that, however, had to await the issuance in the late 1990s and early 2000s of Treasury inflation-protected securities (TIPS) in the United States is the inflation-indexed life annuity. This annuity is essentially a SPIA, with the same features and options as a fixed life annuity, but whose income payments track the Consumer Price Index (CPI). Apparently several companies are now issuing inflation-indexed annuities in the U.S. market. In the United Kingdom, these products have been issued for more than two decades by a few companies, consistent with the greater length of time that the U.K. government has issued "gilt linkers."

More specifically, for one large insurance company in the United States, payments are adjusted each year on January 1 for changes in the nonseasonally adjusted CPI-U, a cost-of-living index. No decrease will ever reduce the payment below the initial benefit amount. Any negative changes in the CPI not applied to the payment, however, will be used to offset future CPI increases. For example, on February 24, 2010, this company quoted over the Internet an initial monthly lifetime payment of $453.39 for an inflation-indexed annuity purchased with $100,000 in a single premium by a 65-year-old man; this may be compared to $626.58 for a fixed SPIA issued by the same company on that date.

Figures 2.5 through 2.8 for the inflation-indexed annuity correspond to figures 2.1 through 2.4 for the nominal SPIA. Clearly a shorter time period is covered as the TIPS market did not exist until the late 1990s. Figures 2.5 and 2.6 show that simulated volatility and scope for regret in initial inflation-indexed monthly payments picked up and the general level of payments declined as the TIPS market itself developed and rates on TIPS declined, particularly following the announcement of the permanence of TIPS issuance by the U.S. Treasury in 2002. During the global financial crisis, the simulations show a significant increase in estimated monthly initial payments on newly issued inflation-indexed annuities during fall 2008 as TIPS bond yields rose in response to a drop in investor demand as deflation developed. Thereafter conditions began to return to normal, with occasional bounces, but overall these movements produced a big jump in volatility and year-over-year differences.

Figure 2.7 shows Internet quotes for inflation-indexed life annuities issued by one large insurance company over the period since its issuance began, in February 2005, while figure 2.8 gives the corresponding money's worth ratios. We see the jump-up in promised payments, inflation-indexed, for newly issued annuities in late 2008, reflecting market conditions. In August 2009, there is a large but short-lived drop in monthly payments for this company. The money's

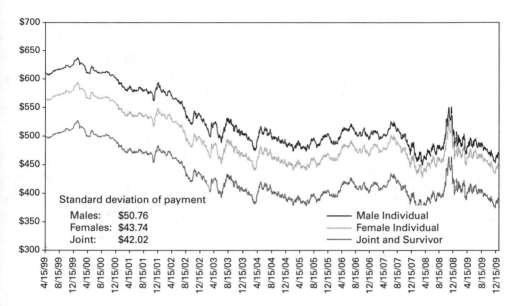

Figure 2.5
Monthly inflation-indexed lifetime payment per $100,000 single-premium, inflation-indexed, immediate life annuity, daily simulations, 4/15/99 to 12/31/09. *Source:* Towers Watson

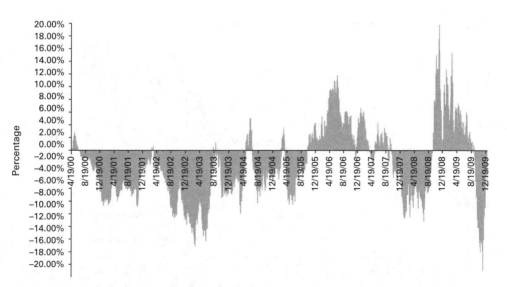

Figure 2.6
One-year differences in monthly inflation-indexed lifetime payments from single-premium joint-and-survivor inflation-indexed immediate life annuity, daily simulations, 4/19/00 to 12/31/09. *Source:* Towers Watson

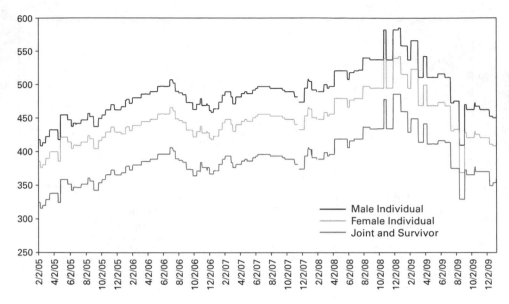

Figure 2.7
Monthly inflation-indexed lifetime payments per $100,000 premium, single-premium inflation immediate life annuity, daily Internet quotes, highly-rated life insurance company, 2/2/05 to 12/31/09. *Source:* Towers Watson

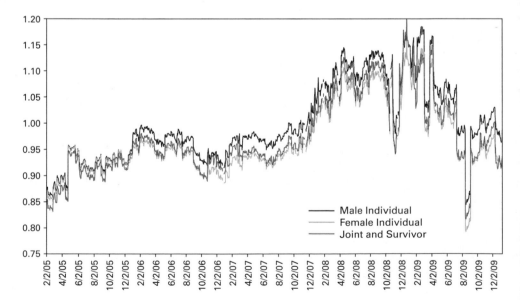

Figure 2.8
Daily money's worth ratios, single-premium inflation-indexed immediate life annuity (actual payment/simulated payment) 02/02/05 to 12/31/09. *Source:* Towers Watson

worth ratio has averaged at 0.98, but there has been a lot of volatility around that, perhaps owing to changes in pricing policy for a new product, some incompleteness in our model, or unstable market conditions. The average ratio, especially if late 2008 and early 2009 are excluded, is consistent with what has been found in the U.K. market for inflation-indexed annuities; that the ratio is lower than in the nominal market may be explained by a lack of inflation-indexed corporate bonds to afford more competitive annuity rate quotes.

Enhanced Liquidity

Another recent innovation in individual immediate life annuity products is the offering of enhanced liquidity, that is, the ability to convert some of the value of the stream of income payments into a lump-sum payment after the start of payment flows. There is the risk to the issuing company of some additional, dynamic, adverse selection from such provisions that presumably are reflected in product pricing (and hence it is unclear how much better in terms of income these products are than partial annuitization), but liquidity is indeed a strong desire among plan participants.

For example, for a fixed life annuity, one insurance company offers a product with the following features. It allows for the withdrawal, on a one-time-only basis, of 30 percent of the expected present value of the remaining payments, based on life expectancy factors set at the time when the annuity was purchased. The option can be exercised only on the fifth, tenth, or fifteenth anniversaries of the first payment from the life annuity or on a significant, nonmedical, financial loss. Once the option is exercised, future income payments are reduced by 30 percent. The insurance company calculates the present value for the withdrawal amount by adjusting the interest rate at the time of purchase so as to pass through to the annuitant, on an approximate basis, any capital gains or losses experienced by bonds held in the general investment account of the insurance company.

Another company gives enhanced liquidity for its variable immediate life annuity only in a qualified plan or IRA. It allows withdrawals of present value through a period set for life expectancy at the time of purchase. The original single premium is divided into two parts representing the present value of annuity payments before and after the year of life expectancy, respectively. The first part is essentially a benefit for a guaranteed period of the length of life expectancy where an acceleration of payments occurs. The second part, which is available only for the first five years of the contract, is a withdrawal of the present value of annuity payments after life expectancy, but on a declining scale over the five years. Because no proof of health status or explicit individual liquidity draw needs to be demonstrated, the company is clearly exposed to some additional adverse selection.

Individual Defined Benefit Pensions

These products are actually deferred annuities, but unlike most other individual deferred annuities currently marketed, individual defined benefit pensions are expected to be distributed as life annuities and not as lump sums. These products have cash values, that is, the market values in the policy can be distributed or transferred to another asset product, unlike pure-form deferred life annuities, which have no cash value and can be distributed as a life annuity only on a set date, age, or retirement.

One company offers a fixed income product, purchased with a single premium or through regularly scheduled premium payments lasting up to thirty years. Income payments will begin on a predetermined fixed date as soon as ten years from the date the annuity was issued, beginning as early as age 55. The level of future income payments is determined based on the age of the annuitant and prevailing interest rates at the time premium payments are made; the interest crediting rate is guaranteed to be at least 3 percent. The interest rate credited on April 4, 2006, for example, was 4 percent. The cash value of the life annuity prior to the start date for income payments is 87.5 percent of premium payments accumulated at 3 percent interest.

Another insurance company offers an annuity product that, in explicit intent, is designed to replicate many of the features of a traditional DB pension plan but is offered as an investment option for a 401(k) plan as a group variable annuity. Each contribution to the product purchases a specific amount of guaranteed retirement income. The income is not received, however, unless the policyholder annuitizes on or after the 401(k) plan's stated retirement age. Transfers and withdrawals are allowed, according to general 401(k) and specific plan rules, but any withdrawals from the annuity reduce guaranteed retirement income in proportion to the account value removed. The guarantee is preserved, however, if there is a rollover to an individual variable annuity offered by the insurance company.

Contributions to this product are invested in a fund that mimics a large corporate pension trust. There is an annual investment charge, as well as annual guarantee charges. Prior to retirement, the account value reflects the investment performance of the funds, less the charges just mentioned. After retirement, the guaranteed income payments are made (there is no cash value then) based on the age of the annuitant and the account balance; the income payments can increase if investment performance exceeds the benchmarks, as in an immediate variable life annuity.

Lifelong Distribution

Lifelong distribution, later called a guaranteed minimum withdrawal benefit, is an increasingly common option offered on individual deferred variable annuities. It is not a life annuity distribution; there is still cash value even in the distribution phase. Nevertheless, there is an aspect of life contingencies for the issuing company that is covered by a separate charge, as will be explained below.[9]

As a prototypical example, one company guarantees a 5 percent annual stream of withdrawals for life or 7 percent for at least 14.2 years based on an account value, which is the greater of:

1. The initial balance compounded at 5 percent for ten years from the initial election of the option or until the first withdrawal, if sooner,

2. The highest anniversary value for the first ten years or until the first withdrawal, if sooner, or

3. The account value at first withdrawal.

Only certain asset investment fund combinations are allowed when the option is selected.

As early as three years after income withdrawals begin, and for every three years thereafter, if investment performance causes an increase in the account value, the protected account value and the withdrawal stream will increase. The protected account value is reduced by the amounts withdrawn until it reaches zero. If the amounts withdrawn are cumulatively equal to the 5 percent stream of withdrawals, then the insured must choose whether to receive 5 percent income payments for life or, at the 7 percent level, for the remainder of the 14.2 years. This insurance company currently charges annually for this distribution option—60 basis points for an individual and 75 basis points for a couple—in addition to the regular insurance and investment charges that a policyholder will have to pay for a variable annuity bought from this insurance company.

An Idea to Integrate the Life Annuity with Long-Term Care Insurance

I have put forward a product innovation idea to reduce the adverse selection inherent in immediate life annuities, while simultaneously improving a market failure of sorts in the market for long-term care insurance (LTCI).[10] This product, called a life care annuity, would integrate an SPIA with a significant pop-up benefit (ideally a cash, and not an indemnity, approach) when the annuitant becomes disabled with the common triggers found in LTCI policies (unable to perform two of the six activities of daily living or cognitively impaired).

This integration would substantially reduce the need for, and the cost of, LTCI underwriting, allowing retirees currently shut out from LTCI—as many as a third of the population—to get coverage. And it is precisely the attraction to the integrated product of those adversely affected by underwriting that enables a reduction in adverse selection for the life annuity segment, thereby increasing the income stream payable by about 5 percent. Empirical research has established these findings. Indeed, this "pooling equilibrium" should be self-sustaining, that is, superior to competing products offered to particular segments of the risk pool. Moreover, some flexibility in product design is appropriate to reflect geographical differences in the cost of care, to add desirable inflation-indexing features, and so on.

The PPA gave this type of combination product a small tax advantage (beginning in 2010) as an after-tax annuity because, essentially, a part of the implied premium for the LTCI segment will become deductible from taxable income. This tax advantage is not yet available in a qualified retirement plan; indeed there are other regulatory and legal hurdles for the life care annuity in a qualified plan or an IRA, such as minimum distribution requirements.

Possible Implications of Empirical Results

It is still the case that activity in the immediate annuity market is quite modest. Yet the interest of public policymakers in this area is growing, evidenced by legislative proposals to incent the choice of a life annuity, by requests for information by government agencies and discussions among policy experts to require the offering of life annuity distributions in DC plans.[11] Moreover, there has been some activity among a few large DC plan sponsors in offering participants annuity buying services. And media attention to this area has increased, as, reportedly, has the interest of the large financial companies providing services in this area. But the case for the individual immediate life annuity would be even more compelling if its deficiencies were also addressed.

There are methods for dealing with the risks arising from the volatility of traditional fixed (or inflation-indexed) life annuity payouts purchased over time, that is, the timing risk of purchase. For example, one could reduce the timing risk by phasing withdrawals from the defined contribution plan and laddering purchases of life annuities over a few years. But this approach, done on one's own, requires discipline and knowledge and, most significant, the ability to finance consumption in retirement from other sources in the phase-in period. Another way to manage timing risk would be to defer annuitization until interest rates peaked. This approach perhaps requires even more discipline, liquidity, hold-out ability, and, especially, market knowledge than the first one.

Alternatively, the plan participant could reallocate assets as retirement draws near, shifting more assets to long-duration bonds, whose prices move inversely to interest rates. This is the defining feature of life cycle or target-date mutual funds, which are indeed becoming more popular investments for participants in DC plans. But, of course, at least in expectation, this method sacrifices return for the lowered risk, as compared to the steadier asset allocations with higher equity positions. Moreover, many life cycle funds also move a substantial share of assets into money market funds as retirement approaches; this feature reduces the natural hedging benefits of the product for the purchase of a life annuity. Variable immediate annuities, whose monthly payouts vary with returns on a participant-chosen underlying asset portfolio, avoid the point-in-time risk of purchasing fixed annuities. The downside, however, is the pushing of income volatility toward the entire retirement period, at the end of the life cycle, where it may be particularly hard to bear. A few plan sponsors allow participants to transfer their 401(k) account balances to the sponsor's DB plan, sometimes on favorable terms, thus securing a life annuity with a fixed payment level. This approach helps avoid marketing costs of individual products, but it still generally leaves the risks arising from interest rate changes to the plan participant.

Policymakers are examining the need to encourage the use of life annuities by participants in defined contribution plans. A small step in that direction was taken in the recently enacted PPA, whereby an old Department of Labor regulation requiring plan sponsors to use the safest available annuity was vacated. It is thought that giving less restrictive standards will engender more competition in the market for life annuities for plan sponsors, thereby encouraging the use of life annuities in defined contribution plans. It is unclear, however, whether this legal change will be sufficient to effect much change in the behavior of plan sponsors, particularly because they are still subject to uncertain, but continual, fiduciary responsibilities in the selection and use of specific annuity providers.

With the passage of time and rising demand by baby boomers, other enhanced formal lifelong distribution programs and products are being created, as we have described, and still others will be created. And these products must be evaluated as to the value of the enhancements and extra features, especially whether these new products are desirable to and understandable by plan participants, compared to their costs and other alternatives.

Notes

1. Even in traditional DB plans, however, there has been a trend away from life annuity payments and toward lump-sum distributions, because, in part, the law prior to the passage of the Pension Protection Act (PPA) in 2006 encouraged lump sums by requiring the use of abnormally low interest rates for purposes of calculating legal-minimum lump-sum distributions if allowed by the plan. Under the PPA, going forward sponsors of defined benefit plans will calculate lump-sum distributions using a corporate bond spot curve rather than long-term Treasury rates. Because corporate bond rates are almost always higher than long-term Treasury rates, lump sums are likely to go lower. When these issues emerge into the awareness of participants, it is possible that life annuity choices in DB plans will increase.

2. See Warshawsky (2001).

3. This tendency increases the cost of annuities by about 10 percentage points compared to a life annuity provided to the entire distribution of mortality expectations (general population), according to several research studies, including Mitchell, Poterba, Warshawsky, and Brown (1999). This is aside from the usual marketing and sales costs and margins for profits and reserves, and the need to search for the best value. Deferred annuities also have extra insurance charges. Some indication of the reliability of the promise by the issuing insurance company to pay future income benefits may be given by the rated claims-paying ability of the company. The insured limits of the various state guarantee funds, where the annuity product is backed explicitly by the general account of the insurance company, are also a relevant consideration.

4. A good demonstration and explanation of the risk-reduction properties for retirement distributions of the fixed life annuity was found at www.fidelityresearchinstitute.com/_pdf/Beyond_Conventional_Wisdom.pdf viewed in November 2006. For a more formal demonstration, see Pang and Warshawsky (2010).

5. The obverse of this trend—that the market value of accrued benefits in traditional defined benefit plans has increased in the last few years as interest rates have declined—was described in Watson Wyatt (2005).

6. See Soares and Warshawsky (2004).

7. That being said, there is still some variance in prices across insurer issuers at any given time.

8. The couples have joint annuities with full benefits payable to the survivor.

9. For a more analytical and current discussion of this type of product feature, see Pang and Warshawsky (2009).

10. See Murtaugh, Spillman, and Warshawsky (2001).

11. See Brown and Warshawsky (2004).

References

Brown, Jeffrey R., and Mark J. Warshawsky. 2004. Longevity-Insured Retirement Distributions from Pension Plans: Market and Regulatory Issues. In *Private Pensions and Public Policies*, ed. William Gale, John Shoven, and Mark Warshawsky, 332–369. Washington, DC: Brookings Institution Press.

Mitchell, Olivia, James Poterba, Mark Warshawsky, and Jeffrey R. Brown. 1999. New Evidence on the Money's Worth of Individual Annuities. *American Economic Review* 89 (5): 1299–1318.

Murtaugh, Christopher, Brenda Spillman, and Mark Warshawsky. 2001. In Sickness and in Health: An Annuity Approach to Financing Long-Term Care and Retirement Income. *Journal of Risk and Insurance* 68 (2): 225–254.

Pang, Gaobo, and Mark Warshawsky. 2009. Comparing Strategies for Retirement Wealth Management: Mutual Funds and Annuities. *Journal of Financial Planning* 22 (8): 36–47.

Pang, Gaobo, and Mark Warshawsky. 2010. Optimizing the Equity-Bond-Annuity Portfolio in Retirement: The Impact of Uncertain Health Expenses. *Insurance, Mathematics and Economics* 46 (1): 198–209.

Soares, Chris, and Mark Warshawsky. 2004. Annuity Risk: Volatility and Inflation Exposure in Payments from Immediate Life Annuities. In *Developing an Annuity Market in Europe*, ed. Elsa Fornero and Elisa Luciano. London: Edward Elgar.

Warshawsky, Mark. 2001. The Market for Individual Life Annuities and the Reform of Social Security: An Update and Further Analysis. *Benefits Quarterly*, Fourth Quarter: 24–43.

Watson Wyatt Worldwide. 2005. Defined Benefit Plans Become Significantly More Valuable. *Watson Wyatt Insider*, September: 13–16.

3 Longevity-Insured Retirement Distributions: Basic Theories and Institutions

with Jeffrey R. Brown

Introduction

The method of funding retirement in the United States is in the midst of a major transition, one that is placing greater responsibility on individuals for managing their own retirement assets. The past two decades have witnessed a large shift away from defined benefit to defined contribution pension plans, a trend that appears likely to continue for the foreseeable future. According to some estimates, the average retiree's balance in 401(k) plans alone will rise tenfold over the next thirty years and will rival Social Security as the major source of retirement wealth.[1]

While defined benefit and defined contribution plans differ along many margins, one of the most important is the method of distributing retirement income. Traditional defined benefit plans typically paid benefits in the form of a life annuity and thus provided retirees with a form of insurance against outliving their resources. According to standard economic life cycle theory, this longevity insurance is quite valuable to consumers, because it provides a higher sustainable level of consumption than is available in the absence of this insurance. Defined contribution plans are much less likely to offer life annuities to retirees. Instead, they offer some form of lump-sum payment or phased withdrawal options, or a combination of these, on retirement. While these

This chapter is composed of "Longevity-Insured Retirement Distributions from Pension Plans: Market and Regulatory Issues," pp. 332–346 and 367–369 in William Gale, John Shoven, and Mark Warshawsky, eds., *Private Pensions and Public Policies* (Washington, D.C.: Brookings Institution Press, 2004) and an updated version of "Dealing with Risks of Outliving Resources in Retirement," pp. 273–276, in Dan McGill, Kyle Brown, John Haley, Syl Schieber, and Mark Warshawsky, *Fundamentals of Private Pensions*, Ninth Edition (Oxford University Press for the Pension Research Council of the Wharton School, 2010). By permission of Oxford University Press. Reprinted with permission of Brookings Institution Press.

alternative distribution methods offer retirees a high degree of flexibility and liquidity, they fail to provide a formal mechanism by which individuals can insure against the risk of outliving their resources, the central issue of this chapter. Individual responsibility for retirement asset decumulation has also emerged as a policy issue in the debate about supplementing or partially replacing the current Social Security system with an individual accounts program. The existing system is currently the primary source of annuitized income for the majority of U.S. households and is the only meaningful provider of inflation-indexed annuities. Any plans to alter the existing Social Security benefit structure could affect the desirability of alternative distribution methods from private retirement plans.

This chapter examines the extent to which individuals can and do insure themselves against longevity risk in defined contribution plans. This issue is of policy concern for several reasons. The distribution method chosen can directly affect the extent to which retirees are able to finance consumption in old age—particularly those individuals who live significantly longer than they anticipated at retirement. Also, increasing average longevity and the trend toward earlier retirement presumably make the problem of ensuring adequate resources throughout individuals' old age more widespread among the population. The adequacy of old-age income directly affects the extent of poverty rates among the elderly, a problem that is especially acute for elderly widows.[2] In addition, if individuals fail to provide adequately for old-age consumption needs, the financial pressure on means-tested social assistance programs such as SSI (Supplemental Security Income) and Medicaid could increase. Finally, the distribution method chosen can significantly affect the size of intergenerational transfers taking place in the economy and thus the wealth distribution of the next generation.

This chapter focuses on three issues. First, we review the welfare gains from annuitization that result from a standard life cycle model. We then discuss several reasons that households may choose not to annuitize despite these theoretical welfare gains, including the presence of Social Security, pricing of annuities in the market, bequest motives, inflation risk, health uncertainty, ignorance, and regulatory impediments. Third, we demonstrate that one result of the shift from defined benefit to defined contribution plans is a reduction in opportunities to annuitize retirement wealth; the majority of defined contribution plans do not offer an annuity payout option.

The Welfare Benefits of Annuitization

Annuities play a central role in the economic theory of wealth decumulation. By trading a stock of wealth for a life-contingent income stream, healthy individuals are able to sustain a higher level of consumption than in the absence of annuities and are assured that they cannot outlive this income.

Individuals who do not have access to annuitization must allocate their retirement wealth in a manner that trades off two competing risks. The first is the risk that if individuals consume too aggressively, they increase the likelihood of facing a future period in which they are alive with little or no income. The second is the risk that if individuals self-insure by setting aside enough wealth to be certain it cannot be outlived, then they risk dying with assets that could have been used to increase consumption while alive.

The economic value of annuitization in a life cycle model with uncertain lifetimes was first demonstrated in 1965, and this framework has been used extensively to value the insurance benefits of annuities.[3] The basic result is that life cycle consumers will always choose to purchase actuarially fair annuities to finance retirement consumption and, absent a bequest motive, will annuitize 100 percent of their resources.[4] The intuition for this result is straightforward: annuities pay a rate of return that is equal to the riskless rate plus a mortality premium. The mortality premium arises from the positive probability that the insured individual will not be alive to receive future payments. Because this mortality premium is always positive, the annuity rate of return strictly dominates the riskless return. In addition, because the annuity income cannot be outlived, individuals are completely insured against an outcome in which they are alive in some future state without sufficient resources to fund ordinary levels of consumption.

The welfare gains from annuitization can be put into dollar terms using an expected utility framework (interested readers will find a more formal treatment of this model in the chapter appendix). Consider a 65-year-old consumer facing an uncertain date of death, who maximizes a lifetime utility function given a fixed amount of retirement wealth. We first allow this individual to fully annuitize in an actuarially fair market, and we calculate the utility level that this individual achieves. We then take away access to the annuity market, and ask: "How much additional wealth must we give this individual to make him as well off (that is, to put him on the same expected utility curve)

Table 3.1
Annuity equivalent wealth without and with preexisting annuities

	Annuity equivalent wealth	
Coefficient of relative risk aversion	No preexisting annuities	Preexisting annuities
1	1.502	1.330
2	1.650	1.441
5	1.855	1.623
10	2.004	1.815

Source: Brown, Mitchell, and Poterba (2001)

in the absence of annuities as he would be if he were permitted to fully annuitize his wealth?"

In previous work, the ratio of nonannuitized to annuitized wealth that puts one on the same expected utility curve has been labeled as annuity equivalent wealth, (AEW).[5] For example, an AEW equal to 1.20 means that an individual would be indifferent between $120,000 of nonannuitized wealth and $100,000 of fully annuitized wealth.

The middle column of table 3.1 reports the AEW for an individual, inflation- indexed annuity purchased by a 65-year-old male with mortality expectations consistent with that of the 1933 birth cohort (which turned 65 in 1998). Because the value of annuitization rises with risk aversion, we report values of the AEW for several different levels of the risk aversion parameter in the utility function.[6] For the case of log utility (CRRA = 1), the AEW is 1.502, indicating that this consumer would be indifferent between obtaining access to a real annuity or having a 50.2 percent increase in non-annuitized wealth. For higher levels of risk aversion, the increase is even more substantial. With risk aversion of 10, having access to an actuarially fair annuity is equivalent in utility terms to a doubling of wealth.

Within this life cycle model, the gains from annuitization are substantial. Given this, economists have been somewhat puzzled by the limited extent of annuitization outside defined benefit plans and Social Security. A substantial literature has examined a number of possible explanations, which we review in the next section.

Why Don't Individuals Fully Annuitize?

Social Security, itself a real annuity, is the major asset in the portfolio of most retired individuals.[7] Because Social Security provides a minimum level of income that lasts for life, recipients are already protected against completely outliving their resources. Therefore, the benefits from additional annuitization are reduced. However, the benefits from additional annuitization do not fall to zero, because in the simple life cycle framework, 100 percent annuitization of retirement assets is still optimal in the absence of bequest motives.

The life cycle model can be adapted to account for the presence of preexisting annuities, such as Social Security. As reported in the last column of table 3.1, the gains from additional annuitization are smaller but still substantial. For example, consider the case of an individual with log utility who has $100,000 of non-annuitized wealth and is also entitled to a flow of Social Security benefits with an expected present value of $100,000. In other words, 50 percent of this individual's net worth is already annuitized. In this case, the person is indifferent between annuitizing the $100,000 of financial wealth or having $133,000 of non-annuitized wealth (or an AEW of 1.330). While this is lower than the 1.502 AEW in the absence of preexisting annuity wealth, it is nonetheless substantial. Thus, while the presence of Social Security and defined benefit pension plans may lessen the value of additional annuitization, that cannot by itself explain why individuals do not choose to annuitize all of their retirement resources.

Individual Annuity Markets Do Not Offer Actuarially Fair Prices

One important explanation for the lack of annuitization is that annuity prices are unattractive for the average person in the population. Price deviations from their actuarially fair level can be expected to arise for two basic reasons. First, insurance companies selling annuities need to cover administrative and marketing expenses and earn a competitive accounting profit. Second, to the extent that individuals who choose to annuitize have longer life expectancies than the general population, insurance companies need to adjust their prices to reflect this fact.

Friedman and Warshawsky were the first to document the extent to which private market annuity prices deviate from an actuarially fair level by calculating a money's-worth ratio using both population and annuitant mortality tables.[8] The money's-worth ratio is a measure of the expected discounted present value of future annuity payments per dollar of premium that individuals can expect to receive if they were to participate in the individual annuity market. This pricing analysis has been extended using more recent data.[9] In 1999 a 65-year-old male (female) with a mortality rate like that of actual annuitants could expect to receive approximately 97 cents (95 cents) on the dollar, when discounted using the Treasury yield curve. This suggests that administrative costs account for a 3 to 5 percent reduction in annuity payouts. However, when an annuity is valued using population-average mortality rates, a 65-year-old male (female) could expect to receive only 85 cents (87 cents) on the dollar. This suggests that adverse selection is responsible for an 8 to 12 percent reduction in annuity payouts. Therefore, to the extent that annuities are priced unattractively, it is attributable to selection effects more so than to administrative costs. Note, however, that the observed load factors are not large enough by themselves to explain the almost complete lack of annuity demand by U.S. households.

Bequest Motives and Risk Sharing within Families

The original life cycle model of annuity valuation recognized that if retirees wish to leave bequests to their children, full annuitization is no longer optimal.[10] Walliser shows that if bequests enter the utility function in a CRRA form and are weighted so that optimal bequests are about four times annual consumption, then with actuarially fair annuity markets and a risk-aversion coefficient of 2, it would be optimal to annuitize only 60 percent of one's wealth at age 65.[11] Furthermore, the optimal allocation to annuities would fall with age. Sufficiently strong bequest motives, combined with the existence of Social Security and the fact that private annuity markets are not actuarially fair, could explain the limited amount of annuitization.

An extremely large economics literature on the subject of bequest and transfer behavior has failed to come to a consensus on whether bequest motives have an important effect on household asset allocation and consumption decisions.[12] For example, Hurd shows that couples with children do not decumulate their retirement assets any slower than couples without children, and he interprets this as evidence against bequest motives.[13] In related work, Hurd estimates a bequest parameter from the consumption patterns of individuals and finds that it is not significantly different from zero.[14] On the other hand, Laitner and Juster report data on TIAA-CREF participants that is suggestive of some limited bequest behavior.[15] Bernheim suggested that individual bequest motives were strong enough that 25 percent of elderly households were overannuitized by Social Security and were purchasing life insurance to undo the effects of mandated annuitization.[16] A recent reexamination of this approach, however, suggests that this is unlikely to be the case.[17] Specific to the context of defined contribution plans, Brown reports on empirical findings from the Health and Retirement Study (HRS) that bequest motives do not appear to affect household decisions about whether to annuitize defined contribution plan balances.[18]

Even if bequests to one's children are not important determinants of annuitization behavior, it may be the case that married couples engage in a form of mortality risk sharing between themselves. Kotlikoff and Spivak show that two individuals sharing a common budget constraint can capture nearly half of the utility gains achievable through actuarially fair individual annuities.[19] Hurd also discusses a life cycle model for couples and the interaction between bequests and family self-insurance.[20] Brown and Poterba demonstrate that as a result of this risk sharing, the utility gains associated with the purchase of joint-and-survivor annuities are substantially lower than the utility gains outlined above for a single individual.[21]

Table 3.2 reports some representative results from Brown and Poterba for a married couple consisting of a 65-year-old husband and a 62-year-old wife.[22] As for the case of a single individual, the annuity equivalent wealth is calculated assuming access to actuarially fair annuities for individuals facing general population mortality tables. The main feature of these results is that the AEW for couples is significantly below that of individuals. For example, a married couple with log utility has an AEW of only 1.175, significantly below the AEW for a 65-year-old single man. Given that most individuals entering retirement are married, within-couple risk sharing may partially explain the lack of annuity demand.

Lack of Inflation Protection in Commercially Available Annuities

The results presented so far have assumed that individuals are able to obtain annuities that are not subject to inflation risk. Although the current Social Security system essentially provides real annuities by

Table 3.2
Annuity equivalent wealth for couples[a]

	Annuity equivalent wealth	
Coefficient of relative risk aversion	Nominal annuities	Real annuities
1	1.175	1.209
2	1.244	1.295
5	1.339	1.446
10	1.407	1.600

Source: Brown and Poterba (2000)
a. Assumes no preexisting annuities and the survivor benefit ratio is 0.5.

indexing benefits to the Consumer Price Index, very few opportunities outside this system to purchase annuities are protected from inflation uncertainty.

Inflation has two undesirable effects on fixed nominal annuity streams.[23] First, even modest rates of inflation will erode the real value of the income stream over time. For instance, at a 3.2 percent annual rate (which is the average U.S. inflation rate over the 1926–1997 period), the real value of a constant nominal annuity will be cut in half in twenty-two years. The erosion from a constant and expected rate of inflation, however, is easily remedied through the use of graded or escalating annuity products that increase the nominal payout by a fixed percentage each year. The second effect arises from the uncertainty about inflation. If inflation varies from year to year, then the real income available to retirees will vary, even in escalating products. When Brown, Mitchell, and Poterba extend the annuity valuation model to account for persistent inflation, they find large differences between the valuation of real versus the valuation of fixed nominal annuities.[24]

Table 3.3 presents results from Brown, Mitchell, and Poterba for single individuals facing inflation uncertainty. They considered two alternative inflation processes: one with independent draws each year (independent and identically distributed) and one in which inflation follows a stylized simple autoregressive [AR(1)] process and thus exhibits some persistence. Not surprisingly, the results indicate that inflation uncertainty reduces the value of a nominal annuity, more so when inflation is persistent. Notice that for more risk-averse individuals, the impact of inflation uncertainty is an even greater consideration.

A caveat should be added to explanations for the lack of annuity purchases invoking market imperfections (as opposed to preferences). Market imperfections can be absolute (i.e., costs of a product are so high as effectively to eliminate its consideration for most households) as well as relative (i.e., other products do the same or almost the same things as the product being examined and are less expensive). Administrative costs and incomplete inflation protection are features of most investment and insurance products and not only annuities. Hence, market imperfection explanations invoking these considerations have to claim that the problems arising from these features are more severe or important for annuities than for other somewhat similar products.

Table 3.4 demonstrates the cumulative impact of the factors mentioned so far. It reports the annuity equivalent wealth for a couple

Table 3.3
Annuity equivalent wealth (AEW) for nominal annuities with uncertain inflation

Coefficient of relative risk aversion	Individual with no preexisting annuity wealth			Individual with half of initial wealth in preexisting real annuity		
	Real annuity	Nominal annuity: i.i.d. inflation	Nominal annuity: Persistent inflation	Real annuity	Nominal annuity: i.i.d. inflation	Nominal annuity: Persistent inflation
1	1.502	1.451	1.424	1.330	1.304	1.286
2	1.650	1.553	1.501	1.441	1.403	1.366
5	1.855	1.616	1.487	1.623	1.515	1.450
10	2.004	1.592	1.346	1.815	1.577	1.451

Source: Brown, Mitchell, and Poterba (2001)

Note: The AEW for the nominal annuity is calculated under the assumption that inflation takes one of six possible values, roughly capturing the distribution of inflation outcomes over the 1926–1997 period. Inflation shocks are independent across periods in the i.i.d. (independent and identically distributed) case, and follow a stylized AR(1) process in the persistent inflation case.

Table 3.4
Annuity equivalent wealth for couples with 50 percent preexisting annuity wealth and a 12 percent load factor (money's worth = 0.88)

Coefficient of relative risk aversion	Nominal annuity with fixed 3.2 percent inflation
1	0.972
2	1.011
5	1.069
10	1.157

Source: Authors' calculations

consisting of a 65-year-old man and a 62-year-old woman who have 50 percent of their total wealth annuitized through Social Security. They are assumed to purchase a joint and 50 percent survivor annuity that is fixed in nominal terms in an environment of 3.2 percent annual inflation. In addition, due to a combination of administrative costs and selection effects, the nominal annuity is assumed to have a money's worth ratio of 0.88, that is, the couple faces a 12 percent load factor on their annuity purchase.

The results indicate that couples with low levels of risk aversion now have an annuity equivalent wealth that is close to one. In fact, for a risk-aversion coefficient of one, complete annuitization would actually lower utility.[25] For higher levels of risk aversion, the gains from annuitization are still positive, but much smaller than the gains found in a simple life cycle model of a single individual purchasing actuarially fair real annuities. These results show that while no single factor may explain the lack of annuity demand, several factors working in combination can substantially lessen or even eliminate the value of annuitization.

Health Uncertainty and the Irreversibility of Annuitization
The annuitization decision is largely irreversible. Insurance companies do not allow individuals to cancel an annuity agreement once it is in place; otherwise, adverse selection would obviously occur as individuals acquire additional information about their expected longevity. Furthermore, annuitization imposes a liquidity constraint on individuals, meaning that in each period, they have access only to that period's annuity income (and any unconsumed previous payments). Thus, if individuals face significant uncertainty about future expenditure needs, they may be reluctant to fully annuitize.

Uninsured long-term care expenditures are arguably the most important source of financial uncertainty facing most elderly retired individuals. Although Medicare, supplemented by Medigap and retiree health insurance, adequately insures a large proportion of medical expenses for most elderly Americans, it covers only 100 days of long-term care and only in certain limited circumstances, leaving this important source of financial risk uninsured for most elderly. Similarly, Medicaid imposes strict income- and asset-based eligibility tests that generally require individuals to exhaust their personal assets and apply all but a trivial amount of their income to cover nursing home expenses.

Among those age 65 and over, an estimated 60 percent will need some long-term care in their remaining lifetime.[26] Long-term care needs include critical care that must be supplied in a nursing home, as well as a less critical need for simple assistance with daily activities. According to Murtaugh and associates, current projections indicate that more than 40 percent of the 65-and-over population will spend some time in a nursing home.[27] The likelihood of spending some time in a nursing home at some point during the remainder of life increases with age (from 39 percent at age 65 to 56 percent at age 85). Murtaugh and associates estimate that the average expected stay in a nursing home among users of all ages is 2.4 years.[28] The expected stay for most is less than a year, but for almost 20 percent of users, it is more than five years. The mean number of years of nursing home use declines with age, from 2.8 years in the 65-to-74 age group to 1.9 years in the 85 and over age group.

According to the Lewin-VHI, Brookings-ICF Long-Term Care Financing Model, the average lifetime home health care use is just over 200 visits.[29] About half of those expected to use home health care will use fewer than 90 visits during their lifetime, while 12 percent can expect to use more than 730 visits.

The escalating cost of typical long-term care services presents a substantial financial risk to individuals and their families. Cohen reports that the average annual cost for a stay in a nursing home rose from $38,000 in 1995 to $44,500 by 1998.[30] Assisted living facilities currently charge, on average, $26,000 a year. It is clear that older Americans recognize health care costs as an important source of financial risk. Venti and Wise report results from the Health and Retirement Study on the question, "In thinking about your financial future, how concerned are you with health care costs?"[31] Fifty-two percent of respondents indicated a high level of concern—a significantly larger proportion than the proportion concerned with other sources of uncertainty such as job loss or financial market collapse.

Although nursing home care represents the greatest source of financial uncertainty for most elderly households, very few are insured against this risk. According to Murtaugh, Kemper, and Spillman, about 30 percent of the elderly population are unhealthy enough that current underwriting criteria would prevent the purchase of long-term care insurance.[32] Warshawsky and associates estimate that less than 8 percent of the elderly population owns an individual long-term care insurance policy, and group employer-sponsored coverage is still quite uncommon.[33] Therefore, retired individuals may be reluctant to fully annuitize their retirement resources because they wish to retain a buffer stock of wealth that they can use to pay for possible future long-term care expenses.[34]

Lack of Consumer Understanding of Annuitization

Thus far, we have been working primarily within the framework of a rational life cycle consumer who chooses an optimal consumption path with full knowledge of his or her own survival probabilities. In 1999, however, the Task Force on Annuity Messages of the American Council of Life Insurers (ACLI) concluded that "consumers have very little knowledge about annuities or understanding of how the product works."[35]

The ACLI task force conducted a number of qualitative focus groups among consumers. These groups indicated that "the term annuity is somewhat familiar to people, but many cannot define it." Furthermore, the focus group findings suggested that "virtually no consumer fully understands how a lump-sum distribution can be converted to an annuity. While older Americans are generally aware that annuities involve some type of payment stream, few really grasp how it works. Most Americans do not know that annuity payments are a combination of principal and investment return or how the insurance feature can promise these benefits for a lifetime."[36]

The report goes on to suggest that the least understood aspect of annuities is how risk sharing can allow insurers to offer lifelong income. Consumers tended to focus on the risk of dying early and therefore receiving less in return from the annuity than they paid in, while overlooking the fact that they may live longer than expected and receive much more than they paid. In fact, some consumer focus group participants equated lifetime annuity payments with gambling on their lives and believed that the odds in the gamble favored the insurance company. Viewing insurance as a source of increased risk is not consistent with the standard economic model of consumers using annuities to reduce risk by equating the marginal utility of consumption across different states of nature.

This qualitative research by ACLI suggests that consumers simply do not understand the longevity insurance benefits provided by a life annuity. Clearly, for any consumer who equates the purchase of longevity insurance with gambling, the life cycle model is unlikely to represent their preferences. Moreover, the strong desire of some individuals to control, manage, and invest wealth for its own sake, and perhaps even for some entertainment value, is not well explained by traditional economic models. Although previous work has shown that the predictions of the simple life cycle model are correlated with intended annuitization decisions on the margin, much of the variation in this decision has been left unexplained.[37] One potentially fruitful area for future research is to consider whether any behavioral models of decision making have the potential to improve our understanding of household decisions about annuitization.

Institutional Barriers and Legal Issues

Federal law categorizes employer-sponsored tax-qualified retirement plans into three categories: pension, profit-sharing, and stock bonus plans. Defined benefit plans and money purchase defined contribution plans are considered by law to be pension plans, while most 401(k) plans and other thrift-type plans are considered profit-sharing plans.[38] This distinction is important because pension plans are required to "provide systematically for the payment of definitely determinable benefits to employees over a period of years, usually for life, after retirement."[39] Defined benefit and money purchase plans typically meet this requirement by providing a life annuity as the normal form of payment.[40]

By contrast, 401(k) plans and other profit-sharing or stock bonus plans are not required to offer an annuity as a payout option. Hence, plans that we generally refer to as defined contribution plans, with the minor exception of money purchase plans, are not required by federal law to offer life annuities to participants. Indeed, as we show in the next section, most defined contribution plans do not offer such an option to their employees.

Although most defined contribution plans are not required to offer annuities, there are no explicit legal constraints against doing so. Several possible reasons arising from the legal and regulatory environment, however, may discourage sponsors of defined contribution plans from offering annuities. The first reason is the increase in administrative complexity that offering an annuity brings. Since 1984 federal law has required all retirement plans that provide life annuities to pay these benefits automatically to married employees in the form of qualified joint-and-survivor annuities (QJSA).[41] The law also requires that pension plans provide a qualified preretirement survivor annuity (QPSA) to the spouse of any participant if the participant dies after becoming entitled to a vested benefit but before the normal annuity starting date. These requirements were put into place in response to concerns that husbands were selecting single life annuities, which pay higher benefits than joint-and-survivor annuities. The selection of single life annuities meant that wives, who typically survive their husbands, were not adequately protected against the loss of pension benefits on the death of their husbands. The joint-and-survivor requirement can be waived with the consent of the spouse, but the consent must be in writing and witnessed by a plan representative or a notary public, and sufficient time before the annuity starting date must be given for this consent to occur.

The law permits the plan sponsor to make actuarially fair adjustments in benefit levels to recoup the cost of survivor annuities, that is, by reducing the benefits for the participant and his or her spouse compared with the benefits in a single life annuity. According to McGill and others, many plans do reduce benefits to reflect approximately the cost of joint-and-survivor annuities, although most do not do so for preretirement survivor annuities.[42] Although actuarial adjustments are allowed, the legal requirements for survivor annuities have added to the costs and potential liabilities of pension plan sponsors by increasing administrative burdens. Overall, there is a sense among professionals who advise plan sponsors, that is, plan practitioners, that the requirements have discouraged sponsors of plans from offering life annuities as a payment form unless they are required to do so.

A second institutional barrier that may limit the offering of annuitization opportunities by plan sponsors is the uncertainty among plan practitioners about the attitude of the Internal Revenue Service (IRS) toward the payment of life annuity benefits from a trust held for participants in a profit-sharing plan. Defined benefit pension plans can be either insured or trusteed; money purchase plans are insured plans, and profit-sharing plans are trusteed plans. If a pension plan is insured, it is funded through contracts with a life insurance company; life annuities made available to participants are underwritten by the insurance company through individual contracts or a group contract. If the defined benefit pension plan is funded through a trust, the plan sponsor's contributions to the plan are invested and reinvested in a variety of assets. In a trusteed defined benefit pension plan, retirement income benefits can be either provided through (individual or group) annuities purchased from an insurance company or paid directly from the trust fund.

The regulatory uncertainty arises about the ability of plan sponsors to offer annuities directly from profit-sharing plan trusts, a possibly desirable arrangement. If an employer sponsors both a pension and profit-sharing plan, the plan participant can transfer assets accumulated in the profit-sharing plan to purchase additional retirement benefits (that is, a life annuity) through the pension plan if the plan sponsor allows such transfers. If the employer does not offer a pension plan, it is nevertheless possible, because of the number and characteristics of plan participants or particular efficiencies and skills possessed by the benefits staff, that a profit-sharing plan itself could offer annuities paying higher rates than available through an insurance company. Because the assets in a trust for a profit-sharing plan are matched to market-value accounts owned, and often controlled, by plan participants, however, it is unclear what security could be offered for the interest and mortality rate guarantees implicit in the payment of determinable annuity benefits. Either the annuities would have to be completely participating (as opposed to nonparticipating) or the plan sponsor or the plan itself would have to guarantee rates, perhaps backed up by a reinsurance contract or through a captive insurance company. The view of the IRS concerning these arrangements is unknown.

A third consideration for plan sponsors relates to the regulatory burden imposing a liability for the evaluation of the claims-paying ability of the insurance company providing annuities. The Department of Labor, in Interpretive Bulletin 95–1, has stated that a plan fiduciary must evaluate a potential annuity provider's claims-paying ability and generally must select the safest annuity available, although the cost of the annuity may also be considered in the final selection. Some plan practitioners have claimed that this requirement has led to a decline in the level of benefits payable, as competition in the market may have been impaired.

Summary of Barriers to Annuitization

The gains to annuitization suggested by the simplest version of the Yaari life cycle model are substantial. When one jointly considers the role of Social Security, risk sharing within families, and health uncertainty, all of which ought to reduce the value of annuities, it is possible to explain why many households do not annuitize. However, it appears that the gains from annuitization should still be large enough to stimulate more demand for annuities than we observe in the private market. To explain the limited market for annuities, one must turn to other factors, including market imperfections, limited consumer understanding of the benefits of annuitization, and institutional and regulatory barriers to the provision of annuities. Importantly, if consumers would benefit from annuitization but are unable to do so because of market imperfections or regulatory constraints, or if consumers fail to understand the risk of not annuitizing, then public policies that encourage annuitization may be welfare improving.

The Current State of Retirement Plan Distributions

Table 3.5 shows the retirement plan benefits disbursed annually from private defined benefit and defined contribution plans, both single employer and multiemployer. From the time of the passage of the Employee Retirement Income Security Act (ERISA) through 1990, disbursements from defined benefit plans predominated. In the early 1990s, however, defined contribution disbursements surpassed those from defined benefit plans, and, more recently, are nearly double.

While some of these benefit disbursements represent preretirement distributions (more common for defined contribution plans), the amounts are mostly paid at or close to retirement. As shown in table 3.5, defined contribution plans have been playing an increasingly important role in delivering retirement benefits to private sector workers. Participants in these plans rarely get annuities for retirement. In part, this is because most defined contribution plans do not offer an annuity option. As seen in table 3.6, a 2009 COMPARISON survey by Watson Wyatt of medium and large private U.S. businesses found that only 25 percent of defined contribution plans offered a life annuity to retiring participants. Moreover, most defined contribution plan

Table 3.5
Retirement plan benefits disbursed by type of plan, selected years, 1975–2007 ($millions)

	Single employer			Multiemployer	
	Total	Defined benefit	Defined contribution	Defined benefit	Defined contribution
1975	$19,065	$10,457	$6,102	$2,446	$60
1980	35,280	18,524	12,961	3,624	171
1985	101,898	47,801	46,991	6,665	441
1990	129,405	56,079	62,147	10,284	894
1995	183,025	70,947	96,302	14,187	1,590
2000	341,041	106,483	211,036	21,027	2,495
2005	354,540	110,062	213,690	26,493	4,294
2006	408,153	121,124	254,465	28,071	4,493
2007	449,253	129,014	286,046	29,490	4,703

Source: U.S. Department of Labor, Private Pension Plan Bulletin Historical Tables and Graphs, March 2010, p. 21

Table 3.6
Annuity distribution options in defined contribution plans

Is an annuity offered?	
No	75%
Yes; life annuity is a distribution option from this plan.	19%
Yes; annuity purchase through a selection of insurance companies arranged by the plan sponsor is an option.	2%
Yes; annuity purchase from the defined benefit plan is an option.	1%
Life annuity is the default form of distribution from this plan.	2%

Source: Watson Wyatt 2009 COMPARISON database of employee benefit plans of medium- and large-size private employers, based on 518 defined contribution plans

participants do not take their benefits in annuity form. Michael Hurd and Constantijn Panis found that about 3.5 percent of older defined contribution plan participants annuitized their benefits on separating from their jobs during each two-year wave of the Health and Retirement Study (HRS) survey during the 1990s.[43]

In addition to the shift toward defined contribution plans, more defined benefit plans have been providing lump-sum benefit options. In particular, there has been a move toward hybrid plans, which are essentially defined benefit plans that are configured to look and act like defined contribution plans from the perspective of employees.

According to the Bureau of Labor Statistics, in 2005, 25 percent of workers enrolled in defined benefit plans were in hybrid plans, that is, cash balance (23 percent) or pension equity (2 percent) plans.[44] One common characteristic of hybrid plans is the default provision of lump-sum benefits, through an individual account balance, although, by law, an annuity distribution must be made available.

The provision of lump-sum benefits, however, is not limited to hybrid plans among defined benefit plans. Watson Wyatt, in its 2009 COMPARISON survey, found that 45 percent of traditional defined benefit plans offered an unrestricted lump-sum benefit. Consistently, in a recent survey of employee benefits in private industry, the Bureau of Labor Statistics found that 52 percent of all workers with private defined benefit plans (both traditional and hybrid) were allowed to take at least some benefits in lump sums at retirement, and that the overwhelming majority of these workers could take their entire benefit in this form. While comprehensive statistical information is limited, experience studies and actuarial assumptions suggest that most participants in defined benefit plans choose the lump sum when the option is available.

The fact that an increasing number of workers are receiving lump-sum retirement benefits at the end of their careers does not necessarily mean that these individuals do not convert their retirement savings into steady and reliable income streams. But the evidence strongly suggests that they are not doing it through annuity programs nearly to the extent many pension experts desire. For example, in table 3.7 (panels a and b), we report the results of the analysis done by Watson Wyatt, updating the earlier work by Hurd and Panis using the HRS survey, on the dispositions of pension plan resources by older workers on job separations over sequential two-year periods.[45] In the HRS questionnaire, defined benefit plan participants could indicate up to five distribution options that they could choose from when they left their jobs: cash out their plan, roll the benefit into an IRA, leave the benefits to a future payment date, take their benefit immediately (as an annuity), or other. Although not all HRS participants were offered all five options, the analysis could not be limited to the universe of workers who had the option of taking a lump-sum distribution. The HRS does tell us, however, that between 1992 and 2004, approximately 42 percent of defined benefit plan participants could choose to take an unrestricted lump-sum distribution when they left their jobs. Defined contribution plan participants had similar choices: cash out their plan, roll the

Table 3.7a
Retirement plan distributions: What older workers did with their defined benefit plans (1992–2004)

Option	Average value of plan at distribution (2004 dollars)	Percentage of population	Percentage of total dollars
Cash out	$64,114	6.65%	2.13%
Roll into IRA	164,034	7.99	7.56
Leave intact	166,892	22.28	22.12
Receive benefit now	206,144	59.23	67.29
Other	102,673	1.54	0.80

Source: Watson Wyatt tabulation of the *Health and Retirement Study*

Table 3.7b
Retirement plan distributions: What older workers did with their defined contribution plans (1992–2004)

Option	Average value of plan at distribution (2004 dollars)	Percentage of population	Percentage of total dollars
Cash out	$27,184	17.55%	7.61%
Roll into IRA	86,794	32.23	41.45
Leave intact	72,679	38.62	39.46
Convert to annuity	75,940	3.55	4.98
Other	64,799	7.10	6.32

Source: Watson Wyatt tabulation of the *Health and Retirement Study*

balance into an IRA, maintain that account, convert the account into an annuity, or other.

Panels a and b in table 3.7 show the decisions that HRS respondents, with defined benefit and defined contribution plans, respectively, made when they left their jobs, the average value of plan resources for each decision, and the percentage of total dollars in each payment category.

As the middle columns show, fewer defined benefit plan participants than defined contribution plan participants cashed out their benefits when they terminated employment—6.65 percent compared with 17.55 percent. Moreover, fewer assets were cashed out from defined benefit accounts than from defined contribution accounts—2.13 percent compared with 7.61 percent. Most defined benefit participants (59.23 percent) were receiving benefits (mostly in annuity form), while many (22.28 percent) were postponing disbursement, presumably to eventually get an annuity. By contrast, most defined contribution participants

(38.62 percent) were waiting until, perhaps, minimum distribution requirements forced them to make withdrawals at age 70 1/2, while many (32.23 percent) sought greener investment pastures and rolled over their accounts to IRAs. Relatively few defined contribution plan participants (3.55 percent), however, converted to an annuity. This result is nearly identical to that of Hurd and Panis.

Taking the annuitization rate of 3.5 percent to be a two-year steady-state hazard of annuitization, Hurd calculated that about 15 percent of defined contribution plan dispositions will eventually be paid out as annuities.[46] Considering the recent movement among defined benefit plans toward hybrid plans and the still relatively small annuitization rate of growing defined contribution plan assets, we definitively see a trend away from the annuitization of retirement plan assets.

Conclusions

Annuities play the important economic role of insuring individuals against the financial risks associated with longevity uncertainty. In the absence of opportunities for annuitization, retirees are required to balance the risk of outliving their resources with the desire to increase consumption while alive. Those who choose to consume conservatively forgo the extra utility they could have achieved from a higher consumption level. Those who consume too aggressively risk finding themselves with insufficient resources at older ages. As a result of their ability to resolve these risks, annuities play a central role in the life cycle theory of wealth decumulation.

One important implication of the shift from defined benefit to defined contribution pension plans is a reduction in opportunities for retirees to annuitize their retirement assets, because relatively few defined contribution plans include a life annuity as one of the payout options. Even in those plans that offer an annuity option, the fact that it is not mandatory means that individuals who choose to annuitize will likely receive lower monthly income due to adverse selection, that is, the lower mortality characteristics of the individual annuitant pool.

Appendix: Calculation of Annuity Equivalent Wealth

The calculation of annuity equivalent wealth begins with a representative individual who is assumed to maximize an expected utility function V, by choosing an optimal consumption path (C_t) from time 0 to time T (the maximum possible life span), given a rate of time preference ρ and a vector of cumulative survival probabilities (P_t):

$$\underset{\{C_t\}}{\text{Max}} \sum_{t=0}^{T} \frac{P_t U(C_t)}{(1+\rho)^t}. \tag{1}$$

The budget constraint facing this individual depends on whether he has access to annuities. In the absence of annuities, the constraint is that the present value of future consumption, discounted using the riskless interest rate r, be equal to the individual's initial wealth, W_0:

$$W_0 = \sum_{t=0}^{T} \frac{C_t}{(1+r)^t}. \tag{2}$$

If this individual is able to purchase actuarially fair annuities, the budget constraint becomes:

$$W_0 = \sum_{t=0}^{T} \frac{P_t C_t}{(1+r)^t}. \tag{3}$$

The difference between equation 2 and equation 3 is the role of survival probabilities. In equation 2, the present value of all future consumption must not exceed the initial wealth level. With annuities in equation 3, the budget constraint is that the expected present value of the consumption must equal initial wealth. This budget constraint assumes that the insurance company provides an actuarially fair annuity whose payout path exactly equals the consumption path chosen by the individual. In actuality, there may be additional constraints on the structure of the annuity path that make it suboptimal in some circumstances.[47]

Even before solving for the optimal consumption path, it is easy to see why annuities will be preferred in this model. One way to view the difference in the two budget constraints is to interpret the survival probabilities in equation 3 as the relative price of future consumption when annuities are available versus when they are not available. Viewed this way, the price of future consumption is always lower when annuities are available, since the value of $P_t < 1$ for all $t > 0$.

It is common to assume that the one-period utility function, $U(C_t)$, exhibits constant relative risk aversion and can thus be defined as

$$U(C_t) = \frac{C_t^{1-\beta}}{1-\beta}, \tag{4}$$

where β is the Arrow–Pratt coefficient of relative risk aversion and $1/\beta$ is the elasticity of intertemporal substitution in consumption.

By maximizing equation 1 subject to equation 2 or 3, one can solve for the individual's optimal consumption path with or without access to annuities. Each optimal C_t^* can be found as a function of W_0, ρ, r, β, and the full set of survival probabilities $\{P_t\}$, as follows:

$$C_t^{no\ annuities} = W_0 \left(\frac{1+r}{1+\rho}\right)^{t/\beta} P_t^{1/\beta} \left(\sum_{j=0}^{T} \frac{(1+r)^{j(1-\beta)/\beta}}{(1+\rho)^{j/\beta}} P_j^{1/\beta}\right)^{-1}, \text{and} \qquad (5)$$

$$C_t^{annuities} = W_0 \left(\frac{1+r}{1+\rho}\right)^{t/\beta} \left(\sum_{j=0}^{T} \frac{(1+r)^{j(1-\beta)/\beta}}{(1+\rho)^{j/\beta}} P_j\right)^{-1}. \qquad (6)$$

To gain some intuition for the difference between these equations, it is useful to consider the special case in which the consumer has log utility ($\beta = 1$) and in which the interest rate and rate of time preference are equal to one another ($r = \rho$). In this case, equations 5 and 6 reduce, respectively, to

$$C_t^{no\ annuities} = P_t W_0 \left(\sum_{j=0}^{T} \frac{P_j}{(1+r)^j}\right)^{-1}, \text{ and}$$

$$C_t^{annuities} = W_0 \left(\sum_{j=0}^{T} \frac{P_j}{(1+r)^j}\right)^{-1}.$$

In this special case, the difference in the consumption at time t is proportional to the cumulative survival probability to time t. Since $P_0 = 1$ by definition, the level of consumption at time 0 is the same whether annuities are available. In the case with no annuities, consumption declines over time due to falling survival probabilities, whereas with annuities, the consumption profile is level for the rest of the individual's life. Thus, consumption with annuities is greater than or equal to consumption without annuities in all periods, and thus utility is higher.

By plugging the optimal consumption rules from equations 5 and 6 back into the lifetime utility function (1), one can construct the indirect utility functions, $V(.)$, that correspond to each budget constraint. These indirect utility functions express the maximum utility the individual can achieve by following the optimal consumption path as a function of the parameters W_0, r, ρ, β, and $\{P_t\}$:

$$V_0(W_0)^{no\ annuities} = \frac{1}{1-\beta} W_0^{1-\beta} \left(\sum_{j=0}^{T} \frac{(1+r)^{j(1-\beta)/\beta}}{(1+\rho)^{j/\beta}} P_j^{1/\beta}\right)^{\beta}, \text{and}$$

$$V_0(W_0)^{annuities} = \frac{1}{1-\beta} W_0^{1-\beta} \left(\sum_{j=0}^{T} \frac{(1+r)^{j(1-\beta)/\beta}}{(1+\rho)^{j/\beta}} P_j\right)^{\beta}.$$

As already indicated, for a given level of wealth W_0, an individual achieves a higher level of utility with annuities than without. It is possible to state this utility gain in dollar terms by determining how much additional wealth would need to be given to an individual without annuities to make him as well off as if he had annuities. This is done by finding the α such that

$$V_0(\alpha W_0)^{no\ annuities} = V_0(W_0)^{annuities}.$$

The α is what we call the annuity equivalent wealth. In the case shown here, it is easy to solve for α analytically. However, once one begins to incorporate additional complexities, such as the presence of preexisting annuities, liquidity constraints, or other sources of uncertainty, solving for α must be done through dynamic programming solution techniques. [48]

Notes

1. See Poterba, Venti, and Wise (2000).

2. See Hurd and Wise (1989).

3. See Yaari (1965).

4. In a simple life cycle model with no other savings motives besides retirement consumption and bequests, an individual with bequest motives will invest the bequest portion of wealth in riskless bonds, and will annuitize the rest.

5. See Brown and Poterba (2000); Brown, Mitchell, and Poterba (2001); Brown (2001b).

6. With CRRA utility, the reciprocal of the risk aversion parameter is the elasticity of substitution in consumption across periods. A low risk aversion coefficient corresponds to a high willingness to substitute consumption intertemporally.

7. See Mitchell and Moore (1999).

8. See Friedman and Warshawsky (1988, 1990).

9. See Mitchell and associates (1999); Brown, Mitchell, and Poterba (2001).

10. See Yaari (1965).

11. See Walliser (2001).

12. A much more complete survey of the bequest and transfer literature is provided by Gale and Slemrod (2001).

13. See Hurd (1987).

14. See Hurd (1989).

15. See Laitner and Juster (1996).

16. See Bernheim (1991).

17. See Brown (2001a).

18. See Brown (2001b).

19. See Kotlikoff and Spivak (1981).

20. See Hurd (1999).

21. See Brown and Poterba (2000).

22. See Brown and Poterba (2000).

23. See Brown, Mitchell, and Poterba (2001).

24. See Brown, Mitchell, and Poterba (2001).

25. This does not necessarily mean that some additional annuitization on the margin would not be valued, only that complete annuitization is clearly not optimal in this case.

26. See Warshawsky, Granza, and Madamba (2000).

27. See Murtaugh and associates (1997).

28. See Murtaugh and associates (1997).

29. As quoted in Health Insurance Association of America (1997, table 1.3).

30. See Cohen (1998).

31. See Venti and Wise (2000).

32. See Murtaugh, Kemper, and Spillman (1995).

33. See Warshawsky, Spillman, and Murtaugh (2002).

34. Warshawsky, Spillman, and Murtaugh (2002) analyze an idea to combine long-term care insurance with the life annuity in order to reduce adverse selection and underwriting, and make both LTC insurance and annuities more attractive and available to middle-class elderly households.

35. See American Council of Life Insurers (1999, p. 16).

36. See American Council of Life Insurers (1999, p. 16).

37. See Brown (2001b).

38. Money purchase plans are funded by employer contributions based on a fixed formula. Profit-sharing and stock bonus plans (which include employee stock ownership plans) have discretionary employer contributions and are therefore not considered to be pension plans (that is, plans meeting a definitely determinable benefit requirement). All of these plans, however, are defined contribution plans in that the ultimate benefits are based upon the accumulated employer contributions and earnings and losses thereon.

39. Treasury Regulation Section 1.401–1(b)(1)(i).

40. See McGill and associates (1996).

41. The qualified annuity must provide income to the surviving spouse that is not less than one-half of the amount of the annuity payable during the joint lives of the participant and his spouse.

42. See McGill and associates (1996).

43. See Hurd and Panis (2006).

44. See U.S. Department of Labor (2007).

45. See Watson Wyatt (2007).

46. See Hurd (2004).

47. See Yagi and Nishigaki (1993).

48. Readers interested in the details of the dynamic programming algorithms should see Mitchell and others (1999) for the case of a single individual, Brown and Poterba (2000) for the case of couples, and Brown, Mitchell, and Poterba (2001) for the case in which returns, inflation, or both are uncertain.

References

American Council of Life Insurers. 1999. "Positioning and Promoting Annuities in a New Retirement Environment." Task Force on Annuity Messages. Washington, DC. ACLI.

Bernheim, Douglas D. 1991. How Strong Are Bequest Motives? Evidence Based on Estimates of the Demand for Life Insurance and Annuities. *Journal of Political Economy* 99:899–927.

Brown, Jeffrey R. 2001a. Are the Elderly Really Over-Annuitized? New Evidence on Life Insurance and Bequests. In *Themes in the Economics of Aging*, ed. D. Wise. Chicago: University of Chicago Press.

Brown, Jeffrey R. 2001b. Private Pensions, Mortality Risk, and the Decision to Annuitize. *Journal of Public Economics* 82 (1): 29–62.

Brown, Jeffrey R., Olivia S. Mitchell, and James M. Poterba. 2001. The Role of Real Annuities and Indexed Bonds in an Individual Accounts Retirement Program. In *Risk Aspects of Investment-Based Social Security Reform*, ed. J. Campbell and M. Feldstein. Chicago: University of Chicago Press.

Brown, Jeffrey R., and James M. Poterba. 2000. Joint Life Annuities and Annuity Demand by Married Couples. *Journal of Risk and Insurance* 67 (4): 527–553.

Cohen, Marc A. 1998. Emerging Trends in the Finance and Delivery of Long-Term Care: Public and Private Opportunities and Challenges. *Gerontologist* 38 (1): 80–89.

Friedman, Benjamin, and Mark Warshawsky. 1988. Annuity Prices and Saving Behavior in the United States. In *Pensions in the U.S. Economy*, ed. Zvi Bodie, John Shoven, and David Wise. Chicago: University of Chicago Press.

Friedman, Benjamin, and Mark Warshawsky. 1990. The Cost of Annuities: Implications for Saving Behavior and Bequests. *Quarterly Journal of Economics* 105 (February): 135–54.

Gale, William G., and Joel Slemrod. 2001. Overview. In *Rethinking Estate and Gift Taxation*, ed. William G. Gale, James R. Hines, Jr., and Joel Slemrod. Washington, DC: Brookings.

Health Insurance Association of America. 1997. *Long-Term Care: Knowing the Risk, Paying the Price*. Washington, DC: Health Insurance Association of America.

Hurd, Michael D. 1987. Savings of the Elderly and Desired Bequests. *American Economic Review* 77 (3): 298–312.

Hurd, Michael. 1989. Mortality Risk and Bequests. *Econometrica* 57 (4): 779–813.

Hurd, Michael. 1999. Mortality Risk and Consumption by Couples. NBER working paper 7048. Cambridge, MA: National Bureau of Economic Research.

Hurd, Michael. 2004. Comment. In *Private Pensions and Public Policies*, ed. William Gale, John Shoven, and Mark Warshawsky, 376. Washington, DC: Brookings Institution Press.

Hurd, Michael, and Constantijn Panis. 2006. The Choice to Cash Out Pension Rights at Job Change or Retirement. *Journal of Public Economics* 90:2213–2227.

Hurd, Michael D., and David A. Wise. 1989. The Wealth and Poverty of Widows: Assets before and after the Husband's Death. In *The Economics of Aging*, ed. David Wise. Chicago: University of Chicago Press.

Kotlikoff, Laurence J., and Avia Spivak. 1981. The Family as an Incomplete Annuities Market. *Journal of Political Economy* 89 (April): 372–391.

Laitner, John, and F. Thomas Juster. 1996. New Evidence on Altruism: A Study of TIAACREF Retirees. *American Economic Review* 86:893–908.

McGill, Dan M., and Associates. 1996. *Fundamentals of Private Pensions*. 7th ed. Philadelphia: University of Pennsylvania Press for the Pension Research Council of the Wharton School.

Mitchell, Olivia S., and James F. Moore. 1998. Can Americans Afford to Retire? New Evidence on Retirement Saving Adequacy. *Journal of Risk and Insurance* 65(3): 371–400.

Mitchell, Olivia S., and Associates. 1999. New Evidence on the Money's Worth of Individual Annuities. *American Economic Review* 89 (December): 1299–1318.

Murtaugh, Christopher, Peter Kemper, and Brenda Spillman. 1995. Risky Business: Long-Term Care Insurance Underwriting. *Inquiry* 32 (3): 271–284.

Murtaugh, Christopher, and Associates. 1997. The Amount, Distribution, and Timing of Lifetime Nursing Home Use. *Medical Care* 35 (3): 204–218.

Poterba, James M., Steven F. Venti, and David A. Wise. 2000. Saver Behavior and 401(k) Retirement Wealth. *American Economic Review* 90 (May): 297–302.

U.S. Department of Labor. Bureau of Labor Statistics. 2007. *National Compensation Survey: Employee Benefits in Private Industry in the United States, 2005*. Washington, DC: Bureau of Labor Statistics.

Venti, Steven, and David A. Wise. 2000. "Choice, Chance, and Wealth Dispersion at Retirement." NBER working paper 7521. Cambridge, MA: National Bureau of Economic Research.

Walliser, Jan. 2001. Regulation of Withdrawals in Individual Account Systems. In *New Ideas about Old Age Security*, ed. Robert Holzman and Joseph Stiglitz. Washington, DC: World Bank.

Warshawsky, Mark J., Lee Granza, and Anna Madamba. 2000. Financing Long-Term Care: Needs, Attitudes, Current Insurance Products, and Policy Innovations. TIAA-CREF Institute *Research Dialogues* 63 (March).

Warshawsky, Mark J., Brenda Spillman, and Chris Murtaugh. 2002. Integrating the Life Annuity and Long-Term Care Insurance: Theory, Evidence, Practice, and Policy. In

Innovations in Retirement Financing, ed. Olivia Mitchell, and Associates. Philadelphia: University of Pennsylvania Press.

Watson Wyatt Worldwide. 2007. Cashing Out: A Threat to Retirement Security? *Watson Wyatt Insider* 17 (9): 35–41.

Yaari, Menahem E. 1965. Uncertain Lifetime, Life Insurance, and the Theory of the Consumer. *Review of Economic Studies* 32:137–150.

Yagi, Tadashi, and Yasuyuki Nishigaki. 1993. The Inefficiency of Private Constant Annuities. *Journal of Risk and Insurance* 60 (3):385–412.

4 Who Prefers Annuities?

with Tomeka Hill

Introduction and Summary

As baby boomers retire, they must decide how to receive payouts from their defined benefit (DB) plans, defined contribution (DC) plans, and personal savings. Many pension experts believe that life annuities are the best way for retirees to ensure that they do not run out of money. But most people do not choose annuities, and experts are wondering why. To find out, Watson Wyatt Worldwide asked a national panel of older workers and recent retirees about their payout and risk preferences, retirement decisions, and related issues. Our observations are based on special surveys sponsored by Watson Wyatt, the *2007 U.S. Surveys of Older Employees' and Retirees' Attitudes Toward Lump Sum and Annuity Distributions From Retirement Plans*.

According to the surveys, several factors influence workers' and retirees' preferences and choices. First, retirees covered by DB plans or by both DB and DC plans are more likely to receive an annuity (although they may also receive a lump sum). Retirees with only a DC plan, however, overwhelmingly receive their benefits in a lump sum. Second, the amount of the lump sum relative to the annuity value affects participants' stated choices and preferences. Third, older employees' preferences differ by gender, marital status, education, and salary level, but the differences are less pronounced among retirees. Fourth, unsurprisingly, people who believe they are in better health and those who expect to live longer are more likely to choose annuities. Fifth, being more risk averse seems to make workers and retirees more likely to prefer an annuity.

From *Watson Wyatt Insider* 18 (4) (April 2008): 12–21, plus an appendix with new regression results. Reprinted with permission. All rights reserved, Towers Watson. For more information, visit towerswatson.com.

Annuity Decisions within Retirement Plans

Plan type exerts a powerful influence on how benefits are paid out in retirement. Table 4.1 shows survey results on the distribution of older workers by plan type and the percentage of older workers who intend to receive at least some of their retirement benefits as an annuity. Because employees from large companies are overrepresented in our survey, many employees are covered by both a DB and a DC plan.

Of older workers who have only a DB plan with their current employer, about 93 percent plan to receive an annuity. Of those with only a DC plan with their current employer, only about 7 percent intend to take an annuity, probably in part because most DC plans do not offer an annuity option.[1] Roughly 79 percent of those with both a DB and a DC plan anticipate taking at least some of their retirement income as an annuity.

We also asked recent retirees how they receive their retirement benefits. Table 4.2 shows the distribution of retirees by plan type and the percentage who receive any retirement benefits as an annuity. Roughly

Table 4.1
Older employees planning to receive annuity by plan type

	Percentage of employees with retirement plan	Percentage of employees planning to receive at least some benefit as annuity
DB plans only	7.4%	92.5%
DC plans only	5.0	6.5
DB and DC plans	76.9	78.6
No retirement plan	10.7	—

Source: Watson Wyatt Worldwide (2007)

Table 4.2
Retirees who receive annuity by plan type

	Percentage of retirees with retirement plan	Percentage of retirees that receive at least some benefit as annuity
DB plans only	17.8%	76.3%
DC plans only	20.8	12.1
DB and DC plans	43.4	74.0
No retirement plan	18.0	—

Source: Watson Wyatt Worldwide (2007)

76 percent of retirees with only a DB plan receive annuity payments, while approximately 12 percent of those with only a DC plan receive annuity payments. Seventy-four percent of retirees who receive benefits from both DB and DC plans receive annuity payments.

Lump-Sum Amounts and Annuity Preferences

To determine the effect of lump-sum size on the annuity choice, we asked participants whether they would rather have an annuity of $1,000 per month or an annuity of $500 per month plus a lump sum. Based on the average ages of older employees and retirees, we determined lump sums on a unisex basis that were actuarially fair and equivalent to an inflation-indexed life annuity.

Figure 4.1 shows the choices older employees think they would make at age 65. Roughly 58 percent would prefer $500 per month plus a $111,000 lump sum, while 42 percent would opt for $1,000 per month.

Similarly, figure 4.2 shows the choices retirees think they would make at age 75 between $1,000 per month and $500 per month plus a lump sum of $80,500. Again, the majority, 56 percent, would prefer a combination of an annuity and a lump sum. Perhaps most employees and retirees believe that receiving both payment types provides a good balance of spending flexibility and security.

We then asked follow-up questions to find out how participants would choose when the lump-sum values were not actuarially equivalent to the inflation-indexed annuity. We asked participants who chose an annuity in the first hypothetical question whether a higher lump sum would change their mind. Similarly, we asked participants who chose the combination of annuity and lump sum in the first

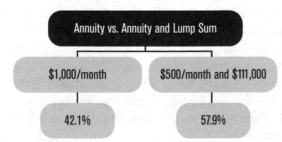

Figure 4.1
Older workers' choices between larger annuity and smaller annuity plus a lump sum.
Source: Watson Wyatt Worldwide (2007).

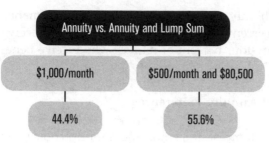

Figure 4.2
Retirees' choices between larger annuity and smaller annuity plus a lump sum. *Source:*
Watson Wyatt Worldwide (2007).

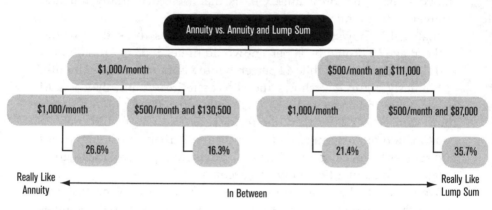

Figure 4.3
Effect of lump sum–annuity amounts on older workers' choices. *Source:* Watson Wyatt
Worldwide (2007).

hypothetical question whether they would have chosen differently had
the lump sum been smaller. Many older employees would still prefer
the annuity-lump sum combination, but for some, their preference
varies according to the lump sum amount. Figure 4.3 shows the results
of all older employees' choices.

Most employees want a lump sum—if it is big enough. The majority
of employees want an annuity—if the lump sum is too small. Only
about 27 percent say they would choose the annuity regardless of the
lump-sum amount, and 36 percent say they would always opt for the
annuity–lump sum combination.

We also asked retirees similar follow-up questions. Again, the size
of the lump sum affected their decisions, although many retirees would

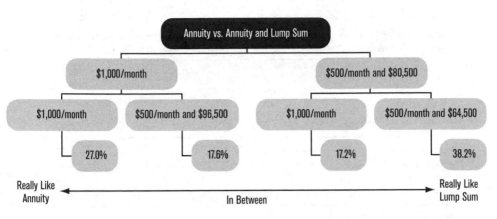

Figure 4.4
Effect of lump sum–annuity amounts on retirees' choices. *Source:* Watson Wyatt World-wide (2007).

prefer both the lump sum and an annuity. Figure 4.4 shows the results for the retirees.

Personal Characteristics and Annuity Preferences

Previously published research on annuities show that people with certain personal characteristics are more likely to choose an annuity over a lump-sum payment, and our study finds similar results. Table 4.3 shows the distribution of older workers by gender, marital status, and education, and the percentages of those who chose the annuity and those who chose the annuity–lump sum in response to our hypothetical survey question. Older workers who are female, are unmarried, and do not have a college degree were more likely to choose the annuity as their only payment method.

When we asked retirees the same question, however, the differences in characteristics between those who chose the annuity and those who chose the annuity–lump sum combination are less significant. Table 4.4 shows the distribution of retirees by gender, marital status, and education and the percentages of those who chose the annuity and those who chose the annuity–lump sum combination based on the hypothetical question. There is no significant difference between males and females or between those with and without a college degree. Unmarried retirees, however, were slightly more likely to choose an annuity than married retirees.

Table 4.3
Comparison of older workers who chose annuity versus those who chose the annuity–lump sum combination by gender, marital status, and education level

	Male	Female	Married	Not married	Have some college experience or less education	Have college degree or higher degree
$1,000/month	38.4%	46.1%	39.4%	48.7%	44.1%	38.9%
$500/month and $111,000	61.6	53.9	60.6	51.3	55.9	61.1
Total	100.0	100.0	100.0	100.0	100.0	100.0

Source: Watson Wyatt Worldwide (2007)

Table 4.4
Comparison of retirees who chose annuity versus those who chose the annuity–lump sum combination by gender, marital status and education level

	Male	Female	Married	Not married	Have some college experience or less education	Have college degree or higher degree
$1,000/month	43.4%	45.6%	42.6%	48.1%	45.5%	42.3%
$500/month and $111,000	56.6	54.4	57.4	51.9	54.5	57.7
Total	100.0	100.0	100.0	100.0	100.0	100.0

Source: Watson Wyatt Worldwide (2007)

Table 4.5 shows the distribution of reported earnings for older workers and annuity choice. Older workers who prefer to receive only an annuity have lower reported earnings than those who prefer the combination. The difference between the median values is $4,000, and the difference between the average reported earnings is $5,124.67.

Longevity, Health Status, and Annuity Choices

As individuals age, they face an increased risk of health shocks and conditions that may shorten life expectancy. Thus, the expected value of an annuity decreases as life expectancy shortens. When the risk of death is substantial because of poor health, an annuity may no longer be the optimal form of retirement income. So the decision between an

Table 4.5
Distribution of salary for older workers who chose annuity and older workers who chose the annuity–lump sum combination

	Reported annual salary			
	25th percentile	50th percentile	75th percentile	Average
$1,000/month	$28,000	$46,000	$71,000	$54,349.26
$500/month and $111,000	32,000	50,000	73,941	59,473.93

Note: All salaries are greater than $5,000.
Source: Watson Wyatt Worldwide (2007)

Table 4.6
Older workers' self-reported expectations of reaching ages 75, 85, and 95

	Expect to live to 75	Expect to live to 85	Expect to live to 95
No chance	2.5%	9.5%	30.2%
25% chance	5.5	17.5	28.6
50% chance	21.0	27.0	24.7
75% chance	24.5	31.0	11.4
100% chance	46.5	15.0	5.1
Total	100.0	100.0	100.0

Source: Watson Wyatt Worldwide (2007)

annuity and a lump-sum payment is greatly influenced by an individual's self-perceived health status and life expectancy.

To determine how optimistic older workers are about their life expectancy and how much they value longevity insurance, we asked them whether they expect to live to ages 75, 85, and 95 (table 4.6). Approximately 47 percent of older workers believe they have a 100 percent chance of living to age 75, while only about 5 percent feel certain that they will make it to 95. These distributions of lifetime expectations seem sensible.

We also look at retirees' expectations of living to ages 85, 90, and 95 (table 4.7). The expectations are more diffuse, but in general and similar to older workers, retirees are less optimistic about their life expectancy at older ages. Although about 18 percent believe they have a 100 percent chance of living to age 85, only 7 percent feel certain they will reach 95. More than half the retirees believe they have no chance of living to 95.

We then cross-tabulate the ways that older employees actually expect to receive their retirement income with their self-assessed

Table 4.7
Retirees' self-reported expectations of reaching ages 85, 90, and 95

	Expect to live to 85	Expect to live to 90	Expect to live to 95
No chance	16.5%	30.2%	52.6%
25% chance	18.6	26.5	16.4
50% chance	28.3	21.2	16.1
75% chance	19.1	16.3	8.0
100% chance	17.5	5.9	7.0
Total	100.0	100.0	100.0

Source: Watson Wyatt Worldwide (2007)

Table 4.8
Older workers' expected payment from retirement plans and probability of reaching age 85

	No chance	25% chance	50% chance	75% chance	100% chance
Receive retirement income as lump sum	34.5%	27.6%	30.7%	30.2%	29.4%
Receive at least part of retirement income as annuity	65.5	72.4	69.3	69.8	70.6
Total	100.0	100.0	100.0	100.0	100.0

Source: Watson Wyatt Worldwide (2007)

probability of reaching age 85 (table 4.8). Older workers who believe they have no chance of reaching 85 are more likely to get a lump-sum-only benefit from their retirement plan than those who believe they have a 100 percent chance of reaching 85 (35 percent versus 29 percent). There is, however, some inconsistency for in-between probabilities.

A similar cross-tabulation for retirees (table 4.9) shows that approximately 55 percent of retirees who do not expect to live to age 85 took a lump-sum payment from their retirement plan. Only about 47 percent of retirees who think they have a 100 percent chance of living to 85 opted, however, for the lump sum only. Here the movement across payment method and life expectancy is more linear than for older workers.

We also look at the effects of current self-assessed health status on actual payment choices from retirement plans. Table 4.10 shows a cross-tabulation between the way older employees plan to receive their retirement benefits and their self-reported health status. Sixty-six percent of older employees in excellent health would prefer to receive

Table 4.9
Retirees' expected payment from retirement plans and probability of reaching age 85

	No chance	25% chance	50% chance	75% chance	100% chance
Receive retirement income as lump sum	55.3%	58.3%	48.5%	47.2%	46.8%
Receive at least part of retirement income as annuity	44.7	41.7	51.5	52.8	53.2
Total	100.0	100.0	100.0	100.0	100.0

Source: Watson Wyatt Worldwide (2007)

Table 4.10
Effect of health status on older workers' expected benefit payment method from retirement plans

	Excellent	Very good	Good	Fair	Poor
Receive retirement income as lump sum	33.6%	29.5%	32.8%	53.6%	46.8%
Receive at least part of retirement income as annuity	66.4	70.5	67.2	46.4	53.2
Total	100.0	100.0	100.0	100.0	100.0

Source: Watson Wyatt Worldwide (2007)

at least part of their retirement benefits as an annuity, compared with 53 percent of older employees in poor health.

Table 4.11 shows the relationship between retirees' retirement benefit payment method choices and their self-reported health status. Fewer than half of retirees in good health or better took all their retirement income as a lump sum (between 45.9 percent and 47.2 percent). However, roughly 77 percent of retirees in poor health opted for a lump sum alone—a significant impact.

Most Older Workers and Retirees Are Risk Averse

Older workers and retirees face several risks that affect their optimal retirement age and form of retirement benefit payment method. These risks include losing a spouse, realizing poor investment performance, being hit with unexpected medical expenses, and outliving their income. To better understand how plan participants think about the unforeseen, we asked some questions whose answers serve as a proxy for aversion to risk.

Table 4.11
Effect of health status on retirees' benefit payment method from retirement plans

	Excellent	Very good	Good	Fair	Poor
Receive retirement income as lump sum	47.2%	47.3%	45.9%	63.3%	76.9%
Receive at least part of retirement income as annuity	52.8	52.7	54.1	36.7	23.1
Total	100.0	100.0	100.0	100.0	100.0

Source: Watson Wyatt Worldwide (2007)

We first asked older employees and retirees to choose between a guaranteed annual salary of $110,000 and a variable annual income with a 90 percent chance of being $90,000 and a 10 percent chance of being $190,000. The answer gives some indication of the individual's tolerance for risk.

Seventy-one percent of employees and almost 73 percent of retirees chose the guaranteed salary. Figures 4.5 and 4.6 show the percentage breakdown for employees and retirees, respectively. It appears that most people are more strongly motivated by security than by a small chance for a lot more money.

We then asked respondents in both risk preference groups to choose between two variable-income jobs, one of which is riskier than the other. Figure 4.7 shows how older employees responded to the two questions. A large majority—more than 60 percent—prefer to have lower-risk income. The retirees' responses are not shown but indicate similar attitudes.

Risk-Averse Older Workers and Retirees Prefer Annuities

Risk-averse older workers and retirees prefer annuities over lump sums, according to the economic and retirement literature. We looked for a relationship in our survey responses between older workers' and retirees' retirement benefit payment method of preference, as represented by their responses to the two levels of hypothetical benefit payment method choices, and their level of risk aversion, as represented by respondents' preferences between either a steady guaranteed income or a possibly higher variable income.

We used three categories to measure types of risk preference: risk loving, mixed, and risk averse. Risk loving describes respondents who chose the variable salary in both levels of job questions. Mixed includes

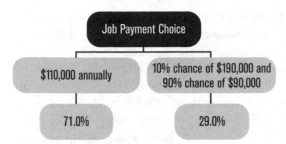

Figure 4.5
Older workers' choices of steady or variable job payments. *Source:* Watson Wyatt World-wide (2007).

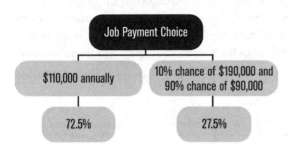

Figure 4.6
Retirees' choices of steady or variable job payments. *Source:* Watson Wyatt Worldwide (2007).

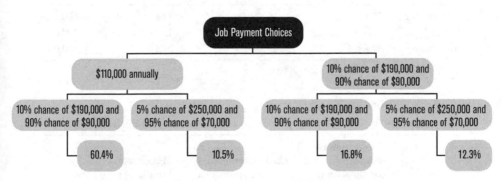

Figure 4.7
Effect of possibly higher risk income on older workers' job payment choices. *Source:* Watson Wyatt Worldwide (2007).

respondents who chose the steady salary in one question level and the variable salary in the other. Risk-averse describes respondents who chose guaranteed salary payments in both question levels.

Older workers who are more risk loving generally prefer the annuity and lump-sum combination payment method, regardless of the amount of the lump sum (see table 4.12). Older workers who are mixed or risk-averse however, tend to prefer the lump sum–annuity combination in one hypothetical situation, but the annuity in another, depending on the lump-sum amount. Roughly 38 percent of mixed risk-preference older workers and about 40 percent of risk-averse older workers are in between: they chose the annuity in one hypothetical situation and the annuity–lump sum combination in the other. Among risk-averse older workers, more (27 percent) chose the annuity in both hypothetical situations than among the other risk-preference types. Among retirees, similar relationships exist, but they are more diffuse. (Table 4.13)

Table 4.12
Effect of older workers' type of risk preference on benefit payment method preferences

	Chose annuity-lump sum combination in both hypothetical situations	Chose combination in one hypothetical situation, annuity in the other	Chose the annuity in both hypothetical situations	Total
Risk Loving	50.1%	25.3%	24.6%	100.0%
Mixed	36.6	37.9	25.5	100.0
Risk Averse	32.4	40.2	27.4	100.0

Source: Watson Wyatt Worldwide (2007)

Table 4.13
Effect of retirees' type of risk preference on benefit method payment preferences

	Chose annuity–lump sum combination in both hypothetical situations	Chose combination in one hypothetical situation, annuity in the other	Chose the annuity in both hypothetical situations	Total
Risk loving	46.2%	30.2%	23.6%	100.0%
Mixed	38.4	35.7	25.9	100.0
Risk averse	37.4	34.5	28.1	100.0

Source: Watson Wyatt Worldwide (2007)

Conclusion

Several factors influence whether employees and workers receive a lump sum or an annuity. Retirement plan type plays an important role: participants with only a DC plan are less likely than those with a DB plan to receive an annuity. As coverage of DB plans becomes scarcer and more workers have only a DC plan, more retirees could be at risk of outliving their resources.

The lump-sum amount generally influences workers' and retirees' decisions about benefit payment method preferences. Risk aversion plays a significant role in people's choices: those who are more risk averse tend to prefer annuities to lump sums. Also, health status and longevity expectations affect the desirability of annuities. We find that people who are healthier and expect to live longer prefer annuities over lump sums.

But many people are subject to various other influences, suggesting that an annuity plus a lump sum is often the distribution form of choice. That option offers a mix of security and flexibility, giving retirees both cash—to deal with unexpected events—and a steady guaranteed income.

One influence that all people are subject to is Social Security. For some workers, Social Security will be a significant portion of their retirement income, while for others, it will constitute a much smaller share. Thus, people might want an annuity that, when combined with Social Security, is sufficient to pay their monthly bills. Also, Social Security is inflation adjusted, while most commercial and pension annuities are not.

As companies become more aware of their employees' needs, they may decide to offer new options, such as making annuities available from DC plans. More annuity products might become available and should be examined carefully by plan sponsors. And employees might choose to purchase commercial annuities to minimize their retirement risks.

Changing pension laws also play a role. The Pension Protection Act of 2006 will effectively reduce the value of lump sums paid from DB plans while holding the value of annuities steady. As intended, lower lump-sum values will likely nudge more workers toward annuities.

Moreover, market volatility in the stock market has made equity investing in DC plans and IRAs less attractive, which could make annuities more attractive as investments. At retirement, lower interest rates make life annuities more expensive—the opposite effect—which could make people less willing to purchase annuities.

Many new DC annuity products allow workers to purchase an annuity while they're still working, which mitigates the interest rate risk at retirement, and some have guarantees that limit the risk of market volatility. And, of course, appropriate diversification limits retirees' equity exposure and can also hedge interest rate risk.

Appendix: Regression Analysis

Tables 4A.1 and 4A.2 show the results of a regression analysis on the survey data of the marginal effects of various independent variables on an ordered dependent variable. They are estimated from ordered logit regression models of survey responses from older workers and retirees, respectively. The value of the dependent variable moves from 1, to 2, to 3 as the survey respondents express a strong preference for the annuity (chooses full annuitization regardless of the quoted hypothetical terms of exchange) to a mixed preference (chooses full annuitization if terms are attractive) to a strong preference for the lump sum (always takes a lump-sum distribution when available). The independent variables are largely self-explanatory in the list and represent a fairly wide array of socioeconomic, preference, and benefit plan influences and characteristics of older workers and retirees discussed in the chapter that are thought to be related to the choice of particular distribution modes. The mixed-risk and risk-averse independent variables are dichotomous and depend on answers to survey questions on hypothetical job offer situations where safe and risky choices are given; the former equal to one means that the respondent has some tolerance for risk if the return is high enough, while the latter equal to one means a high degree of risk avoidance (the missing variable is risk loving). All the variables were weighted for the proportions of the respondents in the relevant national populations of older workers and retirees, respectively.

As seen in table 4A.1, for older workers, the preference for full annuitization is positively and significantly related to being highly risk averse and being covered by both DB and DC plans, while it is negatively and significantly related to expecting to receive an inheritance. For example, if the older worker expects to receive an inheritance, she is 6 percentage points less likely to prefer full annuitization. The coverage relationship may be explained by familiarity with a life annuity

Table 4A.1
Marginal effects of ordered logit regression model: Older workers

	Outcome = Annuity		Outcome = Mixed		Outcome = Lump sum	
	dy/dx	Z-score	dy/dx	Z-score	dy/dx	Z-score
Age 50–54	-0.0005	-0.01	-0.0001	-0.01	0.001	0.01
Age 55–59	0.004	0.11	0.002	0.11	-0.005	-0.11
Female	0.020	0.70	0.008	0.65	-0.028	-0.69
Married	-0.033	-1.04	-0.012	-1.13	0.045	1.08
Good health	0.061	1.59	0.039	1.15	-0.100	-1.40
Longevity	0.074	1.52	0.019**	2.30	-0.093*	-1.74
First quartile income	0.067	1.50	0.017**	2.09	-0.085*	-1.68
Third quartile income	0.014	0.31	0.005	0.34	-0.019	-0.32
Fourth quartile income	-0.022	-0.53	-0.009	-0.49	0.032	0.52
DB plan only	0.094	1.25	0.014	1.41	-0.109	-1.55
DC plan only	0.098	0.84	0.013	0.87	-0.111	-1.06
DB and DC plans	0.082**	2.55	0.051*	1.95	-0.133**	-2.34
Plans to give an inheritance	0.010	0.30	0.004	0.28	-0.014	-0.29
Expect to receive inheritance	-0.057*	-1.70	-0.030	-1.34	0.087	1.58
Less than high school	0.206	0.33	-0.019	-0.08	-0.186	-0.51
Some college	0.010	0.26	0.004	0.27	-0.014	-0.26
College graduate	-0.050	-1.19	-0.024	-0.97	0.073	1.12
Master's, professional, Ph.D. degree	0.076	1.29	0.018**	2.11	-0.094	-1.47
Retiree health insurance	-0.022	-0.64	-0.008	-0.67	0.030	0.65
Confident in having enough resources to live 15 years in retirement	-0.072	-1.56	-0.015**	-2.11	0.087*	1.76
IRA	0.041	1.23	0.018	1.05	-0.060	-1.18
Debt	-0.041	-1.19	-0.014	-1.38	0.055	1.26
No wealth	0.055	0.55	0.013	1.33	-0.068	-0.63
$1–$24,999 wealth	0.176	1.22	-0.002	-0.04	-0.173*	-1.77
$200,000–$499,999 wealth	0.010	0.26	0.004	0.27	-0.014	-0.26
$500,000 or more wealth	0.005	0.11	0.002	0.12	-0.007	-0.11
Mixed risk	0.054	0.82	0.017	1.07	-0.071	-0.88
Risk averse	0.095*	1.88	0.046	1.52	-0.141*	-1.78
Pr(Outcome=?)	0.207		0.437		0.356	

Notes: *** denotes significance at the 1% level, ** at the 5% level, and * at the 10% level. Dependent variable: 1 = annuity-annuity, 2 = mixed, 3 = lump sum–lump sum. *Source:* Authors' calculation, based on Watson Wyatt 2007 Survey.

Table 4A.2
Marginal effects of ordered logit regression model: Retirees

	Outcome= Annuity		Outcome= Mixed		Outcome= Lump Sum	
	dy/dx	Z-Score	dy/dx	Z-Score	dy/dx	Z-Score
Age 60–64	-0.00004	-0.13	-0.00001	-0.12	0.00005	0.13
Age 70–74	0.001	0.04	0.0003	0.04	-0.001	-0.04
Age 75–80	0.019	0.50	0.004	0.59	-0.023	-0.52
Female	-0.016	-0.43	-0.004	-0.42	0.020	0.43
Married	0.028	0.69	0.008	0.61	-0.036	-0.67
Good health	-0.059	-1.15	-0.011	-1.60	0.069	1.23
Longevity	0.057	1.61	0.017	1.35	-0.074	-1.56
DB plan only	0.048	0.86	0.009	1.29	-0.057	-0.92
DC plan only	0.038	0.72	0.008	0.97	-0.046	-0.76
DB and DC plans	0.067	1.62	0.016*	1.69	-0.083*	-1.68
Plans to give an inheritance	-0.122***	-2.79	-0.065*	-1.66	0.187**	2.30
Expect to receive inheritance	0.021	0.55	0.006	0.52	-0.027	-0.54
Less than high school	-0.076	-1.17	-0.035	-0.76	0.112	1.01
Some college	-0.028	-0.67	-0.008	-0.60	0.036	0.65
College graduate	-0.006	-0.13	-0.001	-0.13	0.008	0.13
Master's, professional, Ph.D. degree	-0.008	-0.14	-0.002	-0.13	0.010	0.14
Retiree health insurance	0.025	0.65	0.007	0.61	-0.031	-0.64
Confident in having enough resources to live 15 years in retirement	-0.046	-0.91	-0.008	-1.29	0.054	0.96
IRA	0.008	0.17	0.002	0.17	-0.010	-0.17
Debt	-0.029	-0.80	-0.007	-0.84	0.036	0.81
No wealth	0.102	1.50	0.010	1.40	-0.111*	-1.70
$1–$24,999 wealth	-0.044	-0.69	-0.016	-0.54	0.060	0.65
$200,000–$499,999 wealth	0.002	0.04	0.0005	0.04	-0.003	-0.04
$500,000 or More wealth	-0.049	-1.00	-0.024	-0.90	0.063	0.98
Mixed risk	0.087	1.30	0.015*	1.71	-0.102	-1.39
Risk averse	0.111**	2.11	0.036	1.63	-0.147**	-2.01
Pr(Outcome=?)	0.252		0.361		0.386	

Notes: *** denotes significance at the 1% level, ** at the 5% level, and * at the 10% level. Dependent variable: 1 = annuity-annuity, 2 = mixed, 3 = lump sum–lump sum. *Source:* Authors' calculation, based on Watson Wyatt 2007 Survey.

through the DB plan, while the inheritance relationship is simply explained by the expectation of getting perhaps significant assets just before or during the retirement period. The mixed annuity preference, where there is openness to an annuity at the "right price," is positively and significantly related to longevity, low incomes, being covered by DB and DC plans, and high educational achievement and negatively related to retirement confidence. The relationship to education level may indicate that a positive attitude toward annuities can be encouraged through counseling and financial literacy. Finally, the lump-sum preference is negatively and significantly related to longevity and low income statuses, coverage by DB and DC plans, low wealth, and high risk aversion and is positively related to retirement confidence.

For retirees (see table 4A.2), there are fewer statistically significant results, but they are of similar direction as those for older workers. Plans to give an inheritance, however, are more important for retirees in their distribution mode choice; because death is temporally closer for them, legacies are likely a more salient consideration in their financial and insurance choices and preferences.

Note

1. About 28 percent of DC plans offer any sort of annuity option, according to the Watson Wyatt 2005–2006 COMPARISON survey of plan sponsors.

Reference

Watson Wyatt Worldwide. 2007. *2007 U.S. Surveys of Older Employees' and Retirees' Attitudes Toward Lump Sum and Annuity Distributions From Retirement Plans.* Watson Wyatt Worldwide.

5 Comparing Strategies for Retirement Wealth Management: Mutual Funds and Annuities

with Gaobo Pang

Summary and Introduction

This chapter compares wealth management strategies for individuals in retirement, focusing on trade-offs regarding wealth creation and income security. Specifically, it compares the following six strategies: (1) systematic withdrawal from mutual funds, (2) fixed payout immediate life annuity, (3) immediate variable annuity for life, (4) variable annuity plus guaranteed minimum withdrawal benefit (VA+GMWB), (5) mix of withdrawals from mutual funds and fixed payout immediate life annuity, one-time wealth split at retirement, and (6) mix of mutual fund withdrawals and fixed payout life annuity, gradual annuitization at certain ages.

Systematic withdrawals from mutual funds usually give opportunities for greater wealth creation at the risk of large investment losses and income shortfalls.

Fixed and variable life annuities forgo bequest considerations and distribute the highest incomes.

A variable annuity with guaranteed minimum withdrawal benefit (VA+GMWB) somewhat addresses both income need and wealth preservation.

Mixes of mutual funds and fixed life annuities deliver solutions broadly similar to, and even more flexible than, a VA+GMWB strategy.

From *Journal of Financial Planning* 22 (8) (August 2009): 36–47. Reprinted with permission by the Financial Planning Association, *Journal of Financial Planning*, August 2009, Gaobo Pang and Mark Warshawsky, "Comparing Strategies for Retirement Wealth Management: Mutual Funds and Annuities." For more information on the Financial Planning Association, please visit www.fpanet.org or call 1-800-322-4237.

Defined contribution plan participants should be aware of contract terms, because fees and charges play a nontrivial role in altering wealth creation and income levels. In-plan institutional pricing of funds may provide better opportunities than lump sum purchase on retail terms.

As workers retire with their financial assets predominantly in 401(k) plans and IRAs, they need to select a sound strategy to manage their wealth. The strategy should generate a reliable flow of income in retirement and preserve and grow resources for varied needs at advanced ages, as well as, possibly, a bequest. In short, the strategy should deliver financial security, flexibility, and growth.

We compare six wealth management strategies for retirees. We assess trade-offs for wealth creation and income security. Values are measured in terms of real purchasing power, that is, after adjustment for inflation. Various asset allocations and levels of fees are considered. The analysis focuses exclusively on qualified accounts, for example, a retired middle-class household in which 401(k) plans and IRAs are the main retirement financial assets. We thus ignore the issue of differential tax treatments for mutual fund withdrawals and annuity payouts in non-qualified accounts.[1]

The simulations show that these strategies cater to varying risk preferences or desired priorities. Systematic withdrawals from mutual funds imply opportunities for greater wealth creation, possibly meeting the needs for bequests and emergency liquidity, but this strategy entails large risk of investment losses and bumpy incomes. Absent provisions in their retirement plans, investors may want to use retail fixed or variable life annuities, which distribute the highest life-long incomes. When investors want to address income and wealth needs, a VA+GMWB offers an alternative. This strategy, however, only delivers nominal income stability and does not necessarily dominate systematic withdrawals in real terms. A mix of mutual funds and life annuities works similarly to VA+GMWB and seems to provide more flexibility in striking a balance between the goals of income maximization and wealth preservation. These findings are based on assumptions that are consistent with the generic products on the market and their average levels of fees and charges. Wealth and income generated will vary substantially when different levels of fees apply, arising from factors such as group bargaining, market competition, product differentiation, and so on.

Alternative Building Blocks for Retirement Wealth Management

Strategy 1: Systematic Withdrawal from Mutual Funds

Investors in this strategy are assumed to take a systematic withdrawal as a constant percentage of mutual fund balance in each period.[2] This strategy, by design, will not exhaust the wealth entirely, although it may come close to low or zero dollars in highly adverse situations. It implicitly assumes some self-discipline on the part of investors. The strategy provides liquidity to investors and bequests potential to their heirs. It allows investors to increase consumption when mutual funds perform well, but also exposes them to significant declines in consumption when investment outcomes are poor.[3]

Strategy 2: Fixed Payout Immediate Life Annuity

Retirees in this strategy are assumed to make a one-time purchase of a fixed nominal payout straight life annuity, converting all wealth accumulated. Without an annuity, retirees' income flow and consumption hinge on the speed at which they draw down wealth, in addition to investment success or failure. Retirees may outlive their financial resources if they consume too fast, especially in the context of ever-increasing life expectancy. Or, they may be overly cautious and accept a lower standard of living than their wealth can support. It is a challenge to weigh the considerations. Immediate life annuities, as suggested by various studies, are products that address well the longevity risk and offer a steady flow of income. We use the most widely available annuities that pay fixed nominal benefits for life, and we adjust in our model results the payments for inflation to get real values.[4]

Traditional fixed-payout immediate annuities are subject to adverse selection by groups with low mortality expectations, typically do not allow transfer of wealth upon death of the investors, and face timing risk in the purchase price. Adverse selection increases the cost to investors with average or high mortality expectations. The annuity prices are closely determined by, and thus lifetime payout levels are sensitive to, changes in interest rates at time of purchase.[5] It should be noted that various enhancements are available for fixed (and variable) annuities. Such features as guaranteed periods and death benefits, which are not analyzed here, are designed to meet liquidity and bequest needs. In exchange for these features, the level of income delivered to investors will be reduced relative to straight life annuities.

Strategy 3: Immediate Variable Annuity for Life

In this strategy, retirees are assumed to purchase an immediate variable straight life annuity that delivers variable income for life, with no residual. At the time of purchase, the investor selects an assumed investment return (AIR). This AIR together with the insurer's mortality guarantee determines how many annuity units the investor gets. The annual payout, conditional on survival, is equal to the number of annuity units multiplied by the value of each unit. The number of units remains fixed from the VA issue date onward unless funds are transferred into or out of the VA account. The unit value evolves with the net investment performance of the underlying funds relative to the AIR. The net performance is the gross investment returns net of fund management and insurance fees. The VA payout stream will rise (fall) if the net investment return is higher (lower) than the AIR, or will remain constant if they coincide. The VA investor can deliberately choose a higher AIR to receive larger annuity payouts in earlier years, or choose a lower AIR to tilt the expected benefits to later life.

Strategy 4: Variable Annuity Plus Guaranteed Minimum Withdrawal Benefit (VA+GMWB)

The addition of a guaranteed minimum withdrawal benefit rider to conventional deferred variable annuities is one of the recent innovations in annuity products. VA investors choose among the lineups of underlying mutual funds offered by the VA providers. Many variable annuities also carry a death benefit. To make a consistent comparison, this analysis only considers annuities with a common level of basic death benefits (with the remaining account value paid to beneficiaries) and the corresponding insurance fees.

The appeal of VA+GMWB to investors lies in the protection against market declines and the opportunity to profit when the market booms. The actual withdrawal amounts vary with asset portfolios and returns, but the minimum is guaranteed by the rider to be a certain percentage of the nominal guaranteed income base (GIB). The GIB is non-decreasing and can step up on the rider anniversary date if the market performs well.

For instance, consider a $10,000 investment on VA+GMWB with a 5 percent withdrawal rate; the initial account value and GIB are both $10,000. Suppose there is a 20 percent loss on the investment portfolio in one year, and the account value shrinks to $8,000. The investor is guaranteed the payout of $500 (0.05 times $10,000) in the coming years, regardless of investment losses. If the investment realizes a 20 percent gain instead, the GIB can be reset as $12,000 on the next anniversary date and the investor will get annual payout of $600 (0.05 times $12,000) thereafter. The investor here is assumed to buy the guarantee rider on the bump-up in value. In short, the GIB is the up-to-date highest water-mark of account values and is used to calculate the guaranteed annual income level. The account value is the actual market value of the port-folio that fluctuates with investment performance and may be reduced to zero after subtraction of payouts and fees. Note that the extra GMWB rider fee does not have a direct effect on the GIB or the resulting income payouts. This fee, however, reduces the account value, depresses the likelihood of the GIB step-ups, and therefore has a potential negative effect on the future income stream.

As a variable annuity, this product has the usual mortality and expense charges that are based on the account value. In exchange for the GMWB coverage, investors need to pay an additional rider fee annually on the guaranteed income base. For simplicity, this analysis assumes that investors purchase VA+GMWB for life.[6]

Strategy 5: Mix of Withdrawals from Mutual Funds and Fixed Payout Immediate Life Annuity, One-Time Wealth Split at Retirement

An investor may consider a more complex strategy. Perhaps the most natural composite lineup is a mutual fund systematic withdrawal plus a fixed payout life annuity. Investors adopting such a strategy get a certain percentage of the mutual fund balance in addition to the annuity payout. The former product gives the investors liquidity, flexibility, bequest potential, and opportunities to realize higher returns on the stock market, while the latter guarantees a consumption floor. The specific split of wealth between the two underlying products is essen-tially determined by the investors' levels of risk tolerance, their bequest motives, and the influences of market terms at the time of purchase.

Strategy 6: Mix of Mutual Fund Withdrawals and Fixed Payout Life Annuity, Gradual Annuitization at Certain Ages

To make income levels less skewed by one-time conditions in the annuity market, investors in this strategy allocate wealth to mutual funds in the early years of retirement, escalate the shift to fixed imme-diate life annuities with increasing age, and eventually convert all mutual funds into fixed annuities by a certain age. This phased annui-tization will ease the effect of annuity rate fluctuations over time and may help circumvent the psychological obstacle to the (irreversible) purchase of a life annuity. A large mutual fund portfolio may facilitate greater wealth creation, leaving a potentially larger bequest in the event of early death. Investors, however, face the accompanying risk—they may not make much or may even lose money in the mutual funds if the equity premium fails to materialize. Wealth loss during the transition can be large, as in Strategy 1.[7]

More Details of the Wealth Management Strategies

Investors are assumed to retire at age 65, with stochastic mortality before the maximum lifespan of 100. Assuming an older age for retirement will not change the comparison of strategies. Investors have initial wealth of $1 million, which can be rescaled to assess alternative economic and personal situations. Consistent with legal restrictions for qualified retirement plans, a unisex mortality table is used in the simulations.

Risk Tolerance and Asset Allocations

Reflecting a generally higher risk aversion of the older population, we assume that investors desire an equal proportion of wealth, a 50–50 split, in high-risk assets (equity) and relatively low-risk assets (bonds or annuities). With wealth being annuitized, the equity share in the remaining assets will correspondingly increase (up to 100 percent) so as to maintain the same overall risk exposure. The whole wealth portfolio may nonetheless deviate from this 50–50 ideal and tilt toward low-risk assets when the non-annuitized wealth is a much smaller size as a share of net worth.

Specifically, the equity-bond allocation in Strategy 1 is always balanced at 50–50. Investors in Strategy 2 are life annuity price takers (see below about annuity pricing) and skip asset allocation altogether. The same 50–50 asset split is assumed for the underlying investment of the VA and the VA+GMWB in Strategies 3 and 4, respectively. (We later apply a 70–30 mix in the VA+GMWB strategy to allow investors to deliberately choose more aggressive portfolios given the benefit of downside protections of the GMWB. An increase in rider fees, if tied to the portfolio change, will also alter the results. See more discussions below.) In Strategy 5, we somewhat arbitrarily assume that investors at retirement choose to convert 30 percent of their initial wealth to a fixed payout life annuity and invest the remaining 70 percent in mutual funds.[8] Leveraged by the annuity, the equity-bond split in the mutual fund portfolio is adjusted toward more equity to maintain the 50–50 overall risk exposure. In Strategy 6, investors are assumed to make a phased annuitization from age 65 through 75. As the annuity comprises an increasing share of wealth, the equity-bond proportion is dynamically adjusted toward equity, until the maximum 100 percent of the remaining mutual fund portfolio is in equities. Although returns on life annuities generally improve with age because of the mortality credit, actual total fixed payouts may differ substantially because of the stochastic ups and downs in annuity prices over time owing to changing interest rates.

Asset Returns and Inflation
Equities and bonds are proxied by the S&P 500 and the U.S. Government Bonds Total Return indexes, respectively. Inflation is measured by the change in the CPI-U index. The dynamics of asset returns and inflations are modeled as a vector autoregressive (VAR) process. The VAR coefficients and variance-covariance matrix, estimated on the 1962–2008 quarterly data, are embedded in the simulations to generate a large number of 36-year series of rates and returns. This approach captures the serial correlations among variables and the contemporaneous correlations of market shocks. Moreover, the VAR-based simulations reproduce the persistent structural shifts or long-run mean reversions of variables, the differing short- and long-term correlations between them, and the changing risk-return trade-off of bonds and stocks across investment horizons (a "term structure"). These characteristics are observed prominently in the historical data.[9] The simulated average value is 4 percent for inflation rate (with standard deviation of 2.8 percent), 8.8 percent for equity return (17.1 percent), and 6.4 percent for bond return (6.7 percent). The data-based simulations show equity and bond returns are significantly positively correlated with inflation over long horizons (10-year frequency), though negative correlations hold in the short term (annual frequency).[10]

Annuity Pricing
The underlying assets for fixed life annuities are assumed to be invested in nominal bonds.[11] The calculation of the annuity cost factor uses the government bond yield, which is stochastic through time. Insurance companies also invest in corporate bonds, which have somewhat higher yields, but we assume that the credit spread is used to cover marketing, administration, and other costs as well as bond defaults.

The use of life tables for annuitants, rather than those for general population, in pricing implicitly incorporates a good part of the load, which
reflects adverse selection in the immediate annuity market. In the
pricing of the immediate variable annuity, the same annuitant life
tables apply. The AIR is set equal to the average nominal bond yield.
The VA contracts also charge fund management and insurance fees.[12]

Discretionary Wealth Balance and Income Flows

The wealth at an investor's discretion are the mutual fund balances in
Strategies 1, 5, and 6. It is zero by definition in the case of one-time full
conversion to the fixed life annuity in Strategy 2 or to the VA in Strategy
3. The wealth balance is the account value (if greater than zero) of the
VA+GMWB contract in Strategy 4. Consumptions in each period are
equal to income flows, which are the 5 percent withdrawal of mutual
funds (Strategy 1), or the annuity payouts (fixed in Strategy 2 and variable in Strategies 3 and 4), or a combination of them (Strategies 5 and
6). All data are reported in real terms, that is, inflation-adjusted, as we
explain further below.

Fees and Charges

Mutual funds and variable annuities charge certain fees and expenses.
Based on the average market level of fees for balanced funds sold to
retail investors, say, for their IRAs, as reported in table 5.1a, we assume
that the annual expense ratio for retail mutual funds is 1.2 percent
(rounded, same below). For consistency, this same expense is applied
to the underlying funds in variable annuities. Variable annuities are
assumed to charge an additional 1.2 percent annually on the account
value for mortality, expense, and administrative (M&E&A) fees. For the
GMWB rider, the VA+GMWB product is assumed to charge 0.6 percent
on the GIB, taken from the account balance. These fees are based on
market averages, as reported in table 5.1b. No sufficient public information exists to allow estimates of institutional pricings. Nonetheless,
we discuss group offerings later and illustrate their possible effects if
they result in lower fees.

Simulation Results: Trade-Offs between Success, Gain, and Risk

Baseline Simulations

We run a large number of simulations (100,000 times), each corresponding to a 36-year path (including age 65) of stochastic outcomes of
wealth and income as well as deaths. We assume the investor consumes

Table 5.1
Fees and charges by mutual funds and variable annuities

	a. Mutual fund expense ratios			b. Fees and charges by variable annuities	
	i. Conservative asset allocation	ii. Moderate asset allocation	i and ii together	Insurance charges (M&E&A)	Rider fee for guarantee
Mean (%)	1.28	1.06	1.17	1.22	0.63
Std. Dev. (%)	0.47	0.52	0.50	0.39	0.39
Min (%)	0.15	0.08	0.08	0.25	0.40
Max (%)	2.18	2.21	2.21	1.75	2.00
No. of Obs.	100	100	200	47	29

Notes:
1. Mutual fund expense ratio includes investment management fee, 12b-1 fees, and other expenses. Conservative (moderate) asset allocation reflects the category of mutual funds with relatively low (moderate) risk of fluctuations in asset values and correspondingly lower (higher) return potential.
2. Insurance charges (M&E&A) in variable annuities include mortality and expense risk charges and administrative fees. The calculation in this table considers M&E&As without death benefits or with base death benefits (that is, heirs receive payback of premium if the contract owner dies in the accumulation stage, or account value, but no minimum death benefit guaranteed, in the income stage). Few firms on the market offer plain contracts with no death benefits.
3. This table only considers GMWB rider fees with annual automatic step-up of guaranteed income base. The contract terms of variable annuities on the market vary significantly with regard to maximum issue age, frequency of GIB step-up, rider fee increase upon GIB step-up, guaranteed minimum withdrawal percentage, guarantee coverage period, etc.
Source: For mutual funds, authors' calculations based on the 100 largest balanced mutual funds (by assets) in each category of asset allocation that are covered by www.morningstar.com, March 2008. For variable annuities, the authors' collected data from 15 issuing companies, March 2008.

the withdrawals and annuity payouts (no reinvestment) and the wealth balances plus investment returns carry to the next period.

To evaluate these management strategies, we adjust all wealth and income values by the stochastic realizations of inflation so as to get retirees' real purchasing power. We use several measures of success and risk. First, for real wealth balances among survivors, we identify the average, the 50th percentile (median, most likely), the 5th percentile (bad), and the 95th percentile (good) outcomes. Figure 5.1 plots the results. The mutual fund investment has the highest upside potential (figure 5.1a), with increasing value at possible stake, while the full adoption of annuities, fixed or variable, naturally implies no wealth at

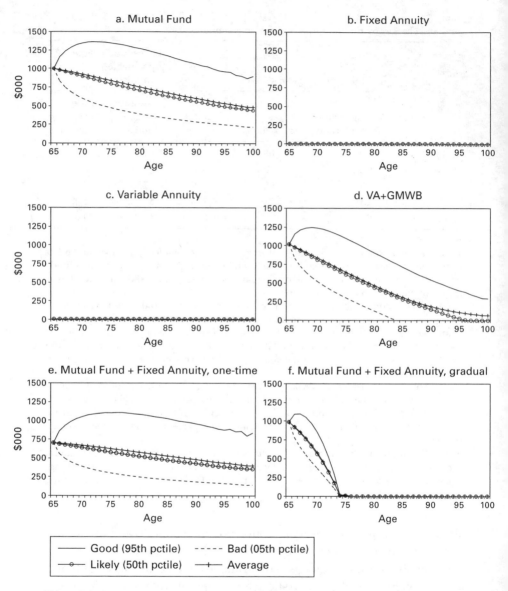

Figure 5.1
Outcomes of real wealth balances for survivors. *Source:* Authors' simulations.

discretion and no bequest (figures 5.1b and 5.1c). The static one-time blending of mutual fund and fixed life annuity in Strategy 5 is more likely to preserve a large wealth principal for investors' flexibility (figure 5.1e), and the dynamic blending in Strategy 6 eliminates wealth self-management beyond age 75 (figure 5.1f). Compared to Strategy 1, the wealth balance in Strategy 5 is noticeably lower by design but remains substantial at most ages—the 50th percentile outcome is in the range of $366,000–700,000 in real terms. Different asset mixes would generate different levels. Nonetheless, these outcomes show the appeal of Strategy 5 to some investors who value the longevity insurance but have some resistance to the illiquid nature of traditional life annuities.[13]

The wealth trajectories of VA+GMWB in Strategy 4 are plotted in figure 5.1d. The end-of-life account values, if greater than zero, are bequeathed to heirs. The wealth balance (the 50th percentile outcome) in this strategy shrinks at a faster rate than it does in Strategies 1 and 5. This outcome suggests investors should think carefully when they use the VA+GMWB product to address wealth needs. Two major factors have come into play: (1) When the GIB steps up in the context of good investment performance, the scheduled wealth withdrawals are boosted too, and so are the GMWB rider charges in dollar terms; and (2) compared to mutual funds, the additional M&E&A and rider fees reduce the retirement wealth nest egg.

In our second assessment measure, there is a great deal of difference among the strategies with regard to income level and stability. Using the same outcome percentiles as above, figure 5.2 shows the levels of real income. As another view of this risk, figure 5.3 plots the likelihood of annual income in real dollars falling below $45,000 (a level slightly below the nominal benefit guaranteed by VA+GMWB at initial wealth).

Mutual funds perhaps give investors more wealth control, but the systematic withdrawal strategy entails risk—more likely than not (over 60 percent probability in many years, figure 5.3a) investors are confronted with real income shortfalls. Compared with mutual funds, the variable annuity generally yields higher payouts and lower (but still substantial) shortfall risk—compare figure 5.2a to 5.2c and figure 5.3a to 5.3c. This is because no bequest is intended in the VA and there exists mortality credit that cannot be replicated by mutual funds. The annuity providers pool both the initial funds and the mortality risks among the annuitants. When some annuitants die, their funds are allocated to survivors in the pool. The extra asset redistribution forms the mortality

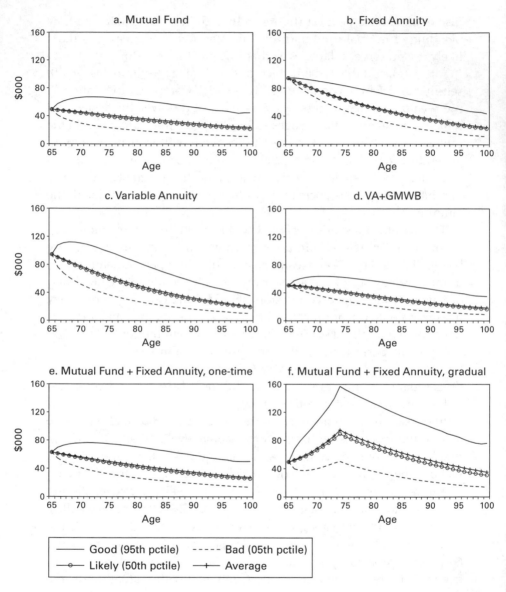

Figure 5.2
Outcomes of real income for survivors. *Source:* Authors' simulations.

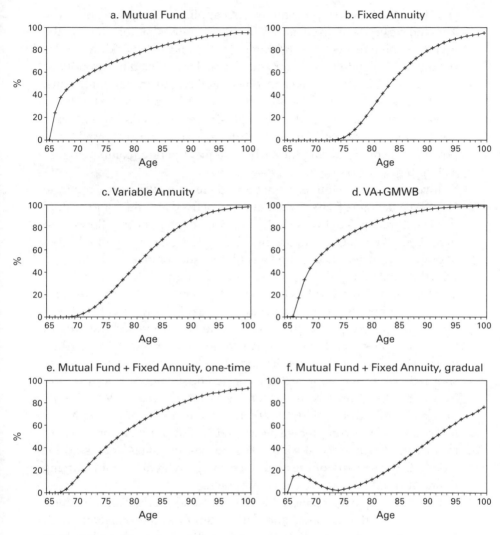

Figure 5.3
Age-specific probability of real income falling below $45,000 for survivors. *Source:* Authors' simulations.

credit. This survivorship premium also applies to fixed life annuities. The choice between fixed and variable annuities simply lies in the investors' preferences over income potential and risk. Seeking regular payouts and spending, investors may consider the fixed life annuity or the VA+GMWB. Both deliver income stability, but in nominal terms, and are exposed to inflation risk (see figures 5.3b and 5.3d). The choice between them hinges on the strength of wealth needs. Absent such needs, the former outperforms the latter in delivering real purchasing power, particularly during the early retirement period (compare figure 5.2b to figure 5.2d).

Investors may wonder whether there are ways to replicate VA+GMWB. Figure 5.2e shows that a mix of fixed annuities and mutual funds in Strategy 5 delivers similar, or even higher, income flows than the VA+GMWB does (compare figure 5.2e to figure 5.2d), in addition to preserving generally the same wealth on hand for investors, although with different time and risk profiles (compare figure 5.1e to figure 5.1d). The VA+GMWB product has the guaranteed and growth portions combined, and imposes M&E&A and GMWB rider fees on the entire allocation. Strategy 5 keeps the guaranteed annuity income and the growth portions separate, and assumes insurance fees (implicit) only on the guaranteed portion. This replication strategy appears to have lower shortfall risk in terms of real income (compare figure 5.3e to figure 5.3d). This result reveals that income stability offered by VA+GMWB only rests at the nominal level. Still, this product may appeal to investors who prefer a comprehensive structure and are wary of losses in mutual funds when the stock market crashes and stays depressed for a period. The security of the insurance company guarantee in extreme financial conditions, however, is unknown.

Emphasizing real income stability, the 10-year gradual annuitization in Strategy 6 offers another alternative. Ignoring the unusually high income (a peak of about $160,000 with a slim 5 percent probability), investors can reasonably expect to receive significantly improved annuity payouts. The median real incomes are greater than those generated by the one-time annuitization strategies (figure 5.2f). The overall inward shift (reduction) of income shortfall risk is substantial (figure 5.3f). By this single standard, Strategy 6 perhaps outperforms other strategies. A modest jump in the shortfall risk is observed in the transition years when the investor is in her late 60s, which can be considered as the price for the accommodation of a potential early-death bequest and less regret for the timing of the annuity purchase.

Table 5.2
Outcomes of real wealth and income with baseline assumptions

	a. Wealth Balance					
Strategy	95%tile ($k)	Median ($k)	5%tile ($k)	Mean ($k)	Std. dev. ($k)	% below $600k
1. Mutual fund	1,272.3	830.7	406.9	829.2	270.5	21.3
2. Fixed life annuity	0.0	0.0	0.0	0.0	0.0	100.0
3. Variable annuity	0.0	0.0	0.0	0.0	0.0	100.0
4. VA+GMWB	1,100.4	642.7	49.2	628.2	328.9	45.8
5. Mutual fund + life annuity, one-time	1,018.1	605.4	278.8	615.2	232.5	49.1
6. Mutual fund + life annuity, gradual	962.0	10.3	0.0	292.5	368.0	73.9

	b. Income					
	95%tile ($k)	Median ($k)	5%tile ($k)	Mean ($k)	Std. dev. ($k)	% below $45k
1. Mutual fund	62.9	41.4	20.5	41.3	13.3	60.0
2. Fixed life annuity	94.3	67.7	31.4	66.0	19.8	17.6
3. Variable annuity	102.2	63.9	25.3	64.4	25.0	25.7
4. VA+GMWB	59.1	41.8	20.1	40.7	12.2	59.7
5. Mutual fund + life annuity, one-time	72.3	50.9	26.7	50.4	14.5	36.3
6. Mutual fund + life annuity, gradual	129.8	65.4	36.0	72.2	30.1	13.0

Source: Authors' simulations.

We further examine realized wealth and incomes in all periods, provided that the survivals have occurred. We also calculate the probability of the real wealth balance falling below $600,000 and the probability of real income below $45,000.

Table 5.2 reports the results. Mutual funds provide opportunities for greater wealth creation, yielding the highest median wealth value ($830,700) among all strategies. The income flow, however, has a high likelihood of falling short (about 60 percent chance of being below $45,000), and the median is relatively low ($41,400). This is owing to the relatively conservative withdrawal percentage that should be set low in practice to avoid outliving resources.[14] Investors may thus enjoy a lower welfare than can be actually supported. The variable annuity forms an alternative with significantly higher income ($63,900) and lower shortfall probability (25.7 percent) for investors who need no wealth. In this direction, the fixed life annuity even performs better, with a median income of $67,700 and a shortfall probability of 17.6 percent.

The VA+GWMB product does a reasonable job in keeping up wealth balances in most periods (median $642,700), but creates only a marginal improvement in real income (median value of $41,800 and shortfall probability of 59.7 percent) over Strategy 1. In contrast to VA+GWMB, Strategies 5 and 6 can generally provide investors with greater purchasing power. Strategy 6 does particularly well in terms of ensuring a minimum of real income. The real income level can be fine tuned at the compromise of adjusted size of wealth. In other words, catering to their risk preferences and specific economic or intra-family considerations, investors have the flexibility to construct comprehensive retirement portfolios to meet their needs using traditional products in the market.

Note that the stochastic simulations incorporate long-run positive correlations between inflation and asset returns. This should give all strategies relative to nominal fixed annuities (Strategy 2) some advantage in hedging against inflation and preserving real consumption over longer horizons.

A Comparison with Alternative Asset Allocations

We now make alternative assumptions regarding the equity-bond mix in the underlying assets: an aggressive 70–30 portfolio and a conservative 30–70 portfolio versus the baseline 50–50. These allocations fall into the "allowable" range, as major VA+GMWB providers typically limit the equity fraction to around 60–80 percent. Such restrictions enable the providers to contain their risk exposure.

Greater equity holdings create higher wealth and income on average but also imply larger swings (standard deviations) of outcomes (table 5.3a). That is, individual investors are more exposed to investment losses as the portfolio grows aggressive. A more conservative portfolio generally leads to a lower level of wealth creation, with a smaller variance (table 5.3b). With an aggressive portfolio, combinations with fixed annuities and the variable annuity with a GMWB rider become more attractive because investors can use these somewhat "market-proof" payouts to establish a minimum consumption floor. The choice between

Table 5.3
Outcomes of real wealth and income with alternative portfolios

	Wealth Balance				Income			
Strategy	Median ($k)	Mean ($k)	Std. dev. ($k)	% below $600k	Median ($k)	Mean ($k)	Std. dev. ($k)	% below $45k
a. Aggressive 70-30 equity-bond portfolio								
1. Mutual fund	860.9	874.0	326.9	20.3	42.9	43.4	16.0	55.4
2. Fixed life annuity	0.0	0.0	0.0	100.0	67.7	66.0	19.8	17.6
3. Variable annuity	0.0	0.0	0.0	100.0	66.6	67.5	27.6	24.0
4. VA+GMWB	659.5	648.0	362.5	44.5	43.8	43.1	13.9	53.6
5. Mutual fund + life annuity, one-time	625.8	660.8	326.1	46.4	52.2	52.6	18.0	34.8
6. Mutual fund + life annuity, gradual	10.6	297.4	376.8	73.7	66.7	74.7	33.8	13.4
b. Conservative 30-70 equity-bond portfolio								
1. Mutual fund	787.0	783.0	245.4	25.3	39.3	39.0	12.0	65.9
2. Fixed life annuity	0.0	0.0	0.0	100.0	67.7	66.0	19.8	17.6
3. Variable annuity	0.0	0.0	0.0	100.0	60.5	61.3	24.1	29.6
4. VA+GMWB	610.9	600.3	315.9	48.9	39.9	38.8	11.5	65.4
5. Mutual fund + life annuity, one-time	570.6	568.4	180.5	55.7	48.7	48.1	13.1	40.9
6. Mutual fund + life annuity, gradual	9.8	286.8	361.5	74.5	63.1	69.2	27.6	14.4

Source: Authors' simulations.

VA+GMWB and some mixing strategies again depends on the investors' preferences.

A Further Look at VA+GMWB

The GMWB rider helps isolate investors from nominal income shortfalls in a down market. This is a "put" option for investors. A more aggressive portfolio gives investors the chance to step up the GIB and correspondingly receive a larger income payout. The difference in expected annual consumption between a 70–30 equity-bond portfolio and a 30–70 portfolio is $3,900, and the wealth balances differ by $48,600, both in real terms.

Is it optimal for investors to select the riskiest portfolio available? The answer depends on two major factors: the size of the rider fee and the bequest motive. Regarding the former, for financial solvency, insurers of VA+GMWB contracts naturally should charge higher rider fees for assuming higher "guaranteed" risk. In theory, neither investors nor insurers should be in an obviously advantageous position.[15] The majority (approximately 70 percent) of the VA+GMWB providers in table 5.1 state in their prospectuses that, upon the automatic step-up or the investor-elected step-up of GIB, the contracts will increase, may increase, or reserve the right to increase the annual rider percentage charges, subject to the contract maximum rates. Changes in market conditions may also trigger such fee hikes.

A strong bequest motive may also keep investors from being too aggressive in investment. VA+GMWB products are presumably more oriented toward generating (or even maximizing) income for consumption. An aggressive portfolio, especially if accompanied by higher fees, can result in the possibility of leaving a smaller bequest. Nonetheless, if investors have set aside a trust for their heirs from other assets, and if they can get the GMWB rider and VA at reasonably low fees, it is rational for them to be aggressive with portfolios.

Let's now further consider the critical role of fees. We use alternative levels of fees for VA+GMWB to examine how wealth and income are affected under different contract terms. The baseline 50–50 equity-bond portfolio applies here. An improvement in contract terms may be attributable to market competition and financial innovation or to the enhanced market power when large defined contribution (DC) plan sponsors collectively bargain for their participants. On the other hand, market power by providers, for instance, through product differentia-

Table 5.4

Outcomes of real wealth and income for VA+GMWB with alternative fees

Fee levels	Wealth Balance				Income			
	Median ($K)	Mean ($k)	Std. dev. ($k)	% below $600k	Median ($K)	Mean ($k)	Std. dev. ($k)	% below $45k
0. Baseline fees (M&E&A 1.20% GMWB 0.60%)	642.7	628.2	328.9	45.8	41.8	40.7	12.2	59.7
1. Max fees (M&E&A 1.75% GMWB 2.00%)	479.0	489.7	356.2	59.7	39.0	38.0	11.6	67.8
2. High fees (M&E&A 1.60% GMWB 1.50%)	532.6	531.4	349.5	55.8	39.7	38.7	11.9	65.6
3. Low fees (M&E&A 0.50% GMWB 0.40%)	717.4	698.2	317.8	37.7	43.6	42.6	12.5	54.3
4. Min fees (M&E&A 0.25% GMWB 0.40%)	738.3	718.5	314.6	35.2	44.1	43.3	12.7	52.7

Source: Authors' simulations.

tion and/or misinformed choices by investors, will probably lead to inferior contract terms to investors.

Table 5.4 reports the simulated results. The maximum and minimum levels of fees are from the market data in table 5.1. As it is typically not the case that investors pay maximum or minimum fees in all categories, we introduce two less extreme scenarios—"high" and "low" fees, which respectively represent the 95th and the 5th percentiles of the fees. Not surprisingly, at lower (higher) fees, investors receive a larger (smaller) share of wealth created and enjoy higher (lower) levels of consumption and welfare. What is striking is the magnitude of wealth and income differences when investors pay high fees compared to when a low-fee option is available, other things equal. For instance, the median wealth balance in the low fees scenario is roughly $184,800 higher than in the high fees case.

An investor in the former situation would enjoy a higher consumption by about $3,900 a year.

A Consideration of Institutional Pricing

Fees might be lower for large DC plans. Institutional pricing, with simultaneous and proportional reductions in fees for all strategies, would not necessarily change the performance comparisons in a qualitative way. First, lower fund expense on underlying assets would equally apply to mutual funds and VA products, leaving the relative positions of Strategies 1, 3, and 4 intact. Second, with heterogeneous populations formed and the adverse selection problem somewhat mitigated in large DC plans, the reduction in insurance fees should equally apply to fixed and variable group annuities, leaving the comparisons of Strategies 2, 3, and 4 unchanged. By transitivity, these in turn imply that group pricings would not otherwise strengthen or weaken the blending strategies of mutual funds plus life annuities. And third, as the only potential source for overturning results, it is not clear whether an institutional GMWB rider fee would be lower than at the retail level. Theory may not suggest a wholesale-retail price difference because VA+GMWB issuers are assuming greater risks, with no obvious gain of risk diversification, in the face of increased subscription to GMWB guarantees.

Nonetheless, we use the following experiment, assuming uneven reductions in fees, to illustrate the benefit of institutional pricings. Absent relevant data, we assume fund management fee and M&E&As are reduced to a quarter of the baseline assumptions. Fees on any actual plan may be higher or lower. We maintain the baseline assumptions about fixed payout life annuity on the premise that its pricing is more determined by the market structure and adverse selection than by group bargaining. Table 5.5 reports the simulation results. In contrast to the baseline results in table 5.2, this experiment by construction makes strategies involving mutual funds and VA products more attractive—higher wealth balance and/or income payout plus lower shortfall risks. Note that the improvements in the profiles of VA and VA+GMWB are even greater because both fund management and insurance fees are reduced. These results illustrate the potential gains to investors when prices are changed in their favor. Whether this would tilt investors' preference for one strategy over another essentially depends on the category and magnitude of fee reductions.

Table 5.5
Outcomes of real wealth and income with lower fees

Strategies	Wealth balance				Income			
	Median ($k)	Mean ($k)	Std. dev. ($k)	% below $600k	Median ($k)	Mean ($k)	Std. dev. ($k)	% below $45k
1. Mutual fund	900.6	904.6	282.1	13.4	45.2	45.3	13.9	49.6
2. Fixed life annuity	0.0	0.0	0.0	100.0	67.7	66.0	19.8	17.6
3. Variable annuity	0.0	0.0	0.0	100.0	75.5	75.2	24.2	11.5
4. VA+GMWB	792.3	771.4	313.0	29.1	45.7	45.1	13.2	47.8
5. Mutual fund + life annuity, one-time	654.9	673.0	254.1	40.3	53.8	53.4	14.9	29.2
6. Mutual fund + life annuity, gradual	8.6	288.0	364.1	74.4	69.2	76.0	31.6	10.5

Note: Mutual fund expense ratio and M&E&As are all 0.30 percent.
Source: Authors' simulations.

Conclusions

With the sponsorship shift toward defined contribution plans by many U.S. employers, more workers will rely on 401(k) plans and IRAs as their primary source of retirement income outside of Social Security. It is a challenge for retirees to foresee future financial needs and precisely allocate resources. Because DC plans are typically self-managed by their participants and lack the automatic withdrawal mechanism featured in most defined benefit (DB) plans, the chances are good that workers may run out of their DC funds or under-consume, given that the length of life is uncertain. To avoid retirement ruin, DC plan participants need to establish a sound wealth decumulation strategy.

This analysis compares wealth management strategies for individuals in retirement, including mutual funds, annuities (fixed, variable, or variable plus a minimum income guarantee), and combinations of them. These strategies each have advantages and caveats, appealing to investors with varying risk preferences and intra-family needs. Those who allocate assets in the underlying portfolios toward equities are generally seeking opportunities for greater wealth creation, at the cost of greater risk of wealth destruction, while those who use fixed payout annuities or guarantees seek income regularity and stability. Nearly all products, however, define income payments in nominal terms and thus leave real consumption subject to the uncertainty and erosion of inflation. DC plan participants should also be alert to contract terms in these strategies, because the fees and charges play a nontrivial role in altering wealth creation and income levels. They may be better off by exploring in-plan institutional pricing of funds and annuities, if available, than taking lump sums from their DC plans to purchase products on retail terms.

None of the strategies obviously dominates, given the confluence of uncertainties in asset returns, length of life, and varied risk and bequest preferences. Perhaps useful advice to DC plan participants, and plan sponsors in educating and assisting their employees with strategy selection, is to start with a dichotomy. Investors may want to first carve out a safe segment of their wealth to establish minimum necessary consumption and a certain level of hedging against longevity risk. This longevity insurance is being lost with the decline of DB plans but can be restored with some annuitization as a welfare-enhancing strategy in DC plans.[16] This can be achieved through a traditional life annuity or an income guarantee in variable annuities. After this top priority, the remaining wealth can be more oriented for growth opportunities. Also, investors should be aware of how much annuity benefits are available to them from DB plans and Social Security and correspondingly optimize their portfolios.

Notes

1. Milevsky and Panyagometh (2001) show that the differential tax treatments significantly alter after-tax wealth outcomes from variable annuities versus mutual funds. Brown and Poterba (2004), however, only find mixed support for the role of tax considerations in generating household demand for variable annuities. We also ignore Social Security, assuming its benefit is used as a floor and protection against poverty.

2. Managed payout funds, that is, some new mutual fund innovations that package an investment and spending mechanism like endowment income funds, can also be modeled as systematic withdrawals.

3. Horneff et al. (2006) show that a fixed percentage withdrawal is appealing to retirees across a wide range of risk preferences, while other phased withdrawal rules of varying percentages are only appropriate to sub-groups of population. As a sensitivity test, we will later consider a fixed dollar withdrawal.

4. There are few inflation-indexed annuities on the U.S. market. Research on the U.K. market (Finkelstein and Poterba, 2004) has shown that these annuities are even a poorer actuarial value than nominal annuities.

5. See Warshawsky (2007).

6. The GMWB rider can also be purchased for a certain number of years, and the rider fee should be generally lower than for lifetime protection.

7. Details about modeling the wealth management strategies are given in a Technical Appendix, which is available from the authors upon request.

8. Pye (2009) shows that annuitizing 25 percent to 50 percent of wealth can effectively reduce the risk of running out of resources and thus retrenching consumption in later life.

9. The VAR specification follows Campbell and Viceira (2004, 2005). Details of the estimation and simulations are described in a Technical Appendix, which is available from the authors upon request.

10. The current financial crisis makes it difficult to predict whether future inflation and asset returns will significantly deviate, upward or downward, from these long-run levels. We make no pre-judgment or modifications on the VAR-based expectations. Pye (2009) offers a summary of the dynamics of inflation and asset returns since the 1960s. He also implements an alternative approach to modeling random shocks and mean reversions of these variables.

11. The current insurance law allows a small fraction of underlying account assets in equity investment.

12. The modeling of conventional variable annuity is similar to the calculation of annuity payouts in the TIAA-CREF prospectus (May 2008) for Single Premium Immediate Annuity with Life Funds and the Statement of Additional Information.

13. Ameriks and Ren (2008) show that income annuities, despite the costs and illiquidity, should be a part of an investment and spending plan for investors who desire regular payments and stable spending in late life.

14. Alternatively, we model a "self-annuitization" strategy, that is, a fixed nominal dollar withdrawal equal to 5 percent of initial wealth. This is consistent with fixed life annuities in that they deliver nominal payouts. The "self-annuitization" exposes investors to greater risk of outliving wealth, particularly at advanced ages. The 5th percentile wealth and incomes are lower compared to the baseline Strategy 1. (A fixed real dollar withdrawal, that is, a nominal withdrawal increasing with inflation, would generate further lower 5th percentile outcomes.) The increase in such shortfall risk is by a smaller margin for Strategies 5 and 6, though.

15. Milevsky and Salisbury (2006) show that the theoretical no-arbitrage cost of GMWB is significantly higher than fees actually charged by most VA+GMWB products in the market. They view the current under-pricing as unsustainable and expect GMWB fees to eventually increase or product design to change.

16. See Watson Wyatt (2007), for instance.

References

Ameriks, John, and Liqian Ren. 2008. *Generating Guaranteed Income: Understanding Income Annuities*. Malvern, PA: Vanguard Investment Counseling and Research.

Brown, Jeffrey, and James Poterba. 2004. "Household Demand for Variable Annuities." Boston College Center for Retirement Research working paper no. 2004–08.

Campbell, John, and Luis Viceira. 2004. Long-Horizon Mean-Variance Analysis: A User Guide. Appendix for "The Term Structure of the Risk-Return Tradeoff." Available at http://www.cfapubs.org/toc/faj/2005/61/1.

Campbell, John, and Luis Viceira. 2005. The Term Structure of the Risk-Return Trade-Off. *Financial Analysts Journal* 61 (1):34–44.

Finkelstein, Amy, and James Poterba. 2004. Adverse Selection in Insurance Markets: Policyholder Evidence from the U.K. Annuity Market. *Journal of Political Economy* 112 (February):183–208.

Horneff, Wolfram J., Raimond Maurer, Olivia S. Mitchell, and Ivica Dus. 2006. Optimizing the Retirement Portfolio: Asset Allocation, Annuitization, and Risk Aversion. NBER working paper no. 12392.

Milevsky, Moshe, and Kamphol Panyagometh. 2001. Variable Annuities versus Mutual Funds: A Monte-Carlo Analysis of the Options. *Financial Services Review* 10:145–161.

Milevsky, Moshe, and Thomas Salisbury. 2006. Financial Valuation of Guaranteed Minimum Withdrawal Benefits. *Insurance, Mathematics and Economics* 38:21–38.

Pye, Gordon B. 2009. When Should Retirees Retrench? Reducing the Need with Part-Time Work and Annuitization. *Journal of Financial Planning* 22 (1): 48–55.

Warshawsky, Mark. 2007. Recent Developments in Life Annuity Markets and Products. Benefits Quarterly. *Second Quarter* 23 (2): 46–57.

Watson Wyatt. 2007. Adding an Annuity to Improve Defined Contribution Plan Options. Arlington, VA: Watson Wyatt.

6 Optimizing the Equity-Bond-Annuity Portfolio in Retirement: The Impact of Uncertain Health Expenses

with Gaobo Pang

Introduction and Summary

With the recent decline of traditional defined benefit (DB) pension plans, there has been a corresponding shift to defined contribution (DC) plans by many U.S. corporate plan sponsors. The Social Security (SS) system may also have reductions in its scheduled benefit payouts in order to move it to sustainable solvency. Because DC plans are typically self-managed by their participants and lack the withdrawal discipline featured in the life annuity distributions of SS and most DB plans, a legitimate concern arises that many retirees may run out of their DC funds or underconsume given that the length of life is uncertain.

To protect people against longevity risk, experts have suggested setting annuitization as a default or mandatory option in DC plans. Despite the superior nature of annuities as insurance against longevity, however, most retired households have historically shown relatively little interest in voluntarily annuitizing their wealth. Various factors have been cited as the potential explanations to this "annuity puzzle." Among them, uncertain health expenses have recently gained particular attention. The literature has thus far offered inconclusive findings. Sinclair and Smetters (2004) and Turra and Mitchell (2008) find that uncertain uninsured health expenses and their negative correlation with life expectancy reduce the attractiveness of annuities. Davidoff et al. (2005), on the other hand, show that uncertain health expenses, if occurring in late life, may actually increase the demand for annuities.

Our study offers a comprehensive stochastic life-cycle framework to address the major risks and choices for households in the

From *Insurance: Mathematics and Economics* 46 (1) (January 2010): 198–209.

retirement phase. We assume that annuitization can be made at any age and in any amount, in contrast to a one-time choice of annuitization upon retirement in many previous studies. We consider jointly the household investment choices of bonds, equities, and annuities. The annuitization decision is modeled as a portfolio allocation choice because a life annuity basically represents a class of financial assets with its own unique risk and return features. Specifically, households in the retirement phase optimize consumption and allocate their financial wealth among stocks, bonds, and annuities, in the context of pre-existing annuities such as SS and DB pension coverage. Households in the model have differential exposure to mortality risks and uninsured health care costs, in addition to facing stochastic capital market returns. They also do or do not have a bequest motive.

Our key findings and the logic are as follows. The uncertainty in uninsured health expenses generally leads to precautionary savings, and rational households should shift their assets from risky equities to riskless bonds for a desired level of risk exposure. The simulated optimal portfolio is similar to the practice of life-cycle (target-date) funds in the retirement phase.

Life annuities are as safe as bonds, though contingent on survival, provide higher returns than bonds due to the embedded survivorship credit that increases with age, and eventually dominate bonds, even with a load, for hedging against longevity risk. Occurrences of health care are also life contingent and the expense magnitudes increase with age, as empirically observed, which makes annuities superior to bonds in also hedging against this health spending risk. The existing annuity payouts can be rolled over to finance new immediate annuity purchases so as to capture higher returns and provide greater old-age insurance.

It is optimal for households to hold precautionary savings in the equity-bond bundle prior to annuitization when the annuity return (considering some load) has not yet exceeded the reference returns on the conventional assets. The shift to annuities also provides greater leverage than do bonds for higher-risk-and-return equity investment in the remaining asset portfolios. The health-spending-uncertainty-enhanced annuitization is compatible with the broader theory about liquidity constraints and precautionary savings because the relatively low uninsured health care costs in the early retirement years are largely buffered by the pre-existing SS and DB coverage.

This chapter proceeds as follows: a brief literature review, the details of the stochastic life-cycle model, the findings from the simulations (focusing on the effect of uncertain health expenses on equity-bond-annuity choices), and concluding remarks.

Literature Review

Our work builds on the relevant literature. One strand examines the relationship between health expenses and general household saving behavior. Palumbo (1999) shows that uncertain health expenses play a potentially important role in generating precautionary saving, which helps explain the slow rates of dissaving among elderly families in retirement. Dynan et al. (2004) posit that the precautionary saving with uncertain health expenses and bequest motives are likely the main driving forces for the non-dissaving in old age and saving variations across income groups. These two saving motives need not be mutually exclusive in that the precautionary savings may end up being part of the bequest eventually left to heirs. De Nardi et al. (2006) find that out-of-pocket health care costs increase quickly with both age and permanent income. Households in higher income groups, compared with the lower-income, need to save more because they have higher probability of living to advanced ages (differential mortality) and tend to face larger health expenses (differential health expenses).

Some studies examine the effects of health status and medical expenditures on equity-bond portfolio choices. Feinstein and Lin (2006) show that a prospect of poor health and substantial medical expense may lead the elderly to a more risk-averse investment behavior (less equity). Love and Perozek (2007) show that the introduction of age-dependent background risks such as health expenses lowers the optimal portfolio shares of risky assets with age for older households.

Another strand of research examines what factors are causing the empirically observed lack of voluntary annuitization, in contrast to general theories that suggest annuities are welfare-improving. The seminal work by Yaari (1965) finds that full annuitization of wealth is optimal if the consumer has no bequest motive. Milevsky and Young (2002) show that there exists a real option value to defer annuitization to an older age because the waiting time gives retirees, if sufficiently risk tolerant, opportunities to gain from higher equity returns, better assessment of the length of one's future lifespan, and more favorable terms on annuity purchase. Kotlikoff and Spivak (1981) and Brown and

Poterba (2000) show that the intra-family risk pooling reduces the benefit of annuitization for married couples. Dushi and Webb (2004) show that the high levels of pre-existing annuities in the retirement phase significantly reduce the need to annuitize further.

Particularly relevant are the studies about how uncertain health expenses affect the demand for annuities. Turra and Mitchell (2008) find that uninsured health expenditures motivate precautionary savings and that this need for liquidity makes annuities less attractive at retirement, especially for those whose life expectancy is shortened by health shocks. They also show, however, that the optimal fraction of wealth annuitized remains large in most situations. Sinclair and Smetters (2004) share a similar view—annuities become less effective in providing financial security if health shocks cause large uninsured expenses and simultaneously shorten life expectancy. Davidoff et al. (2005) show that people without a bequest motive should fully annuitize their wealth under market completeness, so long as a positive premium exists, comparing the annuity return (including mortality credit) to the reference returns on conventional assets. Significant, albeit partial, annuitization remains optimal widely even with market incompleteness or a bequest motive. These conditions for a full or partial annuitization are much less restrictive than assumed by Yaari (1965). Moreover, Davidoff et al. (2005) show that the impact of uninsured health expenses on the demand for annuities is critically dependent on the timing of such expenses. Uncertain health expenses, when occurring early in retirement, call for more liquidity holdings and less (illiquid) annuities, but will make annuities better financial instruments to hedge against such expenses if they occur late in life. Yogo (2008) models health as a durable consumption good and health expenditures as endogenous investments in health, rather than treating them as exogenous negative income shocks. The author finds that the need for precautionary savings essentially disappears because the retiree can invest directly in health and accumulate health capital in place of accumulating liquid assets.

Researchers have recently devoted more effort to integrating equity-bond allocation choices with annuitization decisions to better address the needs and strategies in the wealth decumulation phase. Dus et al. (2005), Horneff et al. (2006a, 2006b, 2007, 2008, 2009), and Maurer et al. (2008) examine various investment portfolios and wealth withdrawal strategies in a life-cycle framework, quantify welfare gains with the addition of fixed or variable annuities, and generally show that a well-designed equity-bond-annuity portfolio will offer retirees the chance to capture the equity premium when younger and exploit longevity insurance and mortality credit of annuities in later life. These studies, however, do not address the impact of uninsured health expenses on asset allocation and annuitization choices, which are considered especially in our analysis.

A Life-Cycle Model Starting at Retirement

Preferences

We set up a discrete-time life-cycle model in retirement with age $t \in \{0,...T\}$, where $t = 0$ indicates the retirement age and T the maximum lifespan. Households in the model are assumed to have Epstein-Zin-Weil-type (EZW) preferences (Epstein and Zin (1989) Weil (1990)) over consumption, and a bequest where applicable. Let $\tilde{C}_{it}$ denote the utility-generating composite consumption adjusted by household size n_t (see below) and M_{it} be the non-annuitized wealth for household i at time t. The EZW preferences are specified by the following recursion:

$$V_{it} = \left\{ (1-\beta)n_t \tilde{C}_{it}^{1-1/\gamma} + \beta \left[E_t \left(\varphi_{it} V_{it+1}^{1-\rho} + (1-\varphi_{it})b(M_{it+1}/b)^{1-\rho} \right) \right]^{\frac{1-1/\gamma}{1-\rho}} \right\}^{\frac{1}{1-1/\gamma}} \quad (1)$$

where V_{it} is the indirect utility value at t, E_t the expectation operator, β the time preference discount factor, φ_{it} the survival probabilities for person i to age $t + 1$ conditional on being alive at age t (see the exposition of differential mortality below), b the strength of bequest motive, M_{it+1} the terminal wealth as a bequest upon death, γ the elasticity of intertemporal substitution (EIS), and ρ the coefficient of relative risk aversion (RRA).

Households gain utility from ordinary consumption C_{it}/n_t on a per capita basis. A certain level of consumption is required on necessities C_0. Households are also assumed to get partial utility from health care spending. Let H_{it} be the stochastic out-of-pocket health care cost for household i at age t and κ_t the age-varying fraction of H_{it} that yields utility. The composite consumption $\tilde{C}_{it}$ is defined as[1]

$$\tilde{C}_{it} = C_{it}/n_t - C_0 + \kappa_t H_{it}. \quad (2)$$

Note that health expenses in this formulation, though partly generating utility, make the utility volatile, thus preserving the disturbance of exogenous spending shocks to ordinary consumption.

Health spending is assumed to generate utility on the premises that these expenses to some degree reflect household choices, that they often include basic living expenses, and that health care can be one of the most valuable items for the elderly. The literature varies in treating the association of use and costs of health care with life expectancy and utility. Sinclair and Smetters (2004) and Turra and Mitchell (2008) focus on the possibility of life expectancy being shortened by health shocks. Hall and Jones (2007), however, posit that health care extends life and that the marginal utility of life extension does not decline while the marginal utility of ordinary consumption falls rapidly. In their view, health spending increases utility both "by increasing the quantity of life through a mortality reduction and by increasing the quality of life" (p. 49). Yogo (2008) models health expenditures as endogenous investments in health. Brown and Finkelstein (2008) state that "we do not consider it reasonable to assume that the individual is receiving no consumption value from institutional care" because of shelter and meals provided (p. 1089). Our formulation here is an intermediate case in that health spending is assumed to partly generate utility but have no explicit impact on life expectancy.

Differential Mortality and Uncertain Health Expenses
The literature documents a substantial heterogeneity in mortality rates and uninsured health expenses among individuals, notably by gender, health status, and permanent income, among other factors. To restrain the complexity of computation, we model the heterogeneity mainly across permanent income levels, based on de Nardi et al. (2006). They show that rich people tend to live longer than the poor and that uninsured health expenses rise quickly with both age and permanent income. The conditional survival rate in equation (1) is specified as a function of age t and permanent income decile z_i: $\varphi_{it} = g(t, z_i)$. The dynamics of the stochastic out-of-pocket health care cost, H_{it}, is given by:

$$H_{it} = \exp(f(t, z_i))P_{it}\varepsilon_{it} \tag{3}$$

$$P_{it} = P_{it-1}\eta_{it} \tag{4}$$

where $f(t, z_i)$ is a deterministic component, P_{it} a permanent shock with innovation η_{it}, and ε_{it} a transitory shock. The logarithms of η_{it}, and ε_{it} are assumed to be independent and identically normally distributed with means zero and variances σ_η^2 and σ_ε^2, respectively.

To avoid tracking the transition of health status, we take the average mortality rates and health expenses estimated by de Nardi et al. (2006) across people in each permanent income decile. The implicit assumption here is that the levels of health expenses do not change otherwise specified survival probabilities. Our model is focused on the situations where general illnesses and treatments do not impose a correlation between morbidity and assumed mortality. That is, we assume that health spending is only undertaken if it is expected to result in support of longevity, at least at the population average levels. If, however, major illnesses are associated with both a shorter life expectancy and a preference for consumption in early life, the demand for annuities may be reduced by health shocks. The correspondingly higher health care cost, apart from the life expectancy consideration, however, would not necessarily justify holding more cash (a self-insuring strategy). Rather, better health insurance coverage, with the premium being perhaps higher but predictable, should be more efficient. An individual can allocate funds for the insurance premium for each age. Life annuities, with returns increasing with age, may well provide such funds. In other words, optimizing health insurance should also be part of the portfolio choice when expensive illnesses and increased mortalities are possible, which is not modeled here due to computational constraint.

Levels of health care spending in our model are (exogenously) linked to permanent income deciles, not directly to wealth balances. We ignore the case that households might choose to draw down their wealth so as to become eligible for the means-tested Medicaid or that they might take more risky portfolios if they were already at the brink of the Medicaid eligibility.

Financial Assets

Households in the model face an investment opportunity set containing riskless bonds, risky stocks, and safe but life-contingent annuities. The real gross bond return is constant, R^b, and the equity return, R^e_{it}, follows a log normal distribution with mean $\bar{R}^e$ and variance σ^2_e. Hence, the investment return R_{it} on non-annuitized wealth is dependent on the household's equity-bond mix:

$$R_{it+1} = \alpha_{it} R^e_{it+1} + (1 - \alpha_{it}) R^b \tag{5}$$

where α_{it} is the share of equity investment and $(1 - \alpha_{it})$ the remaining share of bonds.

We consider only joint and survivor (J&S) life annuities whereby the surviving spouse receives as much payout as the couple receives when both members are alive. That is, with a single premium payment, the same fixed level of annuity payout continues from the purchase time until the death of the last surviving spouse. This set-up is computationally identical to a single life annuity and helps avoid tracking separately the survival of each household member. This construction, however, makes the life annuity relatively more expensive for the surviving spouse because it imposes a longer (joint) than actual life expectancy for the spouse, meaning lower annuity payout each period. This is largely acceptable because the model would therefore not overstate the demand for life annuities. Additionally, the magnitude and likelihood of health spending tend to be greater at advanced ages for couples than for singles, highlighting the need and importance of examining strategies against the spending risk. We later test and confirm the robustness of results by modeling female singles only.

Let $\ddot{a}_t$ denote the annuity factor for a household of husband and wife both aged t; the purchase with a single premium W_{it} at t yields an annual annuity payout $W_{it}/\ddot{a}_t$ starting at $t + 1$. The annuity factor in turn is determined by assumptions regarding the joint survival probabilities among annuitants, φ_t, the expense load, v, and the (constant) investment return on underlying assets, R_a. Specifically, the uniform-pricing annuity factor is given by

$$\ddot{a}_t = (1+v)\sum_{k=1}^{T}\left(\prod_{j=t}^{t+k}\varphi_j\right)R_a^{-k}. \tag{6}$$

Let S_{it} denote the annual payout of annuities "purchased" prior to period t, with S_{i0} being the pre-existing SS and DB payouts, both calculated in real terms. Then, the next period annuity payout S_{it+1} is equal to current payout S_{it} plus payout from any newly purchased annuity, as follows:

$$S_{it+1} = S_{it} + W_{it}/\ddot{a}_t. \tag{7}$$

Annuities are contingent securities in that the annuitant, after paying the premium, receives the pre-determined annuity payout if she or he is alive and nothing if dead. Bonds and equities are non-life-contingent asset classes that in theory should deliver average and typically lower returns than the contingent payout. The insurance providers pool both the annuity funds and the mortality risks among the annuitants. When some annuitants die, their funds are allocated to those alive in the pool.

This extra asset redistribution forms the mortality credit that grows with age. The trajectory of the ever-increasing annuity return becomes clearer if we look at the one-period annuity return implied in equation (6), which is $R_a / [\varphi_t(1+v)]$ for an age t annuitant. As the survival rate φ_t gets smaller as people age, this annuity return increases nonlinearly. The older the annuitants who outlive others are, the greater is the survivorship bonus. For a usual expense load v in the annuity market, the yearly annuity return is initially lower than but will in sequence exceed the return on bonds and the expected return on equities.

Budget Constraints and Wealth Dynamics

Households upon retirement in the model possess pre-annuitized wealth (PAW) and non-annuitized wealth (NAW). The former refers to wealth from SS and DB pensions, which provide a guaranteed income stream of fixed annual payouts to the household for life. The latter broadly refers to the financial wealth accumulated in the working years that can be freely invested in stocks, bonds, or life annuities. Both PAW (annual payouts) and NAW can be used to support consumption, pay health care costs, and purchase additional life annuities when desirable. The dynamics of financial wealth is specified by:

$$M_{it+1} = R_{it+1}(S_{it} + M_{it} - H_{it} - C_{it} - W_{it}) \tag{8}$$

$$M_{it} \geq 0, \forall t . \tag{9}$$

The budget constraint (8) states that annuity payout plus NAW, $S_{it} + M_{it}$, forms the cash-on-hand to cover uninsured health expenses, H_{it}, after which consumption and annuity purchase can be financed in the amounts of C_{it} and W_{it}, respectively. Or, the household can hold assets in equity or bonds with R_{it} being the gross return. The simple liquidity constraint (9) mandates that consumers cannot borrow against future SS or DB payouts or die with debt in any period.[2]

The Optimization Problem and Solution Method

Households optimize over consumption and investment to maximize the expected lifetime utility in (1) and (2), subject to conditions (3) through (9). The state variables constraining decisions are $(S_{it}, M_{it}, P_{it}, t)$. As the number of state variables grows, the required computation increases exponentially, a numerical burden called the "curse of dimensionality." To partially mitigate this problem, following Gomes and Michaelides (2005), Carroll (2006), and Horneff et al. (2006b), we exploit the scale-independence of the maximization problem and normalize all variables by permanent shocks. That is, dividing equations above by P_{it}, using lowercase letters to indicate the ratios (e.g., $m_{it} = M_{it} / P_{it}$), and using the relation $P_{it+1} / P_{it} = \eta_{it+1}$, we reduce the set of state variables to (s_{it}, m_{it}, t). The numerical computation begins by discretizing the continuous state variables (s_{it} and m_{it}). The maximization is then solved from the last period backward to the first period for all combinations of state grid points and distributions of random variables (equity returns, mortality, and health expenses). Given the optimal decision rules recorded along the backward process, Monte Carlo simulations are finally carried out to generate the optimal actions (consumption, asset allocation, and annuity purchase) from the first period forward to the end of life. Numerical integrations are done through the Gaussian quadrature method, and (extra) interpolations are used for points that do not lie on the state space grids.

Parameter Calibration

We set the parameter values for the numerical solution and simulations. Following Gomes and Michaelides (2005) and Scholz et al. (2006), the subjective discount factor β is set to 0.96 to reflect impatience, although some studies also suggest the possibility of larger values. There is a wide range of empirical estimates for the coefficient of relative risk aversion. Within the plausible range, we set ρ to 5, reflecting a moderate- to low-risk tolerance for retired households. The elasticity of intertemporal substitution, γ, is set to 0.5, also commonly used in the literature. We later conduct sensitivity tests on several key parameters.

As a bequest motive is often cited as one of the major reasons for the dearth of voluntary annuitization, we consider no bequest ($b = 0$) and a certain bequest motive ($b = 2$), as in Gomes and Michaelides (2005) and Horneff et al. (2006b). We make no effort to test which parameter value is most justified. Abel and Warshawsky (1988) show that the bequest determined by the model depends not only on the value of the bequest strength parameter in general specifications, but also on other parameter values in the modeled consumer preferences. The real net bond return $R^b - 1$ is set to 3.0 percent and the real net equity return $R^e_t - 1$ to 6.5 percent (mean) with a standard deviation of 16.1 percent.[3] The interest rate in the annuity pricing $R_a - 1$ is set to 3.4 percent.[4] The annuity expense load v is set to 15 percent, based on the empirical estimates in the literature (Mitchell et al. 1999).

Households in the model retire at $t = 0$ and die no later than $T = 35$, corresponding to ages 65 and 100, respectively.[5] The household size n_t, estimated on the Health and Retirement Study (HRS), starts with 1.7 at age 65 and declines to 1.1 at age 100. The utility-generating fraction of heath expenses, κ_t, is assumed to increase linearly from 50 percent at age 65 to 80 percent at age 100. We focus on households in the second, fifth, and eighth income deciles and assume their minimum consumption on necessities, C_0, to be $8,000, $10,000, and $12,000, respectively.

In this analysis, we make no attempt to fit our model to empirically observed annuitization behavior, which is left for future research. Nonetheless, to place the results in the observed household financial situations, we run the simulations based on actual wealth distributions among retiring households. We tabulate the composition of wealth for households from the 1992–2004 HRS survey waves, if the head of household is aged 65 (or 66 if he or she turned 65 before the survey). Table 6.1 shows the average wealth in real terms by household income deciles. The non-annuitized wealth includes financial wealth, half of housing equity, and all of IRA balances and DC account values. The pre-annuitized wealth refers to the present discounted value of SS and DB benefits, both calculated in real terms. There are significant wealth differentials across income deciles. The top decile's total wealth is nearly five times larger than the bottom decile's. More important, most deciles already have their wealth highly annuitized. The first decile has over 70 percent of wealth in SS and DB plans, and the ninth and tenth deciles are the only two groups who have wealth less than half annuitized. This high degree of annuitization, as discussed by Dushi and Webb (2004), could possibly reduce greatly the need to further annuitize, especially when there is liquidity demand and/or a bequest motive.

Survival probabilities for the annuity factor calculation in equation (6) are from the Cohort Life Tables for the Social Security Area (Bell and Miller, 2005). Annuity purchasers thus face a uniform pricing, irrespective of their income groups and differential mortalities. A certain degree of adverse selection may arise by this assumption, which is included, in reduced form, in the expense load. The differential survival rates for the utility maximization in equation (1) are based on de Nardi et al. (2006). For consistency, these differential mortalities are normalized by the above SSA life tables. These normalized mortalities for males and females, by permanent income deciles, are then used to

Table 6.1
Household wealth at age 65 by income decile (average, constant 2004 $000)

Income decile	1	2	3	4	5	6	7	8	9	10
1. Non-annuitized wealth	99.6	141.3	165.2	281.5	238.7	286.8	312.5	438.4	552.0	1,054.8
DC plan + IRA	35.7	47.0	55.3	95.3	71.5	92.9	99.3	127.0	175.4	296.6
Half of housing equity	39.0	48.1	53.8	64.1	69.9	76.2	79.6	114.1	112.6	191.5
Financial wealth	24.9	46.2	56.1	122.1	97.3	117.6	133.5	197.3	264.1	566.7
2. Pre-annuitized wealth	229.6	248.9	284.8	313.4	330.2	370.6	413.4	451.5	499.1	644.6
Social Security	96.4	112.1	119.2	124.2	129.1	132.8	138.6	144.3	148.5	162.1
Defined benefit	133.3	136.8	165.7	189.2	201.1	237.8	274.8	307.2	350.6	482.6
3. Total wealth (= 1+2)	329.3	390.2	450.0	595.0	568.9	657.3	725.9	889.9	1,051.2	1,699.4
4. Annuity share of wealth (= 2/3)	70%	64%	63%	53%	58%	56%	57%	51%	47%	38%

Source: Authors' calculations based on Health and Retirement Study waves 1992–2004

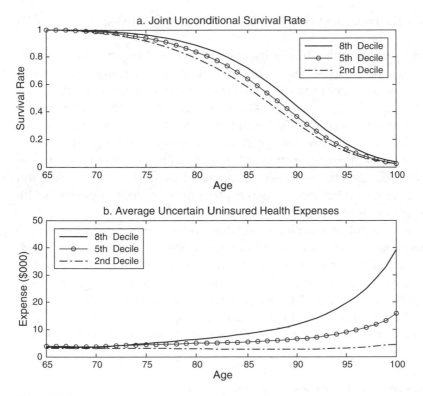

Figure 6.1
Differential mortality and health expenses by income deciles. *Source:* Authors' simulations.

calculate the *joint* survival rates for all ages—the probabilities of at least one household member being alive. Figure 6.1a plots the survival rates.

We use the findings by de Nardi et al. (2006) to gauge the distribution and dynamics of out-of-pocket health care expenses. These expenses include payments for insurance premiums, nursing home care, hospital, doctor/dental/surgery, prescriptions, outpatient care, and so on. The authors find substantial heterogeneity in out-of-pocket health expenses that rise quickly with both age and permanent income. We make two parsimonious adjustments to their estimates: one, because their study only covers ages 70 through 100, we apply their estimated coefficients for age 70 to ages 65–69 in our model; two, we multiply the average of male and female health expenses by the household size n_t. This household size is intrinsically linked to the joint mortality of husband and wife in this later phase of life. When a household member dies, the household size shrinks and so do the health expenses in direct proportion.

Households with higher income tend to face steeper upward trajectories of health expenses, as shown in figure 6.1b. The uninsured health expense averages around $4,000 for all households in their 60s, and it increases rapidly to about $40,000 at age 100 for the eighth decile, modestly to over $15,000 for the fifth decile, and slowly to around $5,000 for the second decile, conditional on survival. These differences may reflect that the quantity and cost of health care are to some extent a choice. Also, the existence of Medicaid as welfare health care and long-term care insurance might explain the lower out-of-pocket health expenses for those with lower incomes.

It is useful to examine more deeply the pattern of the uncertain uninsured health expenses, as shown in table 6.2. First, average health expenses are larger for the well-to-do (with higher income)—the simulated yearly health expenses over ages 65 to 100 are approximately $4,100, $6,500, and $9,100 for households in the second, fifth, and eighth income deciles, respectively. Second, despite the differential dollar values of out-of-pocket costs, the wealthier are faced with a similar

Table 6.2
Simulated annual health expenses (ages 65–100, $000)

Income decile	1	2	3	4	5	6	7	8	9	10
1. Mean of expenses	3.4	4.1	4.9	5.7	6.5	7.3	8.2	9.1	9.9	10.8
2. Std. dev. of expenses	3.4	4.1	4.9	5.9	7.1	8.6	10.4	12.5	15.0	18.1
3. Pre-existing annuity (SS+DB annual payout)	14.6	14.9	17.1	18.8	19.8	22.2	24.8	27.1	29.9	38.6
4. Health expense coverage Mean/ annuity	23%	28%	29%	30%	33%	33%	33%	33%	33%	28%
5. (Mean + 2 * s.d.)/ annuity	70%	82%	86%	93%	105%	110%	117%	126%	133%	121%

Source: Authors' simulations

burden compared to the less wealthy. This point becomes clear when the health expenses are expressed as a share of pre-existing annuity payouts.[6] By row 4 of table 6.2, the average health expense accounts for about 30 percent of SS and DB payouts across income deciles. Third, the variations in health expenses grow with income—the standard deviation of health expenses is $12,500 for the eighth decile, more than triple the $4,100 standard deviation for the second decile. Taking into account the variations, the health-expense-to-annuity ratio gets much higher, and more so for the wealthier, with age. A health care cost equivalent to the average plus two standard deviations, a range that about 95 percent of possible outcomes fall within, would take up a substantially larger share of disposable wealth. An important implication follows: the uncertainty (volatility) of the health care costs may have a greater influence on consumer behavior than does the expected cost level, as will be revealed in the simulations below.

Simulation Results

We build the model step by step until the full optimization and run a large number of simulations—100,000 for each income decile—with initial wealth as reported in table 6.1.

Consumption and Wealth Profiles without Health Expenses and Annuities

We first examine how consumers optimize over consumption and savings, assuming that they are shut out of the annuity market and are immune to the uncertain health expenses. They can invest in equities and bonds. Consumption generally declines with age (plotted later in figure 6.5). This is because households prefer to consume sooner than later as the marginal utility of consumption shrinks with the increase in the effective discount rate (higher mortality rate and a positive time preference).[7] The pace of wealth depletion varies across income deciles, faster for the lower deciles. This reflects that the top income deciles have larger initial NAW and, more important, they need to save for future consumption because they have a greater probability of surviving to advanced ages. Households with a bequest motive choose to depress to some degree their consumption in the early years of retirement. As the wealth stock is nontrivial, the additional wealth generated through equity-bond investment can somewhat lift consumption in later years to a similar or even higher level than without bequest.

Households with more wealth tend to leave greater bequests in dollar terms upon death.

The results show that it is optimal for households to invest significantly in equities (plotted later in figure 6.4). The equity premium induces the utilization of equity investment for wealth creation, as the literature posits (see Mehra and Prescott, 1985, for instance). Psychological hurdles or transaction costs may limit equity investment for some households. Nonetheless, the Survey of Consumer Finances of 2004 shows that equity holdings are substantial for households aged 65 and above. Equity holdings for the second, fifth, and eighth income deciles, respectively, account for about 25 percent, 50 percent, and more than 90 percent of their DC and IRA wealth.

The position of pre-existing annuities alters the equity-bond mix. This is most observable in the case of no bequest motive: as NAW is being depleted with age and the risk-free SS and DB annuities form a greater proportion of total wealth, households choose a larger equity fraction in NAW. This portfolio move does not necessarily entail more risk in the context of increased weight of annuities. The requirement of minimum consumption on necessities induces a portfolio tilt toward bonds. Absent such consumption floors, the optimal NAW equity fraction would be higher across income deciles. With these floors, which are assumed to be lower for households with lower income, the optimal portfolios are more in line with the empirical pattern.

The equity share is generally lower when a bequest motive exists. Larger NAW balances for a potential bequest make the pre-existing annuity leverage relatively smaller, which mandates a lower equity fraction for the same level of overall risk exposure. Also, the equity share declines slightly with age to limit the risk exposure of the bequest as households shift utility weight from consumption to a bequest. The reason for households with a bequest motive to be more cautious is that the uncertainty in equity returns adds randomness to the size of bequest as well as to consumption. This is consistent with Gomes and Michaelides (2005), who show that the presence of a bequest motive decreases the pace of wealth drawdown and the level of equity holdings.

Equity-Bond Portfolio Choices with Uncertain Health Expenses, but without Annuities

We now introduce stochastic uninsured health expenses, but continue to assume no access to the annuity market. The main objective is to identify the impact of the additional background risk on the equity-bond portfolio choice. The uninsured health expenses constitute a drain to the disposable wealth, which naturally lowers non-health consumption at all ages. More important, wealth available for consumption after the deduction of health expenses becomes more volatile. This added uncertainty leads to precautionary savings. That is, households, who face borrowing constraints in a world of incomplete market for lending and insurance, are forced to accumulate or keep a higher level of wealth as a buffer against adverse shocks. Consistent with the theories about precautionary savings and liquidity constraints (Deaton, 1991, and Carroll, 1992), households keep a larger stock of wealth on hand with the presence of uncertain health expenses compared with no expense shocks (figure 6.2). This precautionary motive has a stronger effect on higher-income households because they are faced with a steeper and more volatile path of health expenses. In other words, the magnitude of extra buffer savings is more influenced by the volatility and shape of health expenses than the average cost level per se.

The added uncertainty in health expenses alters the equity-bond composition of savings. Households rebalance assets from risky equities toward riskless bonds so as to have a portfolio consistent with their risk tolerance (results plotted later in figure 6.4). The equity share is flat or declines slightly with age. The optimal level and shape of the portfolio shares are broadly similar to the practice of life-cycle funds in the retirement phase. The simulated optimal equity fraction in the presence of health spending risk, averaged across the deciles for ages 65 through 100, is barely over 40 percent, while the life-cycle funds in the marketplace on average hold about 38 percent of assets in equity for investors at or beyond target retirement age.[8]

Annuitization Choice with Limited Equity Holding
In this subsection, we assume an automatic fraction of equity holdings in NAW and explore the reasons for annuitization, first without and then with uninsured health expenses. Specifically, 40 percent of NAW is automatically placed in equities. This somewhat arbitrary percentage is the average equity fraction derived in the above equity-bond optimization and is similarly observed as a rule-of-thumb for older households in life-cycle funds.

Absent a bequest motive, households in the model start annuitizing their wealth around their mid-70s and fully annuitize in their 80s, when the expected annuity return for the remaining life exceeds those on bonds and equities. The annuity level continues to rise after the

A

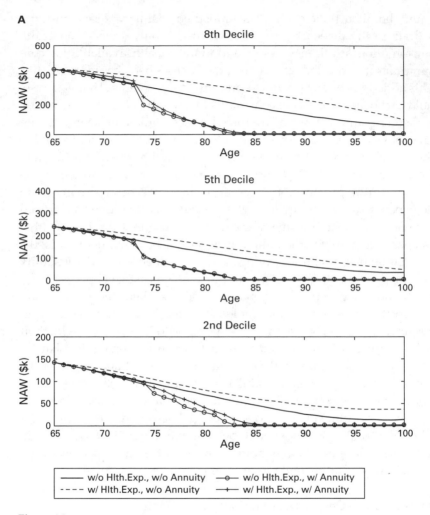

Figure 6.2
Non-annuitized wealth by income deciles: (A) no bequest, (B) with bequest motive (full vs. partial equity-bond-annuity choices.) All graphs depict simulated average non-annuitized wealth: no health expenses and no annuity choice (solid line), with health expenses and no annuity choice (dashed line), no health expenses and with annuity choice (circled line), and with health expenses and annuity choice (plus line). *Source:* Authors' simulations.

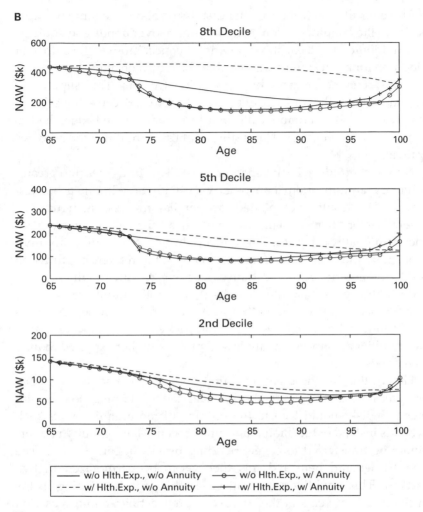

Figure 6.2
Continued

depletion of NAW owing to new annuity purchases financed by existing annuity payouts. With a bequest motive, households keep substantial NAW on hand and reduce voluntary annuity purchases. They also smooth the annuitization over years because the wait may bring better annuity return in terms of greater mortality credit but also because the strategy may end up leaving a bequest in the case of death. This modeled behavior perhaps echoes the actual: most life payout annuities are purchased with guaranteed periods of up to 20 years, partially preserving a bequest potential.

These results confirm the earlier discussion about the ultimate superiority of life annuities as longevity insurance over bonds and equities.
As Davidoff et al. (2005) show, absent a bequest motive, the sufficient
condition for a full annuitization is that the return on annuity is greater
than the reference returns on conventional assets. This superiority
remains valid in the presence of a bequest motive. Because households
now want to hold certain wealth in a form that can be bequeathed to
their heirs, however, partial (and still significant) annuitization becomes
optimal.

Now we introduce health spending risk. This translates into greater
voluntary annuitization than otherwise, with or without a bequest
motive. The results, not plotted, are similar to those in figure 6.3.
Several factors help explain this pattern of change associated with
uncertain health expenses. First, uncertain health spending does not
alter the dominance of annuity returns over the reference returns on
bonds and equities beyond certain ages. Second, both annuity payouts
and health expenses are life contingent, and both annuity returns and
health costs are increasing with age. As the addition of health shocks
would induce households to shift from risky equities to safer assets,
life annuities are more compatible and provide higher expected returns
than bonds.

Finally, this enhanced annuitization does not necessarily contradict
the precautionary savings theory. The theory implies that health
spending risk should lead to the holding of more liquid assets such
as bonds instead of the illiquid annuities because later annuity payouts
cannot be transferred to cover spending pitfalls in earlier years. The
annuity demand here and this theory can be harmonized in two
parts: (i) This liquidity constraint is less likely to be binding in the
early retirement years in the context of pre-existing annuities as well
as cash. The average health expenses over ages 65–75 are in the
range of $4,000–5,000 for the second, fifth, and eighth deciles; account
for approximately 21 percent (with low volatility), 22 percent, and
18 percent of annual SS and DB payouts ($14,900, $19,800, and
$27,100), respectively; and are thus to a large extent buffered by
these pre-existing annuities plus non-annuitized wealth. The SS and
DB payouts also effectively cover the minimum consumption on
necessities. For health expense in later years, the optimal hedging
strategy is to annuitize so as to capture the increasing-with-age
annuity returns (mortality credit). (ii) Nonetheless, the presence of
health spending risk depresses consumption and motivates risk-averse

A

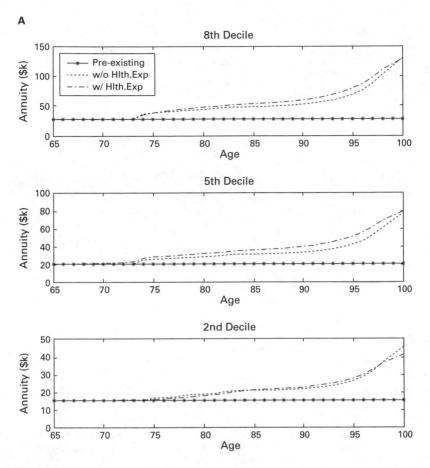

Figure 6.3
Annuity level by income deciles: (A) no bequest, (B) with bequest motive (full vs. partial equity-bond-annuity choices.) All graphs depict simulated average annuity levels: pre-existing annuity (star line), endogenous annuity choice without (dashed line) and with uncertain uninsured health expenses (dash-dotted line). *Source:* Authors' simulations.

B

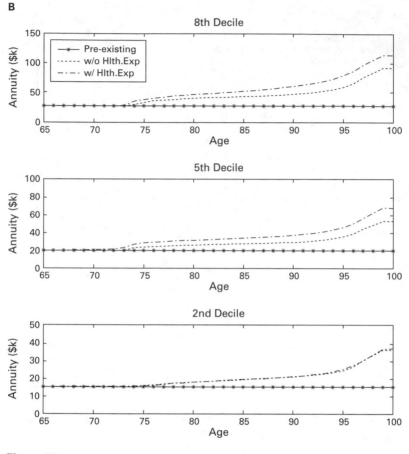

Figure 6.3
Continued

households to build up more NAW in their 60s and 70s to buffer
against adverse shocks. Households eventually annuitize these precautionary savings, at least partially, when the annuity return outperforms bonds and equities, to effectively hedge against future health
spending shocks. Before that time, it is optimal to hold the savings
in the equity-bond portfolio. This strategy also gives households
opportunities to improve their future budget constraint if the associated investment risk is within the tolerable range. In short, the
enhanced annuitization does not necessarily jeopardize the liquidity
needs and serves well as an effective insurance against future life-
contingent health expenses.[9]

This result is consistent with the theoretical conjecture by Davidoff et al. (2005). Our modeling of out-of-pocket health expenses is more sophisticated and empirically based. The health spending risk occurs at all ages and increases with age in terms of both levels and volatilities of these expenses across income groups. In this context, a life care annuity (LCA), though not explicitly modeled here, can be thought to be compatible with this profile of health expenses. Murtaugh et al. (2001) illustrate that an LCA, an integration of a life annuity and long-term care insurance, provides lifetime income to the named annuitant and automatically hikes the periodic payments in the events of physical impairment or disability.

Annuity-Equity-Bond Portfolio Choice with Uncertain Health Expenses

Households in the model are now assumed to fully optimize with access to the complete investment set of annuities, equities, and bonds, against the background of uncertain uninsured health expenses, longevity risk, and stochastic capital market returns. The simulations in the full optimization confirm the major findings in the earlier subsections and also generate important new findings that were not observable in the "limited" optimizations.

It is optimal for households to annuitize their wealth, fully or partially depending on the bequest motive, when the expected annuity return is greater than the reference returns on bonds and equities (compare solid with circled lines in figure 6.2). The addition of the background health spending risk acts to enhance the demand for annuities over bonds. Figure 6.2 also shows that the conversion of liquid precautionary savings to annuities is particularly striking (compare dashed with plus lines). With access to the complete investment set, households have more flexibility when optimizing over consumption and portfolios. The annuitization process is somewhat smoother than when a fixed percentage of their NAW portfolio was exogenously allocated to equity. The simulated average annuity levels are plotted in figure 6.3. It is worth noting that the households with higher income have a greater incremental demand for life annuities when faced with health spending risk. These households face a steeper increase in health spending, as shown in figure 6.1; the health spending is more likely to materialize because they tend to live longer; and the annuity returns similarly increase with age and are thus more compatible with the spending profile, relative to the "static" bond returns.

As the safe and higher-return annuities, albeit life-contingent, account for a larger fraction of wealth, they form a more powerful leverage to accommodate greater equity investment. Figure 6.4 shows that the full optimization allows households, with or without a bequest motive, to increase equity share in their NAW. For instance, the equity weight is higher by more than 20 percentage points for the fifth-decile households with a bequest motive in their late 70s, absent health costs (compare solid with circled lines in figure 6.4). This hike does not necessarily bring additional risk, given the higher degree of annuitization. In the presence of uncertain uninsured health expenses, this annuity leverage for equity holding is even more pronounced. Were households shut out of the annuity market, they would substantially reduce their equity exposure (dashed lines in figure 6.4). With access to annuities, the fifth decile households, for instance, would increase the NAW equity fraction by more than 30 percentage points in their late 70s (plus line in figure 6.4). The magnitude of equity holding varies across income deciles, but they share a similar pattern.

The annuity-leveraged higher equity investment, with realizations of equity premium, in turn helps support an increasing path of annuity purchase. This is more observable when households have a bequest motive and thus hold a significant NAW base for investment. The results suggest that the annuitization and equity-bond portfolio choices are intertwined and should be optimized jointly. A life annuity is not just a passive replacement of bonds as an insurance against risk; it is also an integral part of the asset allocation strategy for wealth creation because of its effective accommodation of higher-risk-and-return portfolios.

Welfare Analysis: Willingness to Pay for Life Annuities
A life annuity improves households' welfare; otherwise they would simply forgo this option. The reshuffles of financial assets to some extent reflect such welfare improvement. More directly, the welfare increase can be measured by the difference between consumption profiles, before and after the access to life annuities, in figure 6.5 (compare solid with circled lines with no health expenses and compare dashed with plus lines with stochastic health expenses). Households enjoy higher late-life consumptions with the support of annuities, and this benefit is particularly valuable when annuities are hedging against life-contingent uninsured health expenses.

A

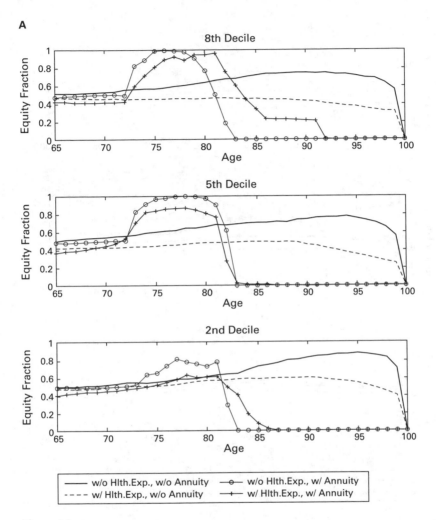

Figure 6.4
Equity fraction of non-annuitized wealth by income deciles: (A) no bequest, (B) with bequest motive (full vs. partial equity-bond-annuity choices.) All graphs depict simulated average equity fraction of NAW: no health expenses and no annuity choice (solid line), with health expenses and no annuity choice (dashed line), no health expenses and with annuity choice (circled line), and with health expenses and annuity choice (plus line). *Source:* Authors' simulations.

B

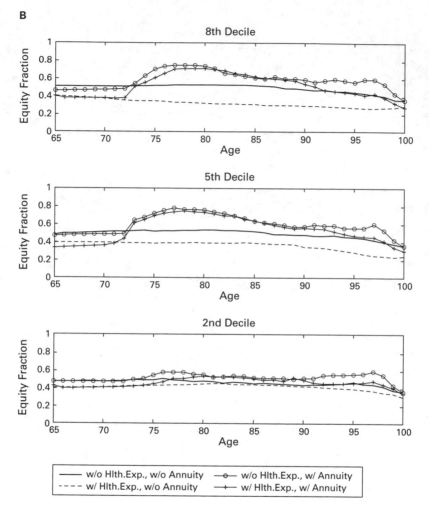

Figure 6.4
Continued

A

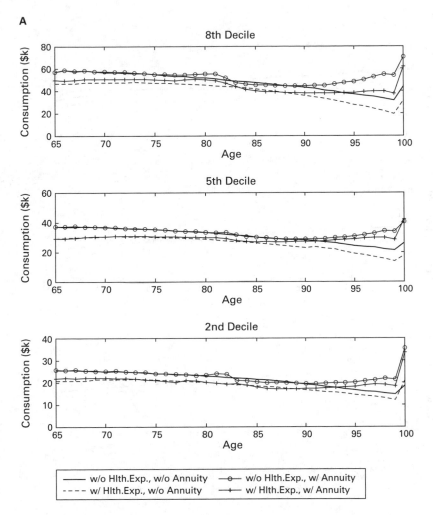

Figure 6.5
Consumption by income deciles: (A) no bequest, (B) with bequest motive (full vs. partial equity-bond-annuity choices.) All graphs depict simulated average consumption: no health expenses and no annuity choice (solid line), with health expenses and no annuity choice (dashed line), no health expenses and with annuity choice (circled line), and with health expenses and annuity choice (plus line). *Source:* Authors' simulations.

B

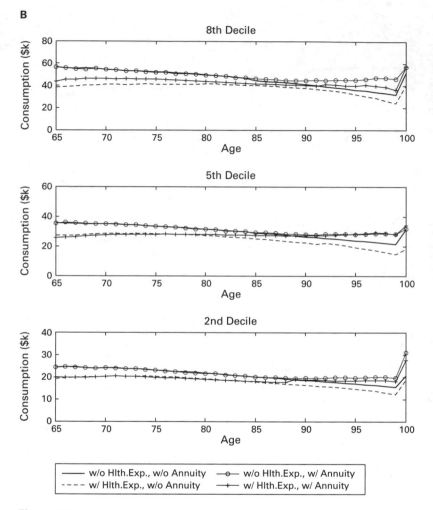

Figure 6.5
Continued

Table 6.3
Willingness to pay for life annuities ($000)

Income decile	2	5	8
1. No bequest motive, no health care spending shocks	11.0	17.6	39.8
2. No bequest motive, health care spending shocks	12.2	25.3	63.7
3. Bequest motive, no health care spending shocks	3.2	7.9	17.1
4. Bequest motive, health care spending shocks	5.2	9.2	93.1

Source: Authors' simulations

We gauge the welfare gain by calculating how much a risk-averse household is willing to pay for a fixed payout life annuity. This measure takes two steps: the maximum expected utility is first derived for a household with full equity-bond-annuity optimization, and then we calculate the increment to initial wealth so that the household achieves the same level of expected utility in a situation of no annuities available. A positive (negative) dollar value suggests that life annuities improve (decrease) consumer welfare. Table 6.3 lists the results. Several observations are worth noting: First, all households benefit from life annuities. Second, a bequest motive decreases the value of annuities. Third, the welfare gain is greater for households in higher-income deciles because they have a lower beginning degree of annuitization. Finally, the uncertainty in health care spending enhances the welfare gain of life annuities, more so for higher-income households because such annuities are more likely to hedge their longer life and higher health spending.

Sensitivity Tests

Alternative Risk Aversion and Elasticity of Intertemporal Substitution
We now conduct sensitivity tests. We first check if our results are affected by the assumed household preferences. We replace the Epstein-Zin-Weil specification with the power function (CRRA form), which is additively separable across time but limits the elasticity of intertemporal substitution to be the reciprocal of relative risk aversion. Comparing results when health spending risk is present versus absent, households in the CRRA utility form similarly significantly increase their demand for life annuities, and the annuitization process starts years earlier than otherwise. The merits of life annuities in hedging against health spending risk are thus not sensitive to the functional forms.

We then change the values of two parameters in the EZW preferences: a lower EIS (0.3) and separately a lower RRA (3.0) versus the
baseline assumptions. All major uncertainties in longevity, asset returns,
and health costs are present. EIS reflects households' willingness to
substitute consumption over time. A lower value of EIS implies that
households are more concerned about the consumption smoothing
from year to year, and relatively less concerned about the long run
hedging against the longevity and health spending risks. The optimal
annuity level is hence lower than the baseline case. A lower EIS has
little impact on equity allocation.

RRA reflects household attitude toward risk. A lower value of RRA
means more risk tolerance, which in turn has two implications. First,
households would hold less precautionary savings in their 60s and
early 70s to buffer against adverse shocks and would hold a larger
fraction of wealth in equity with the hope of capturing risk premium.
Second, the appeal of equity premium mitigates the attractiveness of
annuities to the more risk-tolerant households, and hence less wealth
is annuitized in the later years, with or without a bequest motive.

Single Retirees

There is a general notion that married households may have a lower
demand for annuities owing to their intra-family risk pooling, while
single retirees are more likely to need longevity insurance through
annuities. We model single female retirees whose individual wealth
and pre-existing annuity at age 65 are converted from household levels
using an equivalence scale of 1.25, following Brown and Finkelstein
(2008). The simulations show that the equity-bond-annuity portfolios
for singles are remarkably similar in shape to those for married households. Because single annuities are less expensive than J&S annuities
(owing to lower survival rates for singles), the annuity return starts
exceeding equity and bond returns several years earlier, triggering an
earlier annuitization process. The uncertainty in health care spending
similarly induces singles to shift their assets from equity to bonds and
particularly to annuities aiming to cover longevity and health care
spending in advanced ages.

Lower Pre-existing Annuities

In the context of the ongoing shift from DB pensions to DC plans and
possible reforms of the SS system, we conduct a counterfactual experiment in which all DB coverage has been replaced with DC-type plans

and the SS system has been partially carved out via personal retirement accounts. That is, we assume households have the same level of initial wealth upon retirement as above but all DB wealth and one-third of SS wealth is now in the form of cash (non-annuitized wealth) rather than the pre-existing annuities.[10]

The simulated optimal annuity profiles are similar in shape to the baseline case, but at lower levels. This level difference is because of the assumption that the commercial annuity market has a 15 percent load. It does not indicate that the pre-existing annuity level is higher than otherwise desirable. In this alternative scenario, it is optimal for households to hold a lower NAW equity fraction compared with the baseline, given the lower annuity leverage for risky portfolios.

More Favorable Annuity Pricing

Another sensitivity test is on the annuity expense load. Potential annuity buyers may have private information about their health status and mortality rate. Given uniform annuity pricing, people who find life annuities desirable and buy such annuities tend to be those with longer life expectancy, which makes the life annuity product less profitable from the perspective of insurance providers. Insurance providers impose an annuity load to cover the loss associated with this adverse selection problem. It is possible, however, that this problem and the annuity load will be reduced with certain new approaches and products. Particularly, as more DC plans set annuitization as a default or voluntary option, a larger pool of heterogeneous life expectancies may form. Or, as mentioned above, according to the Murtaugh et al. (2001) proposal, an integrated product combining life annuity with long-term-care insurance will probably appeal to a larger population and serve as a market solution to the adverse selection problem. We therefore conduct an alternative experiment assuming a lower expense load—7.5 percent versus the 15 percent in the benchmark.

A lower annuity load has some important implications compared with the benchmark. First, the year-to-year annuity return would exceed the reference returns on bonds and equities sooner so that retirees would initiate the annuitization several years earlier. Second, given a lower annuity load, a higher annuity level affordable, and thus greater leverage for equities, a higher NAW equity fraction becomes optimal. Third, because the same desirable level of annuity now requires a lower premium, more resources could be used to boost consumption or bequest.

Conclusions

This chapter sets up a life-cycle model and derives the optimal equity-bond-annuity portfolios for retired households, who have differential exposure, by income deciles, to mortality and uninsured health spending in addition to the uncertainty in asset returns, in the context of differential SS and DB plan coverage. For simplicity, we limit the annuitization choice to the joint and survival annuities whereby the same level of annuity payout continues from the annuity purchase time until the death of the last surviving spouse. With the flexible equity-bond-annuity choices, households would annuitize their wealth sometime during retirement, fully or partially depending on their bequest motive. The superiority of annuities in hedging against longevity risk is attributable to their eventually higher returns, with mortality credit incorporated, than the reference returns on conventional assets.

Consistent with the findings in the literature, the uncertainty in health expenses generally leads to precautionary savings and an asset allocation shift from risky equities to riskless bonds, absent annuitization choice. The superiority of annuities over bonds in hedging against longevity risk similarly applies to the hedging against uncertain health expenses because both annuity returns and health expenses are life-contingent and rise with age. As the health spending shocks induce a portfolio shift toward safer assets, annuities are more efficient and eventually dominate bonds. This higher degree of annuitization also provides a greater leverage for more equity holdings in asset portfolios, ceteris paribus, without increasing the overall investment risk exposure. In other words, annuitization is not just a passive replacement of bonds as an insurance against risk—it is also an integral part of the asset allocation strategy for wealth creation because it accommodates higher-risk-and-return portfolios.

This health-spending-uncertainty-enhanced annuitization is not contradictory to the theories about liquidity constraints and precautionary savings. On the one hand, the pre-existing annuities such as SS and DB payouts to a large extent have served as a buffer against adverse shocks. On the other hand, extra savings are noticeable in the liquid equity-bond form in the retirement years when bond and equity returns are yet to be dominated by annuities. With the superiority of annuities in hedging against both longevity and health spending risks, households would be better off by eventually converting these precautionary savings, at least partially, to annuities. Life annuities support late-life consumption and significantly improve household welfare.

As a limitation, our model abstracts from the consideration that major illnesses may affect life expectancy and induce preference for consumption in early life. Emphasizing the liquidity needs and reduced demand for annuities in these situations, however, would be biased without due consideration of health insurance. Holding cash as a self-insuring strategy is costly. Rather, optimizing health insurance should also be part of the portfolio choice when illnesses and mortalities are modeled to be closely linked, which is a direction for future research.

Our analysis suggests the importance of annuitizing retirement wealth for households covered by DC plans or IRAs if the decline in DB plans continues or if Social Security is to be (partially) converted to personal accounts. The (offsetting) voluntary annuitization would not only utilize a life annuity's fundamental insurance against longevity risk but also would improve household welfare by concurrently hedging against other life contingent costs such as health care expenses. This indicates the merits of embedding the annuity feature into DC-type retirement plans if they are to be the mainstream plans. As more DC plans adopt the annuitization option and hence the annuity pool expands, and also as the development of new products such as life annuities integrated with long-term-care insurance helps circumvent market inefficiencies, one may project that there will be an increased demand for life annuities.

Notes

1. This additive functional form assumes that health and non-health consumptions are substitutes. Assuming them as complements would probably strengthen the results.

2. This analysis does not consider life insurance for a bequest or the potential development of annuities as collateral for borrowing. See Sheshinski (2007) for a discussion of annuity innovations.

3. The distributions of asset returns are based on Watson Wyatt 2007 U.S. Asset Return Assumptions, which are in turn derived through a blend of economic theory, historical analysis and the views of investment managers. Similar, higher or lower returns can be found from Shiller (2006) for various time periods. We make no judgment whether future returns will significantly deviate from these historical patterns.

4. It is implicitly assumed that 90 percent of the underlying assets in fixed-payout life annuities are invested in bonds and the remaining in equity earning the average equity return. This 10 percent equity exposure is consistent with stipulations of current U.S.

insurance law and market practice. Simulation results are robust to alternatively larger bond fractions, say, 100 percent. When investors are able to choose the stock-bond mix in variable annuities, as analyzed by Horneff et al. (2009), the demand for annuities is not necessarily reduced by the presence of income shocks. Rather, investors should still annuitize so as to receive mortality credit but increase the bond fraction in the annuity assets.

5. It is straightforward to expand the retirement phase to an earlier age or a longer lifespan. However, the detailed estimates of health expenses are available only up to age 100 in de Nardi et al. (2006).

6. For consistency in our modeling, these annuity payouts, constant for ages 65–100 conditional on survival, are calculated using the household *joint* survival rates based on SSA life tables. This may to some extent understate the buffer effect of SS and DB payouts in early retirement years because the household receipt of SS and DB payouts generally starts with a higher value but shrinks after one member passes away.

7. The consumption in the last period is boosted because uncertainty of life is resolved and no wealth should be saved, absent a bequest motive. Note that the model assumes certain death at age 100 but the joint survival rate at age 99 remains relatively high directly based on the SSA life tables.

8. The market average asset allocations are based on the fifteen largest life-cycle funds in the retirement phase available at www.morningstar.com on November 6, 2007.

9. As a double check, we conduct an experiment assuming little initial assets for households—the only income is Social Security benefit. Simulations show that they would first build up a certain cash balance and then eventually buy additional annuities in the presence of stochastic health expenses.

10. Currently, the combined contribution to Social Security by employer and employee is 12.4 percent of the employee's earnings up to a cap. President Bush's reform proposal would have diverted 4 percent payroll tax (i.e., one-third of the total contribution) into personal accounts.

References

Abel, Andrew, and Mark Warshawsky. 1988. Specification of the Joy of Giving: Insights from Altruism. *Review of Economics and Statistics* 70:145–149.

Bell, Felicitie C., and Michael L. Miller. 2005. "Life Tables for the United States Social Security Area 1900–2100." Social Security Administration actuarial study no. 120.

Brown, Jeffrey R., and Amy Finkelstein. 2008. The Interaction of Public and Private Insurance: Medicaid and the Long-Term Care Insurance Market. *American Economic Review* 98 (3): 1083–1102.

Brown, Jeffrey R., and James M. Poterba. 2000. Joint Life Annuities and Annuity Demand by Married Couples. *Journal of Risk and Insurance* 67 (4): 527–553.

Carroll, Christopher D. 1992. The Buffer-Stock Theory of Saving: Some Macroeconomic Evidence. *Brookings Papers on Economic Activity* 2:61–156.

Carroll, Christopher D. 2006. The Method of Endogenous Gridpoints for Solving Dynamic Stochastic Optimization Problems. *Economics Letters* 91 (3): 312–320.

Davidoff, Thomas, Jeffrey R. Brown, and Peter A. Diamond. 2005. Annuities and Individual Welfare. *American Economic Review* 95 (5): 1573–1590.

De Nardi, Mariacristina, Eric French, and John Bailey Jones. 2006. Differential Mortality, Uncertain Medical Expenses, and the Saving of Elderly Singles. NBER working paper no. 12554.

Deaton, Angus S. 1991. Saving and Liquidity Constraints. *Econometrica* 59:1221–1248.

Dus, Ivica, Raimond Maurer, and Olivia S. Mitchell. 2005. Betting on Death and Capital Markets in Retirement: A Shortfall Risk Analysis of Life Annuities versus Phased Withdrawal Plans. *Financial Services Review* 14:169–196.

Dushi, Irena, and Anthony Webb. 2004. Household Annuitization Decisions: Simulations and Empirical Analyses. *Journal of Pension Economics and Finance* 3 (2): 109–143.

Dynan, Karen E., Jonathan Skinner, and Stephen P. Zeldes. 2004. Do the Rich Save More? *Journal of Political Economy* 112 (2): 397–444.

Epstein, Larry G., and Stanley E. Zin. 1989. Substitution, Risk Aversion, and the Temporal Behavior of Consumption and Asset Returns: A Theoretical Framework. *Econometrica* 57 (4): 937–969.

Feinstein, Jonathan S., and Ching-Yang Lin. 2006. Elderly Asset Management. Working paper, Yale University.

Gomes, Francisco, and Alexander Michaelides. 2005. Optimal Life-cycle Asset Allocation: Understanding the Empirical Evidence. *Journal of Finance* 60 (2): 869–904.

Hall, Robert, and Charles Jones. 2007. The Value of Life and the Rise in Health Spending. *Quarterly Journal of Economics* 122 (1): 39–72.

Horneff, Wolfram J., Raimond Maurer, Olivia S. Mitchell, and Ivica Dus. 2006a. Optimizing the Retirement Portfolio: Asset Allocation, Annuitization, and Risk Aversion. Pension Research Council working paper no. 2006-10.

Horneff, Wolfram J., Raimond Maurer, Olivia S. Mitchell, and Ivica Dus. 2008. Following the Rules: Integrating Asset Allocation and Annuitization in Retirement Portfolios. *Insurance, Mathematics and Economics* 42:396–408.

Horneff, Wolfram J., Raimond Maurer, Olivia S. Mitchell, and Michael Z. Stamos. 2007. Money in Motion: Dynamic Portfolio Choice in Retirement. Pension Research Council working paper no. 2007–07.

Horneff, Wolfram J., Raimond Maurer, Olivia S. Mitchell, and Michael Z. Stamos. 2009. Asset Allocation and Location over the Life Cycle with Investment-Linked Survival-Contingent Payouts. *Journal of Banking and Finance* 33 (9): 1688–1699.

Horneff, Wolfram J., Raimond Maurer, and Michael Z. Stamos. 2006b. Life-Cycle Asset Allocation with Annuity Markets: Is Longevity Insurance a Good Deal? University of Michigan Retirement Research Center working paper no. 2006-146.

Kotlikoff, Laurence, and Avia Spivak. 1981. The Family as an Incomplete Annuities Market. *Journal of Political Economy* 89 (2): 372–391.

Love, David A., and Maria G. Perozek. 2007. Should the Old Play It Safe? Portfolio Choice with Uncertain Medical Expenses. Working paper, Williams College.

Maurer, Raimond, Christian Schlag, and Michael Z. Stamos. 2008. Optimal Life-Cycle Strategies in the Presence of Interest Rate and Inflation Risk. Pension Research Council working paper no. 2008-01.

Mehra, Rajnish, and Edward C. Prescott. 1985. The Equity Premium: A Puzzle. *Journal of Monetary Economics* 15:145–161.

Milevsky, Moshe, and Virginia Young. 2002. Optimal Asset Allocation and the Real Option to Delay Annuitization: It's Not Now-or-Never. Pensions Institute working paper no. 0211.

Mitchell, Olivia S., James M. Poterba, Mark Warshawsky, and Jeffrey R. Brown. 1999. New Evidence on Money's Worth of Individual Annuities. *American Economic Review* 89:1299–1318.

Murtaugh, Christopher, Brenda Spillman, and Mark Warshawsky. 2001. In Sickness and in Health: An Annuity Approach to Financing Long-term Care and Retirement Income. *Journal of Risk and Insurance* 68 (2): 225–254.

Palumbo, Michael G. 1999. Uncertain Medical Expenses and Precautionary Saving Near the End of the Life-cycle. *Review of Economic Studies* 66 (2): 395–421.

Scholz, John Karl, Ananth Seshadra, and Surachai Khitatrakun. 2006. Are Americans Saving "Optimally" for Retirement? *Journal of Political Economy* 114 (4): 607–643.

Sheshinski, Eytan. 2007. *The Economic Theory of Annuities*. Princeton, NJ: Princeton University Press.

Shiller, Robert. 2006. Life-Cycle Personal Accounts Proposal for Social Security: An Evaluation of President Bush's Proposal. *Journal of Policy Modeling* 28 (4): 427–444.

Sinclair, Sven H., and Kent A. Smetters. 2004. "Health Shocks and the Demand for Annuities." Technical paper series 2004-9, Congressional Budget Office.

Turra, Cassio M., and Olivia S. Mitchell. 2008. The Impact of Health Status and Out-of-Pocket Medical Expenditures on Annuity Valuation. In *Recalibrating Retirement Spending and Saving*, ed. John Ameriks and Olivia Mitchell, 227–250. New York: Oxford University Press.

Weil, Philippe. 1990. Non-Expected Utility in Macroeconomics. *Quarterly Journal of Economics* 55 (1): 29–42.

Yaari, Menahem E. 1965. Uncertain Lifetime, Life Insurance, and the Theory of the Consumer. *Review of Economic Studies* 32:137–150.

Yogo, Motohiro. 2008. Portfolio Choice in Retirement: Health Risk and the Demand for Annuities, Housing, and Risky Assets. Finance Department working Paper, University of Pennsylvania.

7 Good Strategies for Wealth Management and Income Production in Retirement

with Gaobo Pang

Introduction

Defined contribution (DC) plan participants need to select good strategies for wealth distribution in retirement. Broad options include self-management strategies, such as systematic withdrawals from mutual funds, and market products, such as fixed payout life annuities. Pang and Warshawsky (2009) recently examined the trade-offs of wealth preservation and income security for a variety of strategies and products. Here we focus on one particularly promising strategic approach: the combination of withdrawals from mutual funds with a series of immediate life annuity purchases. We examine the optimal split of wealth between them and the exact process of fund-annuity conversion. This analysis searches for good distribution strategies for DC participants at retirement, considering variations in risk tolerance, income-wealth preferences, ages of retirement, and whether the household is an individual or a couple.

There is a rich financial economics literature on dynamic asset portfolios for wealth management. These studies assume that sophisticated investors conduct full optimizations throughout life. Our analysis here instead assumes that investors at retirement make a one-time search among wealth distribution strategies and thereafter stick to the chosen strategy in retirement. This is perhaps more practical, relative to the theoretical models, from the perspective of financial planning for older households of moderate means and declining mental agility and, moreover, is consistent with popular products, such as life cycle funds, which specify to investors a particular fixed investment path over a sometimes lengthy horizon.

The success criterion for the strategy search is to minimize the shortfall risk, which is defined as a weighted probability of real income and wealth balances falling below certain thresholds, in a stochastic model. This objective somewhat departs from the conventional analytical assumption that investors maximize their expected utility over consumption and bequests. The former is motivated by, and perhaps better represents the efforts among professional advisors and retirement plan sponsors to address, the common concerns that retirement security is mostly threatened by the downside risks that retirees face.

Searching for Good Strategies for Wealth Distribution

Systematic Withdrawals Plus Purchases of Immediate Life Annuities to Minimize Shortfall Risks

Individuals in the model seek wealth distribution strategies in retirement to support consumption spending while minimizing income and wealth shortfall risks. The former risk is defined as income falling below a threshold (C_0) so that a specific consumption floor is not sustained. The latter risk is wealth balance falling below a certain level (W_0) so that future flows covering uninsured contingencies or the ability to leave a bequest are at jeopardy. These two shortfall risks compete because actions to reduce one usually increase the other. This is the typical trade-off faced by individuals who have to choose the level of fund withdrawals or annuity payout levels so as to both support consumption in the current period and preserve wealth for the future. Representing the necessary compromise, we assume that the individual's objective at retirement is to find a distribution mechanism that minimizes the weighted probabilities of shortfall risks as follows, subject to financial resources available:

$$\alpha^* \, \text{Prob}(\text{income} < C_0) + (1 - \alpha) * \text{Prob}(\text{balance} < W_0),$$

where a higher α, within the range of [0,1], indicates a stronger desire for income safety and correspondingly weaker preference for balance preservation.

Retirees can take a systematic withdrawal from a mix of mutual funds invested in equities and bonds as a constant percentage.[1] The strategy provides liquidity to investors and bequest potential to their heirs. It allows retired investors to increase consumption when mutual funds perform well, but also exposes them to significant declines in consumption spending when investment outcomes are poor.[2]

Retirees can also purchase fixed nominal payout straight life annuities, making a one-time complete or partial conversion of accumulated wealth or a phased annuitization over several years. Immediate life annuities, as suggested by various studies, are products that address longevity risk and offer a steady flow of income. Life annuities, however, may be viewed as expensive by average investors, especially in the retail market, because of the extra costs owing to adverse selection and marketing. Prices of fixed-payout immediate annuities are determined by, and thus payout levels are sensitive to, changes in interest rates at the time of purchase (see Warshawsky, 2007, for a discussion of the sensitivity of annuity payouts to interest rate levels and Smith and Judd, 2009, about the selection of cash-bond investment accumulation mixes for hedging lump-sum withdrawals versus annuity purchases).

An investor may instead consider a particular, more complex strategy. The most natural composite lineup is a mutual fund systematic withdrawal plus a series of purchases of fixed payout life annuities. Investors adopting such a strategy annually get a certain percentage of the mutual fund balance in addition to the annuity payout. The former strategy gives investors liquidity, flexibility, bequest potential, and opportunities to realize higher returns from the stock market, while the latter product guarantees a consumption floor.

To make income levels less skewed by one-time conditions in the annuity market, investors can allocate a larger fraction of wealth to mutual funds in the early years of retirement and escalate the shift to fixed life annuities with age. Under one strategy, they can eventually convert all mutual funds into fixed annuities by a certain age. This phased annuitization will ease the impact of annuity rate fluctuations over time and may help circumvent the psychological obstacle to the (irreversible) purchase of life annuity. An initially larger mutual fund may also facilitate greater wealth creation, leaving a potentially larger bequest in the event of early death. Investors, however, face the accompanying risk: they may not make much or may even lose money in the mutual funds if the equity premium fails to materialize or equity prices fall. Wealth loss during the transition can be large.

Because the immediate annuities comprise an increasing share of wealth, we impose that the equity-bond proportion in funds dynamically adjust toward equity, until up to the maximum 100 percent of the remaining mutual fund portfolio is in equities. This allocation strategy is intended to maintain the original risk exposure of the retiree because annuities have the same general risk characteristics as bonds, excluding the consideration of mortality. After the 100 percent maximum, however, the whole wealth portfolio, including the present value of annuity income flows, tilts toward low-risk assets at older ages, when nonannuitized wealth is small and declining, as a share of net worth. Also, although life-contingent returns on life annuities purchased later generally improve with age due to the growing mortality credit, actual total fixed payouts may differ substantially because of the stochastic ups and downs in annuity prices over time owing to changing interest rates.

Stochastic Asset Returns and Bankruptcies of Insurance Providers

Asset rates and returns are simulated here based on a stochastic model that allows for standard market randomness (also called "shocks") in normal times and low-probability, large-magnitude rare economic disasters ("fat tails"). Rates and returns in normal times are modeled as a vector autoregressive (VAR) system, following Campbell and Viceira (2004, 2005). The VAR specifies current asset returns as a function of lagged returns and current-period shocks. Rare economic disasters are simulated based on the framework of Barro (2006). As advantages over conventional models, this comprehensive modeling captures the persistence of market shocks and both the contemporaneous and serial correlations of asset classes.

Equity, bond, and cash returns in the spirit of Campbell and Viceira (2004, 2005) are proxied by the S&P 500 total return, the ten-year government bond total return, and ninety-day Treasury bill rate, respectively. The VAR regression is based on 1962–2009 quarterly data. When economic disasters strike, equities contract, government bonds can default or inflation explode, and cash rates may drop with certain probabilities and by varying degrees. These probabilities and value shrinkages are estimated in Barro (2006) based on sixty economic events (examples are World Wars I and II, the Great Depression, and postwar depressions) in the twentieth century in thirty-five countries.

Bankruptcy of insurance (annuity) providers may take place in both normal times and rare disasters (rare events alone would likely understate the insolvency risk). For the former, it is assumed that an insurance provider fails with a probability of 0.15 percent per annum (uniform distribution), based on Moody's global analysis of the default probability for corporate bonds rated A for 1970 to 2005. In disasters, the probability of insurer bankruptcy is assumed to be twice that of government bond default. Value losses of insurance contracts in normal times and disasters are each assumed to be stochastic, in the empirical range of the losses in economic contractions found in Barro (2006).[3]

Table 7.1
Summary statistics of simulated rates and returns (%)

	Equity return	Bond return	Bond yield	Inflation
No disasters	Real rates and returns			
Mean	4.0	2.5	2.4	—
Std. dev.	17.8	5.8	2.3	—
With disasters				
Mean	2.7	1.7	1.9	—
Std. dev.	21.8	11.2	6.1	—
No disasters	Nominal rates and returns			
Mean	7.6	6.1	6.0	3.6
Std. dev.	17.4	5.1	2.4	2.7
With disasters				
Mean	6.8	5.8	6.1	4.1
Std. dev.	19.2	6.7	2.4	6.2

Source: Authors' simulations, based on 1962–2009 data

Out of the simulations, the likelihood of rare economic disasters and thus large equity contraction is about 1.7 percent per annum. The probability is about 0.7 percent for government bond default and 1.5 percent for insurer bankruptcy. Loss in bankruptcy varies in the range of about 20 to 85 percent of original contract value. Table 7.1 reports the summary statistics of simulated rates and returns. The incorporation of rare economic disasters significantly lowers the expected asset returns and increases their volatility.[4]

Mutual funds charge certain fees and expenses that significantly affect wealth and income delivered to investors. Mutual funds here are assumed to charge 1.2 percent annually on account balances, regardless of asset compositions, which is the average level of expense ratio of balanced funds on the market.[5] This analysis compares outcomes net of these expenses. Wealth and income values would be higher if institutional pricing (lower fees) were assumed.

The underlying discount rates for annuity pricing are proxied by the yields on ten-year Treasury bonds, which are jointly simulated in the VAR model. Insurance companies invest mainly in corporate bonds, getting somewhat higher yields, but we assume that the credit spread is used to cover investment expenses and any losses from bond defaults.

The annuity pricing uses the annuitant life table to reflect adverse selection in the voluntary immediate annuity market, and there is an additional load of 10 percent to cover administration, marketing, and other costs. A unisex mortality table is used, reflecting the legal requirement for employer-sponsored retirement plans. The probability distribution of annuity payouts reported below reflects possible bankruptcies of annuity providers, which reduce payouts by the randomly realized magnitudes, permanently for the annuitant's remaining life. These assumptions about life annuities may be regarded as exaggerating the probability and extent of insurer losses and therefore biasing the analysis somewhat away from the use of annuities.

The survival of retirees is simulated based on a general population unisex life table. Observations of account balance and income are ignored in the years following the simulated death of an investor.

Good Strategies for Wealth Distribution in Retirement

Results with Baseline Assumptions

As a baseline case, we first assume that an individual retires at age 65 with $1 million accumulated in her 401(k) account or IRA. She initially holds a 50-50 equity-bond mix in wealth, which reveals her preferences toward investment risks. The preference weight on income shortfall probability α is set to two-thirds and correspondingly one-third on balance shortfall risk. The real consumption floor C_0 is set to be $45,000, and the real balance threshold W_0 is $250,000. Minimizing the weighted shortfall risk, the individual at age 65 searches for an income mechanism that consists of a systematic withdrawal from mutual funds and an annuitization schedule. The withdrawal rate, with a 1 percentage point increment for choice at retirement, remains constant over life. The annuitization process can take a course of five to thirty-five years, with a five-year increment, and the purchase can start and end with any percentage of retirement wealth, with a 5 percentage point increment.

Using both immediate fixed annuities and mutual funds, we discover in the stochastic simulation model that the good distribution strategy for the individual retiree is to annuitize 10 percent of wealth initially and 100 percent eventually over a course of twenty years (that is, through age 85) and simultaneously make a fixed 5 percent annual withdrawal from the remaining wealth in mutual funds. The equity allocation in mutual funds increases from 50 percent initially at age 65 to 100 percent at age 74. As reported in panel A of table 7.2, the strategy

Table 7.2
Good strategies for wealth distribution for individual retirees: Baseline assumptions, $000, inflation-adjusted

Real $000	95th percentile	50th percentile	5th percentile	Mean	Std. dev.	Shortfall probability (%)
A. Life annuity plus systematic withdrawal						
Balances	900.0	316.1	0.0	370.8	312.9	44.1
Income	80.5	51.5	18.4	50.9	18.1	32.2
B. No economic disasters						
Balances	900.0	342.4	0.0	385.1	309.1	41.3
Income	83.9	53.1	33.4	55.1	15.8	23.8
C. No annuitization choice, 50-50 equity-bond mix						
Balances	1019.7	581.6	123.4	588.8	295.4	15.1
Income	70.7	41.2	9.1	41.5	20.3	55.7
D. No annuitization choice, 70-30 equity-bond mix						
Balances	1074.5	577.9	99.7	591.8	317.9	17.1
Income	74.6	41.0	7.4	41.7	21.9	55.6

Notes: Baseline assumptions: initially $1 million at age 65 with 50-50 equity-bond mix, weight on income shortfall probability $\alpha = 2/3$, real consumption floor $C_0 = \$45,000$, and real balance threshold $W_0 = \$250,000$.
A. With economic disasters, weighted shortfall risk 36.2 percent, withdrawal 5 percent, annuity initial 10 percent, ending 100 percent by 20 years.
B. Weighted shortfall risk 29.7 percent, withdrawal 5 percent, annuity initial 10 percent, ending 100 percent by 20 years.
C. With economic disasters, weighted shortfall risk 42.2 percent, withdrawal 7 percent.
D. With economic disasters, weighted shortfall risk 42.8 percent, withdrawal 7 percent.
Source: Authors' simulations

implies an income shortfall probability of about 32 percent and a balance shortfall probability of about 44 percent, thus a weighted shortfall risk of about 36 percent. This is the lowest shortfall risk for the assumed options and parameters and therefore a good strategy. Higher numbers mean greater shortfall risks and thus lower "utility."

Panel B of table 7.2 shows the choice of distribution strategy when economic catastrophes are not considered in the model. Without such disasters, higher asset returns would materialize, leading to greater wealth accumulation through mutual funds (higher levels and lower standard deviations). The lower risk of insurer bankruptcy (still possible in normal times) also enhances the annuity payoff to investors. Both forces help generate higher and more stable incomes and lower shortfall risks. The optimal distribution strategy and equity realloca- tion over time underlying panel A remain good, however, in this no- disaster scenario. This is because the added risk of disasters does not turn equity investment more favorable compared to annuity purchase and vice versa. Results and discussions hereafter reflect the analytical inclusion of the possibilities of economic catastrophes and insurer bankruptcies.

If the retiree for some extraneous reason shuns annuities, a fixed 7 percent withdrawal from mutual funds is a good rule for wealth dis- tribution under the assumed parameters (panel C). The mutual fund portfolio is maintained at the 50-50 equity-bond asset mix. This rule keeps a larger fund balance, as indicated by the greater median and mean balances, as well as the lower balance shortfall risk (about 15 percent). A certain balance serves to maintain the capacity to generate future income. Income levels, however, are lower by about $9,000 on average than when life annuities were utilized. The income shortfall risk increases to about 56 percent. The weighted risk of balance and income shortfalls is about 42 percent.

As a slight detour from the discussion, we show the results in panel D for a more aggressive 70-30 equity-bond portfolio. This isolates and clarifies the impact of asset allocations on the probability distributions of income and balance, absent annuitization choice. With a larger equity position, faster wealth creation may occur, as indicated by the larger means of balance and income. The 95th percentile outcomes of panel D, owing to realizations of exceptional equity returns, look attractive. This, however, is no guarantee. Investment outcomes spread over a wider range in case D and the 5th percentile outcomes are significantly worse than in case C. Aiming for greater wealth by virtue of equity exposure thus bears the greater risk of shortfalls.

Contrasting outcomes in cases A and C shows the merits of the strategy of systematic withdrawals plus annuitization: First, the gradual annuitization maintains a good level of liquidity for early years in retirement. Figure 7.1a shows that the probabilities of balances falling below the W_0 threshold in the investor's 60s and early 70s are largely similar to the desirable outcomes when no annuities are considered. The cash in hand can be used to finance unexpected large spending, while future annuity payouts cannot be cashed out to meet current emergencies. The cash can also form a bequest if the investor dies

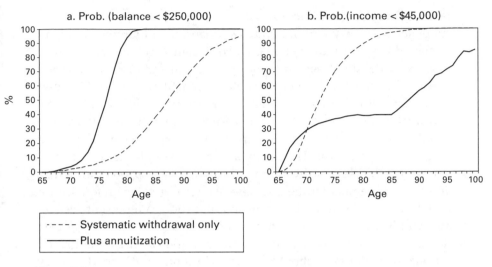

Figure 7.1
Age-specific shortfall probabilities in good distribution strategies. Balances and income are in real terms (i.e., inflation adjusted). *Source:* Authors' simulations

earlier than expected. The likelihood of balance shortfalls increases in later years with the conversion of wealth into annuities. This risk, however, is compensated by the increased security of income and higher income levels.

As the second and more important feature, the "combined" strategy takes advantage of the longevity insurance of immediate life annuities. As shown in Figure 7.1b, the risk of income falling below the consumption floor is considerably lower than in the case of no annuities. "Mortality credit" is the answer. The insurance providers pool both the annuity funds and the mortality risks among the annuitants. When annuitants die, their funds are in essence allocated to those alive, remaining in the pool. This extra asset redistribution forms the mortality credit, which grows (nonlinearly) with age. The older are the annuitants who outlive others, the greater is the survivorship bonus. Annuity purchases at advanced ages are especially rewarding, contingent on survival.

Life annuities eliminate the risk of outliving resources. The purchasing power of annuity payouts (fixed nominal), however, is subject to inflation risks, equally as applicable to systematic withdrawals. The erosion of inflation is apparent in figure 7.1b as the income shortfall risk trends upward after age 85 because nominal payouts are constant but their real values shrink over time.[6]

Results for Alternative Scenarios

As preferences vary with individuals' financial and family situations, so should the distribution strategies. For instance, some investors may place a greater emphasis on liquidity if they already receive a steady stream of income from a generous defined benefit plan. Table 7.3 shows the results with alternate preferences. An equal weight on real income and wealth balances ($\alpha = 1/2$) would suggest that the investor annuitize 20 percent of her wealth over five years and make a 6 percent systematic withdrawal. The equity allocation would increase from 50 percent to 62.5 percent during the transition over ages 65 through 70 and then is maintained there for life. An even greater preference for liquidity ($\alpha = 1/3$) would eliminate annuitization. A 6 percent systematic withdrawal from mutual funds is the good strategy. This strategy depresses consumption by construction, as indicated by the greater income shortfall risk of about 61 percent. In contrast, the good strategy in the baseline case (panel A of table 7.2) may be more appealing to retirees who are covered solely by a DC plan and are more concerned about income security.

Asset portfolios hinge on individuals' attitude toward investment risks. We alternatively assume the initial asset allocations to be a more aggressive 70-30 equity-bond mix and then more conservative 30-70 and 20-80 splits. The shortfall weights hereafter are reset to the baseline assumption ($\alpha = 2/3$). The larger equity portion presumes that

Table 7.3
Good strategies for wealth distribution: Alternative preferences, $000, inflation adjusted

Real $000	95th percentile	50th percentile	5th percentile	Mean	Std. dev.	Shortfall probability. (%)
A. Equal priority for balance and income ($\alpha = 1/2$)						
Balance	1,000.0	518.2	114.3	540.4	277.9	16.8
Income	67.4	43.0	11.4	41.8	17.7	53.5
B. Priority for a larger balance ($\alpha = 1/3$)						
Balance	1,058.3	641.5	147.8	636.2	292.9	10.9
Income	62.9	38.8	9.2	38.3	17.2	61.3

Notes: Assumptions the same as in table 7.2, with economic disasters.
A. Weighted shortfall risk 35.2 percent, withdrawal 6 percent, annuity initial 0 percent, ending 20 percent by 5 years.
B. Weighted shortfall risk 27.7 percent, withdrawal 6 percent, annuity 0 percent.
Source: Authors' simulations

the individual is more risk tolerant. The portfolio has the potential of realizing more equity premium and delivering returns greater than the annuity return, especially in early years when the mortality credit is small. In contrast, the latter asset mixes reveal a greater degree of risk aversion, and the expected return on this portfolio is lower.

Several observations emerge from the results in table 7.4. First, the initial asset composition marginally affects the annuitization pace but maintains an eventual full annuitization. For instance, the 70-30 equity-bond mix has a higher return and a larger balance in expectation than the 30-70 portfolio, other things equal, which is consistent with the comparison of panels C and D results in table 7.2. The 70-30 asset mix here goes with an initial annuitization of 15 percent of wealth while the 30-70 mix has 10 percent in initial annuitization. This result suggests that the annuitization may start with a larger (smaller) fraction of existing wealth when the mutual funds are expected to be faster (slower) in creating new wealth for liquidity. Note that the greater

Table 7.4
Good strategies for wealth distribution: Alternative initial asset allocations, $000, inflation-adjusted

Real $000	95th percentile	50th percentile	5th percentile	Mean	Std. dev.	Shortfall probability (%)
A. Initial 70-30 equity-bond mix						
Balances	850.0	285.4	0.0	351.5	307.9	46.8
Income	84.9	51.6	17.1	51.3	20.1	34.9
B. Initial 30-70 equity-bond mix						
Balances	900.0	319.9	0.0	365.9	302.2	43.5
Income	75.0	51.3	20.3	50.2	15.7	30.1
C. Initial 20-80 equity-bond mix						
Balances	900.0	320.8	0.0	365.7	298.2	43.1
Income	72.2	51.2	20.8	49.9	14.5	29.0

Notes:
A. Weighted shortfall risk 38.9 percent, withdrawal 5 percent, annuity initial 15 percent, ending 100 percent by 20 years.
B. Weighted shortfall risk 34.5 percent, withdrawal 5 percent, annuity initial 10 percent, ending 100 percent by 20 years.
C. Weighted shortfall risk 33.7 percent, withdrawal 5 percent, annuity initial 10 percent, ending 100 percent by 20 years.
Source: Authors' simulations

annuitization by 5 percentage points makes the balances in panel A smaller than in panels B and C. Also consistent with the contrast of panel D to C in table 7.2, the more aggressive portfolio here may realize excellent income outcomes (the 95th percentile) but takes the increased risk of falling short instead. Over time, the annuity return with implicit mortality credit dominates returns on the conventional equity/bond assets, which leads to 100 percent annuitization in twenty years.

Second, lower expected returns on mutual funds have an ambiguous effect on the annuitization choice. On one hand, a somewhat slower pace of annuitization becomes desirable in order to meet the balance threshold or liquidity need, as just analyzed. On the other hand, the fund returns are more likely to be exceeded by the annuity return, which demands a faster annuitization. For instance, the effects net out; when the mutual fund is further tilted to a 20-80 equity-bond mix, the annuitization is not further delayed.

Third, the initially more aggressive portfolio may produce higher income, but the gain from realizations of equity premium is likely to be only modest. There is only a narrow difference between the 70-30 case and the 30-70 case by their 50th percentile outcomes of income. With annuitization of wealth, mutual funds constitute an increasingly smaller share of total wealth, which mitigates the influence of the equity exposure.

And fourth, the bigger bond position forms a better hedging against the annuity price fluctuations that owe to interest rate changes. Bond returns increase when interest rates drop. The 30-70 and 20-80 cases deliver more secure wealth and income outcomes (lower standard deviations). They have a weighted shortfall risk of about 35 percent and 34 percent, respectively, compared to 39 percent for the 70-30 case.

Table 7.5 reports the good distribution strategies if the individual instead chooses to retire earlier at age 60 or later at 70. For the same amount of initial wealth, an earlier exit from the labor force means a longer life in retirement and naturally a greater likelihood of income and balance shortfalls (a weighted probability of about 47 percent versus 36 percent in case A of table 7.2), while the opposite holds for a later retirement (about 25 percent) as the budget constraint loosens relatively. More important, it is preferable for an early retiree to expand the annuitization process to twenty-five years so as to get better terms at older ages owing to the higher mortality credit. For the retirement at age 70, a twenty-year phased fund-annuity conversion toward an ultimate full annuitization remains a good wealth distribution strategy.

Table 7.5
Good strategies for wealth distribution: Alternative retirement ages, $000, inflation-adjusted

Real $000	95th percentile	50th percentile	5th percentile	Mean	Std. dev.	Shortfall probability (%)
A. Retirement at age 60						
Balances	900.0	302.0	0.0	364.8	310.2	45.2
Income	70.3	45.6	13.6	44.3	17.0	48.3
B. Retirement at age 70						
Balances	850.0	393.4	0.0	410.7	291.3	36.2
Income	90.8	56.9	25.7	57.9	19.4	19.1

Notes:
A. Weighted shortfall risk 47.3 percent, withdrawal 5 percent, annuity initial 10 percent, ending 100 percent by 25 years.
B. Weighted shortfall risk 24.8 percent, withdrawal 5 percent, annuity initial 15 percent, ending 100 percent by 20 years.
Source: Authors' simulations

At the same time, the investor can enjoy a higher expectation of consumption and wealth balance with lower shortfall risks.

We also search for the good distribution strategies for married couples who are assumed to purchase joint and survivor (J&S) annuities with 75 percent benefit for survivors. For consistency with this preset living standard, the income shortfall threshold is reduced to 75 percent of $45,000 for the simulated cases of only one survivor remaining. Single annuities for following years will be used when only one member is alive.

According to the results shown in table 7.6, the good strategy for the couple is a 5 percent systematic withdrawal plus a lengthened time frame (thirty years) for annuitization. This strategy concurs with the notion that couples benefit from intrafamily risk pooling and thus desire slower annuitization in the expectation of better annuity terms.[7] The J&S annuity return exceeds expected bond and equity returns at generally older ages compared to the single life annuity. The couple still needs to annuitize fully eventually for longevity protection because they jointly are more likely to reach advanced ages. The equity share in mutual funds starts with 50 percent and reaches 100 percent at age 80.

This distribution strategy remains good for couples who prefer a larger wealth threshold of $350,000, say, except that the full

Table 7.6
Good strategies for wealth distribution: Couples, $000, inflation adjusted

Real $000	95th percentile	50th percentile	5th percentile	Mean	Std. dev.	Shortfall probability (%)
A. Wealth threshold (W_0 = $250,000)						
Balances	1000.0	402.2	17.9	450.8	323.7	44.2
Income	68.8	43.9	13.8	42.9	16.4	41.5
B. Wealth threshold (W_0 = $350,000)						
Balances	1000.0	342.4	0.0	407.4	332.2	64.3
Income	71.8	45.3	13.9	44.4	17.1	38.0
C. Equal priority for balance and income (α = 1/2)						
Balances	1049.1	594.8	125.7	602.8	296.2	16.7
Income	62.4	36.1	7.9	36.4	17.4	57.9
D. Initially 30-70 equity-bond mix						
Balances	950.0	380.6	21.9	424.0	295.7	45.0
Income	63.4	44.1	15.4	42.7	14.2	38.9

Notes:
A. Weighted shortfall risk 42.4 percent, withdrawal 5 percent, annuity initial 0 percent, ending 100 percent by 30 years
B. Weighted shortfall risk 46.8 percent, withdrawal 5 percent, annuity initial 0 percent, ending 100 percent by 25 years.
C. Weighted shortfall risk 37.3 percent, withdrawal 6 percent, annuity 0 percent.
D. Weighted shortfall risk 41.0 percent, withdrawal 5 percent, annuity initial 5 percent, ending 100 percent by 30 years.
Source: Authors' simulations

annuitization should be achieved five years sooner. The likelihood of falling short gets larger by construction, and the ambitious balance threshold becomes especially hard to meet at advanced ages. As the result, a heightened focus on income security in later life through the utilization of annuities would be the strategy to minimize the overall shortfall risk as defined in the objective function.

The life annuity loses its appeal when the couple attaches equal importance to wealth balances (α = 1/2) in the evaluation of distribution strategies. In the good strategy, the couple makes a 6 percent systematic withdrawal from mutual funds, which have larger balances than otherwise with annuities. Some income security is thus sacrificed, as indicated by the higher income shortfall probability (about 58 percent).

The optimal annuitization pace becomes somewhat faster if the couple starts with a more conservative portfolio, for example, a 30-70 equity-bond mix initially. The weight on income shortfall risk here is again reset to the baseline $\alpha = 2/3$. This portfolio has a lower return in expectation, and the J&S annuity is more likely to exceed that at relatively younger ages. As indicated by the results in table 7.6, the couple would benefit from starting the annuitization at age 65 with 5 percent of wealth.

Conclusions

We search for good strategies for wealth distribution in retirement, among varying combinations of systematic withdrawals from mutual funds and fixed payouts from life annuities. The objective is to minimize shortfall risks, weighing trade-offs between income flow and wealth in hand. In the stochastic simulations, we give due consideration to the uncertainties in asset returns and low-probability large-magnitude economic catastrophes such as equity market crashes and bond defaults, as well as bankruptcies of annuity providers.

The results show that a phased annuitization scheme over a number of years should be a sensible pillar for retirement wealth management. This gradual process works to smooth over fluctuations in annuity purchase prices and captures the benefits of risk pooling (i.e., mortality credit) and thus longevity insurance for advanced ages. The annuity payouts establish a consumption floor to cover basic living needs throughout an individual's life.

The results also reveal the merits of a fixed percentage systematic withdrawal scheme from the remaining portfolios. It complements the annuity component by continually allowing the possibilities of greater wealth creation and liquidity in hand. This systematic withdrawal strategy, however, requires certain risk tolerances and presumes the ability of an investor to weather storms such as market crashes. This downward risk is in turn mitigated by the annuity layer, even though the annuity contract itself is subject to some bankruptcy risk from the insurer. Still, risk can never be eliminated entirely, and these strategies are good overall to achieve desirable outcomes and avoid bad ones.

Notes

1. A constant dollar withdrawal would be a case of "self-annuitization," which is similar to fixed payout life annuities in terms of income pattern but forgoes the mortality

credit that is inherent in annuities through risk pooling. Moreover, with a fixed dollar withdrawal, compared to a fixed percentage, there is a significant and higher chance of running out of money before death.

2. Another possible strategy is to spend the portfolio income and not liquidate the principal. Implicitly we assume that the desired level of consumption prevents individuals from pursuing this heavy weighting on and perhaps inefficient way of preserving wealth balances.

3. Implicitly, these value losses are net of recoveries provided by state guarantee funds.

4. A technical appendix of the estimation and simulation details is available from the authors upon request.

5. See Pang and Warshawsky (2009, table 1), which is based on the 200 largest balanced mutual funds with conservative and moderate asset allocations by Morningstar's categorizations, March 2008.

6. Inflation-indexed annuities are not considered here because they are new and still relatively rare in the U.S. marketplace. Evidence from the United Kingdom shows them to have higher loads (see Brown, Mitchell, and Poterba, 2001).

7. See discussions by Kotlikoff and Spivak (1981) and Brown and Poterba (2000), for instance.

References

Barro, Robert. 2006. Rare Disasters and Asset Markets in the Twentieth Century. *Quarterly Journal of Economics* 121 (3): 823–866.

Brown, Jeffrey R., Olivia Mitchell, and James M. Poterba. 2001. The Role of Real Annuities and Indexed Bonds in an Individual Accounts Retirement Program. In *Risk Aspects of Investment-Based Social Security Reform*, ed. John Y. Campbell and Martin Feldstein, 321–360. Chicago: University of Chicago Press.

Brown, Jeffrey R., and James M. Poterba. 2000. Joint Life Annuities and Annuity Demand by Married Couples. *Journal of Risk and Insurance* 67 (4): 527–553.

Campbell, John, and Luis Viceira. 2004. Long-Horizon Mean-Variance Analysis: A User Guide. Appendix to Campbell and Viceira 2005. Available at http://www.cfapubs.org/toc/faj/2005/61/1.

Campbell, John, and Luis Viceira. 2005. The Term Structure of the Risk-Return Trade-Off. *Financial Analysts Journal* 61 (1): 34–44.

Kotlikoff, Laurence, and Avia Spivak. 1981. The Family as an Incomplete Annuities Market. *Journal of Political Economy* 89 (2): 372–391.

Pang, Gaobo, and Mark Warshawsky. 2009. Comparing Strategies for Retirement Wealth Management: Mutual Funds and Annuities. *Journal of Financial Planning* 22 (8): 36–47.

Smith, Gary, and Carole Judd. 2009. Managing Risk around Retirement, Improving DC Design. Thinking Ahead Group technical paper. London: Watson Wyatt Worldwide.

Warshawsky, Mark. 2007. Recent Developments in Life Annuity Markets and Products. *Benefits Quarterly*, Second Quarter 23 (2): 46–57.

8   In Sickness and in Health: An Annuity Approach to Financing Long-Term Care and Retirement Income

with Christopher M. Murtaugh and Brenda C. Spillman

Introduction

As the baby boom generation nears retirement, concerns are increasing as to how the larger and longer-lived cohorts that will be turning 65 over the next 20 to 30 years will finance their long-term care needs. Retirement health and income security policies typically are considered separately. Disability requiring long-term care is an issue that links the two because it can result in catastrophic costs but generally is not insured. Median family income for those age 65 or older in 1998 was $23,000 to $33,000 for married couples and $16,000 for unmarried persons (Social Security Administration, 2000). Although two-thirds of retirees received some income from assets, asset earnings at the median were only about $2,000 and accounted for only 20 percent of aggregate income for those age 54 and older (Social Security Administration, 2000). With private rates for nursing home care averaging between $35,000 and $50,000 per year in 1997, depending on the level of care and type of facility (Gabrel, 2000), a lengthy stay could be a financial disaster for many retirees. Home care can be a lower-cost and more desirable long-term care solution when appropriate. However, it also can pose a substantial threat to financial security, particularly for those with more severe disability or complex medical conditions requiring expensive skilled care.

Although Medicare and private supplementary health coverage reduce the financial risks associated with acute healthcare for nearly all elderly people, no similar, nearly universal public or private coverage exists for long-term care. The welfare-oriented Medicaid program is the primary public funder of long-term care, but it reaches only those

From *Journal of Risk and Insurance* 68 (2) (June 2001): 225–254.

with the lowest income and assets. Medicare finances long-term care only under limited circumstances. Private long-term care insurance still plays a minor role. No more than 5 to 7 percent of the elderly hold policies (Coronel, 1998; American Academy of Actuaries, 1999). Numerous proposals for extending public coverage for long-term care were unsuccessful during the 1980s and as part of reform efforts of the early 1990s. More recently, policy has focused on private solutions for all but those poor enough to qualify for Medicaid.

Meanwhile, although Social Security continues to be a mandatory inflation-adjusted annuity paid out over the lives of retired workers and their spouses, employer-sponsored pension plans are shifting from the defined benefit form to the defined contribution form. A life annuity traditionally was the only payment option in defined benefit plans but typically is not even offered as a distribution method in defined contribution plans. Even among defined benefit plans, lump-sum distributions are increasingly offered and taken by plan participants. Proposed partial privatization of Social Security could imply a further shift away from automatic annuitization at a time of increasing longevity and the resulting higher risk of outliving accumulated assets. In this article, we analyze a method for explicitly linking planning for long-term care and income security. Although a number of factors appear to contribute to the relatively small markets for private long-term care insurance and immediate income annuities, an important factor appears to be adverse selection, which increases the cost of income annuities and limits through medical underwriting the number of persons who can purchase long-term care insurance. In this study, we examine an annuity that provides jointly for income and disability payments. We simulate its potential for reducing adverse selection in both products and thereby expanding their markets. Although the analysis is framed in terms of a private product, the results also have implications for the underlying distributional properties of public programs.

Adverse selection is the tendency of those who have reason to expect greater-than average benefits to be more likely to purchase any insurance-type product priced for the average risk. Without a mechanism to control this tendency, premiums are driven upward and become increasingly less attractive to average and below-average risk purchasers. Adverse selection occurs in immediate annuities because they primarily attract purchasers with above-average expected longevity.

This situation makes annuities more expensive than if purchasers had average longevity. Similarly, insurers believe that long-term care insurance appeals more to those with greater expectation of disability. To protect themselves from poor risks, insurers use medical underwriting to identify and exclude purchasers with preexisting disabilities or other health conditions that are believed to result in higher near-term claims costs. These conditions also result, however, in shorter-than-average survival (Murtaugh, Kemper, and Spillman, 1995).

The central hypothesis of this analysis is that pooling the two opposing risks—long life versus short life with disability—in theory has the potential to reduce both adverse selection in the income annuity and the need for underwriting in long-term care insurance. If that is true in application, such a combined product could be priced more cheaply than separately purchased products and could be made available to more people.

We investigate these propositions empirically using data from the 1986 National Mortality Followback Survey (NMFS) projected to represent hypothetical purchasing pools at ages 65 and 75 in 1995. We simulate the number of persons eligible to purchase a combined product with minimal medical underwriting for the disability benefit and estimate implied premiums for the combined product relative to those for separate purchase of stand-alone products. Our results are estimated single premiums paid at purchase.

Background

Income annuities and long-term care insurance are potentially relevant for most retirement-age persons. The exception is those with the lowest income and assets, who are likely to qualify for medical assistance through Medicaid if they become disabled and need long-term care, particularly nursing home care. They are unlikely to have sufficient income from pensions or accumulated assets to purchase private long-term care insurance or annuities. Excluding these low-income persons, most retired persons face a risk of outliving their assets, and nursing home and home care costs represent major threats to financial security. For the most part, these persons have incentives to avoid Medicaid eligibility, which requires "spenddown" to minimal assets, to avoid financial dependency, limited choice of long-term care providers, and potentially poor quality of care.

Life Annuities

The essential characteristic of a life annuity is that payments continue for the lifetime of the purchaser—it is insurance against running out of money. Drawing income directly from assets provides no insurance against fluctuations in asset returns or against outliving accumulated savings. As a result, the standard of living may need to be lower as a precaution against running out of money. Annuity payments may be either guaranteed (fixed or increasing) or variable depending on the underlying investments. The annuity frequently offers a guaranteed period over which benefits will be paid even if the purchaser does not survive. In this analysis, we simulate only annuities with a guaranteed period—one with a level lifetime payment and one with payments that increase for inflation at a fixed rate.

One disadvantage of a life annuity is illiquidity, because assets cannot be recovered after purchase, regardless of special needs, for example, long-term care costs. A second major disadvantage attributed to individual life annuities is that they are "expensive," primarily because of the cost of adverse selection. Previous studies have estimated this cost to be about 10 percentage points on premiums for straight life annuities, that is, immediate annuities without guaranteed periods (Warshawsky, 1988; Friedman and Warshawsky, 1990; Mitchell, Poterba, Warshawsky, and Brown, 1999; and Poterba and Finkelstein, 1999). Reducing adverse selection would reduce the price and therefore increase the value of life annuities.

Long-Term Care Insurance

The risk of needing long-term care after retirement and the cost of care are substantial, but as noted, such care is largely uninsured. More than 40 percent of those age 65 or older are expected to spend some time in a nursing home, and almost one in ten will spend five or more years there before they die (Kemper and Murtaugh, 1991). A larger proportion of people will need some long-term care, including home care, in their remaining lifetimes. About 17 percent of those age 65 or older had disability requiring some type of human help in 1994, and only 29 percent of them were in nursing homes (Spillman and Pezzin, 2000). The average annual cost for a stay in a nursing home in 1997 was about $35,000 for residential care, $40,000 for intermediate care, and $50,000 for skilled care (Gabrel, 2000). Home care visits cost $50 to $100 on average in 1996, depending on the skill level of services provided, according to data from the National Association for Home Care. Nationally, long-term care spending exceeds $115 billion a year, at least 40 percent of which is paid privately (Braden et al., 1998). Much of public long-term care spending is focused on those with very low incomes.

A number of reasons have been put forth for the small market penetration of private insurance. There is a theoretical argument and some empirical evidence that the existence of Medicaid, even though it is a welfare program, dampens the market for private insurance (Pauly, 1989; Sloan and Norton, 1997), as well as a behavioral argument that parents do not purchase insurance as a strategy to ensure help from their children (Pauly, 1990). Low market penetration also may reflect reluctance to purchase in a relatively immature market, where both insurance products and the delivery system are changing significantly (Cohen, 1998). Most long-term care insurance adopts the classic indemnity approach, paying only eligible expenses for specified services so that even currently well-designed policies can become outdated quickly. Some argue that long-term care insurance may be beyond the means of most of the elderly. Estimates of the percentage of the elderly who could afford coverage, in which affordability is defined as meaning that purchasers should spend no more than a specified percentage of income, tend to range between 10 and 20 percent; those estimates that also consider assets indicate that affordability is more widespread (Wiener, Tilly, and Goldenson, 2000). The value that would-be purchasers place on insurance also affects whether a given level of income and assets leads to purchase. Cutler (1993) has suggested that the fixed or nominally adjusted benefits found in current long-term care insurance products leave purchasers exposed to the risk of long-term cost increases, reducing the value placed on the coverage.

However, another more directly measurable factor limiting private insurance and the one most relevant to the present analysis is medical underwriting. Murtaugh, Kemper, and Spillman (1995) estimated that between 12 and 23 percent of the population would be rejected for private long-term care insurance for health reasons if everyone applied at age 65, and 20 to 31 percent would be rejected at age 75. Although some insurers are now offering risk-rated premiums, underwriting remains a substantial impediment to expansion of private long-term care insurance (Collett, 1999). Moreover, the underwriting process itself is expensive and difficult.

Combined Life and Disability Annuity

The idea of combining income and disability protection has currency in the private market and has been discussed in a preliminary way in academic literature. Since this research was completed, trade press accounts indicate that five or six insurers have begun offering various forms of a combined life annuity and disability policy. In addition, after completing this research, we became aware of one company that has been marketing an individual disability-escalating annuity for several years, based on research conducted by Christopherson (1992). With one exception, a deferred annuity platform is used to avoid the adverse selection that would otherwise arise from the lack of underwriting for the disability component. All the combined annuities seem to take the cash disability payment approach, as opposed to the indemnity approach nearly universal in stand-alone long-term care insurance policies. The commercial success of these products is unknown. To our knowledge, no insurer has yet employed the central insight that combining an immediate life annuity and disability benefits could reduce adverse selection and increase the number of persons qualifying to purchase insurance against the risk of needing long-term care.

The idea of combining lifetime income and long-term care disability protection has also appeared in academic literature. Pauly (1990) asserted that an annuity of this form (which did not then exist in the market) would maximize lifetime expected utility, although this result came in the context of exploring rational reasons for not purchasing long-term care insurance in the absence of such an annuity. In the mid-1990s, one economist proposed a related partially public approach through which a small percentage of Social Security benefits (essentially a public life annuity) would be set aside for a basic long-term care benefit (Chen, 1994). There has been, however, little empirical research into the properties of this combination.

The specific form we estimate is a fixed immediate life annuity with payments that increase upon the determination of a chronic disability. The basic product is a life annuity that pays $1,000 a month for life with a guaranteed ten-year minimum payout, combined with a disability annuity that pays an additional $2,000 a month if the purchaser becomes chronically disabled in at least two activities of daily living (ADLs) or cognitively impaired, and an additional $1,000 a month if the purchaser becomes disabled in four ADLs. We also estimate premiums for this basic product with increasing payments meant to provide some protection against inflation. We chose the benefit amounts to be such that, combined with Social Security, they would cover both basic consumption needs and the average cost of nursing home care at most skill levels and in most regions at the higher benefit level and in some cases at the lower benefit level. Average annual costs ranged from $30,000 for residential care to $45,000 for skilled care in the South and Midwest; only skilled care in the West and intermediate and skilled care in the Northeast, all of which exceeded $50,000 on average, exceeded the estimated annuity benefits at the higher disability level (Gabrel, 2000).

Data and Methods

Our data are from the 1986 National Mortality Followback Survey (NMFS), a nationally representative sample of adults who died in 1986 (Seeman, Poe, and Powell-Griner, 1993). The 1986 NMFS is one survey of a series conducted by the National Center for Health Statistics to study causes of death and disease, demographic trends in mortality, and other healthcare issues.

For the 1986 survey, death certificates of 18,733 United States residents 25 years of age or older, representing approximately 1 percent of all deaths of U.S. residents age 25 or older in 1986, were drawn from the 1986 Current Mortality Sample. A survey of the next of kin supplements information on the death certificate. Respondents were asked to provide information about, among other things, the decedent's health history, limitations in physical and mental functioning, lifestyle (e.g., history of smoking, diet), socioeconomic characteristics, and use of nursing homes. The overall response rate to the questionnaire was 89 percent, leaving an unweighted sample of 16,587. For this analysis, we used data on subsamples of persons dying at age 65 or older (9,181 unweighted cases) and at age 75 or older (6,083 unweighted cases) to make estimates for simulated pools of persons likely or eligible to purchase annuity and disability products at those ages. Both the health and functioning variables are critical to our simulation of prospective purchaser pools. The data on limitations in ADLs and cognitive impairment also are key for our benefit calculations because they are used as the criteria for receiving benefits in virtually all current long-term care insurance. The ADL limitations included in the 1986 NMFS were eating, toileting, dressing, bathing, and walking. A "limitation" was defined as receiving help or using special equipment for these activities during the last year of life. For each ADL, the survey asked the lifetime duration of the limitation. The age at which each ADL limitation began was calculated by subtracting this duration from age at death. Regarding cognitive impairment, the respondent was asked whether a doctor ever said that the decedent had Alzheimer's disease, chronic brain syndrome, dementia, senility, or any other serious memory impairment and when the diagnosis first was made. The chapter appendix provides more information on the disability measures and how our estimates compare with estimates from other surveys.

Explanation of Risk Category Groupings

To define this study's hypothetical pools of persons eligible and ineligible to purchase long-term care insurance, we used a simulation of underwriting for private long-term care insurance developed in previous research (Murtaugh, Kemper, and Spillman, 1995). A variety of sources of information were reviewed to obtain information on underwriting practices, which were then approximated using the NMFS data.

We determined whether each person met any of the following six conditions associated with greater likelihood of being rejected for long-term care insurance at the prospective purchase age: (1) any ADL limitation; (2) cognitive impairment; (3) a major illness (e.g., chronic obstructive pulmonary disease, emphysema, or cancer that eventually led to death); (4) stroke; (5) heart attack within the past two years or any heart attack complicated by other factors; or (6) an unhealthy lifestyle defined as a history of heavy drinking or obesity as an adult. Individuals meeting more than one criterion appear in all relevant risk groups.

Definition of "Purchase Pool" Classifications

The foundation of our analysis is simulation of "prospective purchasers" of separate income annuities and long-term care policies under current long-term care insurance underwriting practice and prospective purchasers of a combined income and disability annuity under a scheme of minimal underwriting. We used those who had none of the underwriting characteristics, and whom we also knew had above-average longevity (Murtaugh, Kemper, and Spillman, 1995), to represent prospective purchasers under current underwriting practice. Their complement, those who had any of the underwriting characteristics, was used to proxy nonpurchasers, who would find income annuities less attractive because of their below-average longevity and who would be ineligible to purchase long-term care insurance under current underwriting practice. To simulate minimal underwriting, we defined a second, expanded prospective purchaser pool as all persons except those who already would qualify for disability benefits under a combined income and disability annuity at purchase. Their complement is those who would be immediately eligible for disability benefits. They make up the nonpurchaser pool under minimal underwriting.

Reweighting for Projections

Because weighted estimates from the NMFS are for persons dying in 1986, the sample differs from individuals who currently make up the market for annuities and long-term care insurance, in two significant ways. First, the cohort of 1986 decedents has an over-representation of deaths at young ages because the number of persons turning 65 over the past several decades has increased. Second, there have been substantial gains in life expectancy, and these improvements are expected to continue. To adjust for these differences, the NMFS sample was reweighted, following the methodology in Kemper and Murtaugh (1991).

Reweighting Method

Our analysis examines two age groups: those turning 65 in 1995 and those turning 75 in 1995. Social Security Administration (SSA) cohort life tables for the appropriate birth cohorts (1930 and 1920) were used to adjust the distribution of elderly decedents age 65 or older and age 75 or older in 1986 by age at death and gender so that their mortality experience matched SSA Alternative II projections for these two age groups. Weights were then further adjusted so that the weighted totals for each projection age matched the number of persons of that age in 1995, using NCHS data.

Table 8.1 summarizes the effect of the reweighting for decedents age 65 or older in 1986. The estimate of mean years of life remaining for persons age 65 is 3.0 years greater after reweighting, consistent with the overrepresentation of younger deaths in the cohort of 1986 decedents and with increases in life expectancy after age 65. The reweighting also increases the proportion of persons meeting disability criteria and the average length of time disabled individuals would be eligible for benefits. The former is because of the strong positive correlation between disability and age, and the increase in the relative size of the weights of persons dying at older ages as a result of the reweighting. The latter reflects a longer period of time, on average, between

Table 8.1
Effect of reweighting to make projections for persons age 65 in 1995

	Before reweighting	After reweighting
	All persons dying at age 65 or older in 1986	All persons turning 65 in 1995
Number of persons	1,470,110	2,070,000
Mean years of life after age 65	14.8	17.8
Meeting 2 + ADL disability criterion		
Number of persons[a]	950,794	1,417,950
Percent of all persons	64.7	68.5
Mean years with 2 + ADL benefits	1.9	2.2
Meeting 4 + ADL disability benefit criterion		
Number of persons[b]	695,491	1,049,490
Percent of all persons	47.3	50.7
Mean years with 4 + ADL benefits	1.1	1.3

a. Persons meeting the 2+ ADL benefit criterion have 2+ ADLs *or* cognitive impairment starting after age 65 and lasting 120 days (90 days to qualify for benefits plus a 30-day waiting period).
b. Persons meeting the 4+ ADL benefit trigger have 4+ ADLs starting after age 65 and lasting 90 days (90 days to qualify for benefits with no additional waiting period).
Source: Authors' calculations

the onset of disability and death among disabled persons dying at older ages.

Mortality Estimates for Purchasers of Annuities

Besides the simulated eligibility to purchase long-term care insurance, a key factor for the validity of our estimates is the life expectancy of "prospective purchasers," under current underwriting practice, which should reasonably resemble the life expectancy of those who currently purchase annuities at prices reflecting the effects of adverse selection. Therefore, we compared our estimates of mortality beginning at age 65 for this group with actuarial estimates of mortality at age 65 for actual purchasers of immediate annuities. The data on the mortality of annuitants in 1995 are based on the Annuity 2000 mortality table published by the Society of Actuaries (Mitchell et al., 1999).

The difference in mortality rates between our prospective purchasers under current long-term care underwriting practice and annuitants is relatively small at each age until about age 95. For women, remaining life expectancy at age 65 was 22.6 years for annuitants and 21.2 years for our prospective purchasers, a difference of 1.4 years. When persons dying after age 95 are excluded, the difference in remaining life expectancy is only 0.3 years. The results are similar for men, although differences are somewhat larger. Remaining life expectancy at age 65 was 19.7 years for male annuitants and 17.4 years for our prospective purchasers, a difference of 2.3 years, which declines to a difference of 1.1 years when men dying after age 95 are excluded.

These differences in mortality may, in fact, be less than estimated because the mortality rates in the annuitant life tables have been "smoothed," with the last hypothetical annuitant not dying until age 115. The smoothing may have resulted in artificially low mortality rates until very extreme ages. The difference also could be due to the positive relationship between socioeconomic status and longevity (Rogers, 1992; Pappas et al., 1993). Current annuitants are likely to be, on average, of higher socioeconomic status than our prospective purchasers because we do not control for socioeconomic status. Nevertheless, if our prospective purchasers under current practice are shorter-lived than current annuitants, the cost of a stand-alone annuity will be underestimated, which is a conservative bias that works against finding the hypothesized results.

Premium Estimates

We estimate premiums for both the immediate income annuity and for the disability coverage as a lump sum paid at purchase. Long-term care insurance premiums currently are most often level premiums paid monthly or quarterly. This practice makes the timing of eligibility for benefits more important because it affects both the amount of prefunding through premium accumulations and the amount of benefits when they include inflation protection. For comparability, we modeled all premiums as lump sums paid at purchase. We estimated the premiums for both the annuity and disability benefits by calculating present discounted benefits from the age of purchase to death for each individual and then taking the mean over individuals. The general form of the expected present discounted value of benefits paid for each member of the kth group is given by

$$E(PV\ Benefits_k) = \frac{1}{n_k}\sum_{j=1}^{n_k} PV\ Benefit_j = \frac{1}{n_k}\sum_{j=1}^{n_k} B\sum_{t=0}^{d_j} \theta_{jt} \left[\frac{1+i}{1+r}\right]^t,$$

where n_k is the number of persons in the kth risk group; d_j is the number of years between purchase and death for the jth person; B is the initial annual benefit at purchase; θ_{jt} is the proportion of the tth year after purchase that the jth person receives benefits ($\theta = 1$ in all years except the fractional year of death for the simplest case of a life annuity paid from purchase to death, and $0 \le \theta = \le 1$ in each year for the disability benefits); i is the rate of inflation protection; and r is the nominal interest rate.

Because our base policy has a minimum ten-year benefit period, the life annuity payout is computed as the benefit for ten years or for the actual number of years survived, whichever is larger. Premiums for the life annuity were marked up 3.5 percent, and those for the disability coverage were marked up 18 percent to reflect a conventional level of expense loading for annuities and long-term care insurance, respectively, excluding marketing and sales commissions. Long-term care insurance is currently sold both directly and through agents. When sold through agents, commissions are generally similar in pattern and level to those for term life insurance: a large first-year commission, about 50 percent of premium, and lower renewal commissions for the next few years, about 3 percent of premium.

For the basic disability benefit, we used the duration of disability in two or more ADLs or cognitive impairment to calculate when benefits would begin. The disability benefit is modeled with a 30-day waiting period, and a disability must be chronic to qualify for benefits. We defined "chronic" as lasting 90 days. Thus, benefits begin 120 days after the onset of the second ADL or cognitive impairment, as reported on the survey. We modeled no second waiting period for the four-ADL supplemental benefit so that those benefits begin 90 days after the reported onset of the fourth ADL. The nominal interest rate used to discount benefits is 6 percent. There is no inflation protection for either the annuity or the disability benefit in the base policy. We also estimated premiums including inflation protection of 3 percent compounded for the life annuity and 5 percent compounded for the disability benefits.

Our base case is purchase at age 65 on a unisex basis. We also compute premiums by gender and for purchase at age 75. Finally, as a sensitivity analysis, we compute premiums in which we assumed that the presence of benefits would induce earlier claims for disability benefits than would have occurred in the absence of benefits, and in which we assumed that everyone entering a nursing home would obtain immediate certification of qualifying disability.

Results

Table 8.2 profiles life expectancy and disability for prospective purchasers and nonpurchasers under our two underwriting assumptions. Prospective purchasers under current underwriting practice can buy stand-alone income and disability policies at prices reflecting their life expectancy and disability experience. The larger pool of prospective purchasers under minimal underwriting can buy a combined product at a price reflecting their mortality and disability experience. We do not assume that all persons eligible to purchase do so. Rather, we implicitly

Table 8.2
Mean survival, risk of meeting benefit criteria, and number of years receiving benefits for hypothesized purchasers and nonpurchasers of an immediate annuity and disability benefits at age 65

	Percent in risk category	Mean survival (years)	Percent meeting 2 + ADL benefit criterion	Expected years of 2 + ADL disability	Percent meeting 4 + ADL benefit criterion	Expected years of 4 + ADL disability
All persons	100.0	17.8	68.5	1.5	50.7	0.7
Prospective purchasers						
Current long-term care (LTC) underwriting	77.1	19.5	69.0	1.5	51.6	0.7
Minimal underwriting only	98.0	18.0	67.9	1.4	50.2	0.6
Nonpurchasers						
Current LTC underwriting	22.9	11.7	66.8	1.5	47.7	0.6
Minimal underwriting only	2.0	5.9	100.0	5.8	74.2	2.0

Note: The estimates for current LTC underwriting practice exclude those who at the purchase age already have at least one ADL limitation, cognitive impairment, a major illness, a history of heart problems, a history of stroke, or an unhealthy lifestyle, defined as being a heavy smoker or drinker or being obese. Those excluded under minimal underwriting include only those who already have two or more ADLs or cognitive impairment at purchase age.
Source: Authors' calculations

assume random purchase within the two pools of prospective purchasers so that risk characteristics of actual purchasers would be the
same as those for all eligible purchasers.

Impact of Minimal Underwriting on Risk Characteristics

Minimal underwriting dramatically increases the pool of eligible
purchasers to 98 percent of persons at age 65, from 77 percent under
current underwriting practice. The expansion has relatively modest
impacts on mean risk and expected duration of disability in the prospective purchaser pool under minimal underwriting but reduces
average survival by 1.5 years. The lack of significant difference in risk
and duration of disability between the purchaser pools is consistent
with the positive relationship between age and disability and with
previous research showing that expected nursing home use among
those who would be accepted for long-term care insurance at age 65
was higher than for most groups excluded by underwriting (Murtaugh,
Kemper, and Spillman, 1995). The key to the higher cost of long-term
care insurance for the excluded groups in that study of nursing home
use was the lack of adequate prefunding of benefit costs because their
service use was more likely to happen in the near term. This pattern
also applies to the onset of disability, with the prospective purchasers
under current practice who ultimately become eligible for benefits
doing so 17 years in the future, compared with generally ten years or
less for the excluded groups (not shown).

Nonpurchasers under current practice differ from prospective
purchasers primarily in mean survival, which is just under 12 years
compared with 19.5 years for prospective purchasers. Risk and expected
duration of disability are similar to those of prospective purchasers. In
contrast, minimal underwriting excludes persons whose survival is
only six years on average and whose expected duration of disability is
about four times that of prospective purchasers.

Impacts on Premiums

Table 8.3 shows the individual premium estimates for the three levels
of benefit and a combined premium resulting from the risk patterns in
table 8.2. The estimates in the top panel include no protection against
inflation, while those in the lower panel include inflation protection.

The premium for the life annuity of $139,827 for the expanded
purchaser pool under minimal underwriting is 3.6 percent lower than
that for prospective purchasers under current practice because of the

Table 8.3
Premiums at age 65 for income annuity with disability benefits: Current LTC underwriting practice versus minimal underwriting

	$1,000 monthly life annuity only	$2,000 monthly 2+ ADL disability benefit	$1,000 monthly 4+ ADL disability benefit	Combined premium
Without inflation protection.				
All persons	$139,098	$ 15,950	$ 3,155	$158,203
Prospective purchasers				
Current LTC underwriting	$145,041	$ 13,900	$ 2,843	$161,784
Minimal underwriting only	$139,827	$ 13,723	$ 2,777	$156,326
Nonpurchasers				
Current LTC underwriting	$119,051	$ 22,866	$ 4,207	$146,124
Minimal underwriting only	$104,147	$122,764	$ 21,293	$248,203
With inflation protection[a]				
All persons	$177,238	$ 35,649	$ 7,630	$220,517
Prospective purchasers				
Current LTC underwriting	$187,102	$ 35,258	$ 7,791	$230,151
Minimal underwriting only	$178,426	$ 33,122	$ 7,220	$218,768
Nonpurchasers				
Current LTC underwriting	$143,963	$ 36,969	$ 7,086	$188,018
Minimal underwriting only	$120,268	$156,864	$ 27,295	$304,427

Note: Base income annuity policy is $1,000 per month for life with a minimum ten-year benefit.
a. Income annuity inflates at 3 percent per year compounded, and disability benefits inflate at 5 percent per year compounded, consistent with long-term care insurance industry standard for inflation protection.
Source: Authors' calculations

expanded pool's lower average survival. This is lower than the 10 percent estimate of the cost of adverse selection in the current annuity market cited earlier (Warshawsky, 1988; Friedman and Warshawsky, 1988, 1990; Mitchell et al., 1999; Poterba and Warshawsky, 1999; and Poterba and Finkelstein, 1999). The difference is in part due to the ten-year minimum benefit in the estimates, which increases income annuity benefits disproportionately among groups excluded from our prospective purchaser pool under current practice because of their shorter survival. The straight life annuities on which the 10 percent estimate was based did not include a minimum benefit. For more direct comparison, the cost of adverse selection in our income annuity with no minimum benefit would be about 6 percent (not shown).

The premiums for disability benefits, like the risk and duration of disability, are similar for the two purchase groups. This is because after minimal underwriting excludes the 2 percent of persons representing the worst disability cost risks, the remaining "poor risks" actually have lower disability costs than those currently accepted for long-term care insurance and reduce the average for the expanded pool. Combined with the lower annuity costs of prospective purchasers under minimal underwriting, the premium for the combined product is $156,326, about 3.4 percent lower than that for an immediate life annuity and equivalent stand-alone long-term care insurance under current underwriting practice.

This pattern is similar when inflation protection is added, in the lower panel of table 8.3, but differences are larger because of the greater impact of the inflation protection on both life annuity and long-term care benefits received further in the future by prospective purchasers under current underwriting practice. In particular, this can be seen in the premium for two-ADL disability with minimal underwriting, which is $33,122, or 6 percent lower than under current practice. With inflation protection, the premium for the combined benefits for the expanded pool is about 5 percent below the premium for the stand-alone products under current underwriting practice.

Both with and without inflation protection, the overall premium for a combined life annuity and disability policy for the entire cohort of persons turning 65 is only slightly higher than that for the expanded pool. This is because the impact of lower average survival on the life annuity premiums partially offsets the higher costs of the disability benefits. While a private insurer might not be willing to immediately cover persons already in claim, the implication is that the small group excluded by minimal underwriting would have little impact on costs for a mandatory public program, in which there is pooling over all risks. A private insurer might, however, be willing to issue coverage to those persons already in claim if their eligibility for disability payments were deferred for two or three years.

Relative Benefits by Risk Group

A key issue is whether a combined product offered at a lower price would attract the expanded purchase pool on which the lower premium is based and, if so, whether the product would be appropriate for the marginal groups purchasing. This would depend on the value that various groups receive directly from benefits and indirectly from the value of insurance protection. To examine this issue, table 8.4 compares ratios of fair premiums for prospective purchasers and nonpurchasers under current underwriting practice to fair premiums for prospective purchasers under minimal underwriting. Those excluded under current practice are also broken out according to their underlying risk categories. The ratios show the proportion of the premium under minimal underwriting that would be attributable to direct income and disability benefits. Where the ratio is less than one, it would not be advantageous for members of that group on average to purchase unless they perceived value (in an expected utility sense) from having insurance protection sufficient to bring their perceived direct and indirect benefit ratio to at least one.

Prospective purchasers under current practice would receive direct income and disability benefits greater than the premium for prospective purchasers under minimal underwriting. Overall, ignoring any value perceived from having insurance, this group would receive direct benefits on average about 3.5 percent above the premium it would have to pay. This group's direct long-term care benefits would be 1.3 percent higher than the premium under minimal underwriting for the two-ADL benefit and 2.4 percent for the four-ADL benefit.

Among the groups excluded from long-term care insurance purchase by current underwriting practice, only those with cognitive impairment at age 65, all of whom also would be excluded under minimal underwriting, and those with at least one ADL limitation at age 65, some of whom would be excluded, would have expected direct benefits higher than the premium under minimal underwriting for the combined benefit. This is because their extremely high average disability benefits more than make up for their low mean annuity benefits.

Table 8.4
Relative premiums at age 65 for income annuity with disability benefits

Premium ratio: Risk group relative to expanded purchase pool

	$1,000 monthly immediate annuity only	$2,000 monthly 2+ ADL disability benefit	$1,000 monthly 4+ ADL disability benefit	Combined premium
Without inflation protection				
All persons	0.995	1.162	1.136	1.012
Purchasers				
Current LTC underwriting	1.037	1.013	1.024	1.035
Minimal underwriting only	1.000	1.000	1.000	1.000
Nonpurchasers				
Current LTC underwriting	0.851	1.666	1.515	0.935
ADL limitation	0.775	5.509	6.066	1.285
Cognitive impairment	0.741	8.532	3.655	1.477
Major illness	0.827	1.306	1.008	0.872
Heart attack	0.789	0.688	0.793	0.781
Stroke	0.853	1.981	2.076	0.974
Lifestyle	0.865	1.219	1.181	0.902
Minimal underwriting only	0.745	8.946	7.669	1.588
With inflation protection[a]				
All persons	0.993	1.076	1.057	1.008
Prospective purchasers				
Current LTC underwriting	1.049	1.064	1.079	1.052
Minimal underwriting only	1.000	1.000	1.000	1.000
Nonpurchasers				
Current LTC underwriting	0.807	1.116	0.981	0.859
ADL limitation	0.712	3.028	3.086	1.141
Cognitive impairment	0.670	4.444	1.817	1.279
Major illness	0.778	0.872	0.663	0.789
Heart attack	0.728	0.433	0.489	0.675
Stroke	0.810	1.299	1.234	0.898
Lifestyle	0.822	0.899	0.872	0.835
Minimal underwriting only	0.674	4.736	3.780	1.392

Note: Base income annuity policy is $1,000 per month for life with a minimum ten-year benefit.
a. Income annuity inflates at 3 percent per year compounded, and disability benefits inflate at 5 percent per year compounded, consistent with long-term care insurance industry standard for inflation protection.
Source: Authors' calculations

The remaining groups all have premium ratios for the combined product less than 1, indicating that they would have to perceive enough indirect value from insurance protection to bring perceived direct and indirect benefits up to the level of the premium they would pay under minimal underwriting. The "worst off" are those with heart problems, who would receive less-than-average benefits for the life annuity and both disability benefits, resulting in an overall direct benefit of 78 percent of premium, slightly below their direct benefits for the life annuity alone. For the remaining excluded groups, however, adding long-term care benefits improves the direct benefit to premium ratio for the combined product relative to the life annuity alone.

For purchase to be advantageous to the groups with direct benefits below premium, they would have to perceive indirect value from insurance ranging from about 3 percent of premium for those who had suffered a stroke by age 65 to 22 percent for the heart attack group. In dollar terms, the perceived value of being insured for life would have to be about $4,000 in the first case and $34,000 in the second for these groups to be willing to purchase. It should be noted that, because the risk categories are not mutually exclusive, ratios of benefits to premium for all groups containing some members who would be excluded under minimal underwriting are somewhat overstated, so that required perceived insurance value is somewhat understated. More than 60 percent of those in the ADL limitation and cognitive impairment groups also appear in one or more of the other excluded categories, but a majority of persons in the remaining excluded groups appear in only one group.

Adding inflation protection to the policy increases the direct benefits of the prospective purchaser group under current underwriting for both the life annuity and stand-alone long-term care coverage because of the higher cost of benefits in the distant future. Consistent with the findings in Murtaugh, Kemper, and Spillman (1995) for nursing home coverage, inflation protection reduces the relative cost of disability benefits for the excluded groups because their disability generally occurs in the nearer term, as well as reducing the relative value of the life annuity. As a result, the excluded groups receive lower direct benefits from the combined product. In this case, those with heart problems would receive benefits of 67.5 percent of the premium paid for the combined product. With inflation protection, direct benefits are below premium for both the life annuity and the disability coverages for all except those with ADL limitation, cognitive impairment, and history of stroke. Perceived indirect value of insurance protection would have to be 10 percent of premium for those with a history of stroke and 32.5 percent for those with heart problems for purchase to be advantageous.

Our estimates include expense loadings of 3.5 percent on the income annuity and 18 percent on the disability benefit, for an average 5 percent on the combined product. Although these loadings cancel out of the ratios showing the percentage of premium going to direct benefits, in practice, the indirect benefits perceived from insurance would also have to be sufficient to cover these insurer expenses, as well as additional sales and marketing costs in some cases.

Although there is no direct empirical evidence on the indirect benefits that people receive from a life annuity and long-term care insurance, there are formal models that attempt to simulate willingness to pay for life annuities. For example, Mitchell et al. (1999) use an explicit individual utility function and compare the expected utility from purchasing an annuity with that from nonannuity methods of decumulating assets during retirement. They use realistic mortality, interest, tax, and inflation rates and estimates of risk-preference parameters gathered from the literature. The simulated expected utility gains suggest the value of an annuity to individuals is between 23 and 31 percent of wealth. Presumably, consideration of the risk of incurring long-term care expenses would not reduce and likely would increase the indirect insurance value of a combined income and disability annuity.

Results by Gender

Table 8.5 disaggregates results for our base policy at age 65 without inflation protection by gender to examine differences in the effect of minimal underwriting on the size of the expanded purchase pool and premiums for the combined coverages. Although employer-sponsored benefit plans are not allowed to vary premiums or payouts by gender, other insurance products may. Substantial evidence shows that women, who have greater life expectancy than men, also have higher long-term care costs, a greater rate of chronic disability, and longer survival with disability (Kemper and Murtaugh, 1991; Manton, 1997; Guralnik et al., 1997). Besides women's greater rate of disability, other factors suggest long-term care costs would be higher for women than those for men. Because of their greater longevity, women are more likely to be available to provide informal long-term care if their husbands become disabled and are also more likely to be widowed and thus without a spouse to provide informal long-term care if they themselves become

Table 8.5
Results by gender for purchase at age 65: Base policy[a] with no inflation protection

Risk group category	Number of persons	Percent in risk category	Combined premium: immediate annuity plus disability	Premium ratio: Relative to expanded purchase pool			
				Immediate annuity	2+ ADL disability	4+ ADL disability	Combined premium
Women							
All purchasers	1,109,000	100.0	$167,542	0.995	1.114	1.098	1.009
Current LTC underwriting	898,418	81.0	$170,688	1.030	1.010	1.023	1.028
Minimal underwriting only	1,090,009	98.3	$166,040	1.000	1.000	1.000	1.000
Nonpurchasers							
Current LTC underwriting	210,582	19.0	$154,122	0.847	1.557	1.420	0.928
ADL limitation	25,880	2.3	$208,689	0.757	4.953	5.066	1.257
Cognitive impairment	6,320	0.6	$247,549	0.728	7.744	4.283	1.491
Major illness	85,573	7.7	$140,806	0.808	1.171	1.004	0.848
Heart attack	24,795	2.2	$122,824	0.756	0.610	0.645	0.740
Stroke	47,070	4.2	$159,598	0.872	1.597	1.766	0.961
Lifestyle	62,480	5.6	$147,681	0.870	1.031	1.039	0.889
Minimal underwriting only	18,991	1.7	$253,790	0.726	7.642	6.728	1.528

Table 8.5
(continued)

Risk group category	Number of persons	Percent in risk category	Combined premium: immediate annuity plus disability	Premium ratio: Relative to expanded purchase pool			
				Immediate annuity	2+ ADL disability	4+ ADL disability	Combined premium
Men							
All purchasers	961,000	100.0	$147,425	0.995	1.251	1.207	1.016
Current LTC underwriting	698,262	72.7	$150,327	1.041	0.988	0.993	1.036
Minimal underwriting only	937,708	97.6	$145,035	1.000	1.000	1.000	1.000
Nonpurchasers							
Current LTC underwriting	262,738	27.3	$139,714	0.871	1.951	1.777	0.963
ADL limitation	28,614	3.0	$193,695	0.803	6.634	7.886	1.336
Cognitive impairment	10,776	1.1	$221,041	0.770	10.464	3.627	1.524
Major illness	117,956	12.3	$133,063	0.859	1.599	1.126	0.917
Heart attack	55,786	5.8	$121,674	0.834	0.864	1.043	0.839
Stroke	39,900	4.2	$143,508	0.828	2.668	2.639	0.989
Lifestyle	84,492	8.8	$136,036	0.879	1.560	1.474	0.938
Minimal underwriting only	23,292	2.4	$243,648	0.774	11.353	9.559	1.680

Note: Base income annuity policy is $1,000 per month for life with a minimum ten-year benefit.
a. Immediate annuity benefit of $1,000 per month, two-ADL disability benefit of $2,000 per month, and four-ADL disability benefit of $1,000 per month

Source: Authors' calculations

disabled. This could contribute to a differentially greater demand for benefits by women with long-term care needs. Ratios of premiums for the various risk groups relative to those for the expanded purchase pool are given for the life annuity and the two levels of disability protection, as well as for the combined coverage. The ratios are calculated within the gender grouping.

Minimal underwriting has a larger effect for men than for women, because of their earlier onset of conditions associated with the excluded groups under current underwriting practice. More than a quarter of men would be excluded at age 65 from purchase of long-term care insurance under current practice compared with 19 percent of women. Under minimal underwriting, 97.6 percent of men and 98.3 percent of women would be eligible to purchase a combined life annuity and disability benefit.

Consistent with their greater longevity and chronic disability, women would have premiums for the combined product that are higher than those for men. Women in the two purchaser pools would pay premiums about 14 percent higher than men for the combined coverage. Among those excluded under current underwriting practice, women on average would have premiums about 10 percent higher than those for men, with a range from about 1 percent higher for those with heart problems to about 12 percent for those with cognitive impairment. Premiums for women excluded under minimal underwriting are only about 4 percent higher than those for men.

Considering the premium ratios, the cost of adverse selection in the life annuity is slightly lower for women. The cost of the annuity for female prospective purchasers under current underwriting practice is about 3 percent higher than that for the expanded pool under minimal underwriting, compared with 4 percent higher for men. For women, disability benefit premiums under current underwriting practice are also higher than under minimal underwriting—1 percent higher for the two-ADL benefit and 2.3 percent higher for four-ADL benefits. Conversely, for men, premiums for both disability benefits are slightly lower under current practice than under minimal underwriting. If priced by gender, the premium for combined coverage under current practice is 2.8 percent higher for women and 3.6 percent higher for men than it would be under minimal underwriting.

For the groups excluded under current underwriting practice, direct benefits would represent a smaller percentage of the premium under minimal underwriting for women than for men. This implies that if the combined product were to be priced separately by gender, women in these groups would have to perceive more indirect benefit from insurance value than men for purchase to be advantageous. For both men and women, those who already have ADL limitations or cognitive impairment at age 65 would receive direct benefits exceeding the premium under minimal underwriting. For the remaining groups, women purchasing the combined product would have to perceive insurance value ranging from 4 percent for those with history of stroke to 26 percent for those with heart problems. For men, the range is 1 percent to 16 percent for the same conditions.

These gender differences confirm the potential for adverse selection by gender if products are priced for the full population. Women in the expanded purchasing pool would have a gender-specific premium for the combined annuity and disability benefits about 6 percent higher than the gender-neutral premium for all persons, while the gender-specific premium for men would be about 7 percent below that for all persons.

Results for Purchase at Age 75

Many persons currently postpone considering long-term care insurance for several years after retirement, and they sometimes find that their health precludes them from purchase. Our estimates are that by age 75, over 30 percent of persons would be underwritten out of long-term care coverage under current practice (table 8.6). Minimal underwriting would expand the potential purchasing pool for a combined life annuity and disability product to 94.5 percent of persons at age 75 and reduce the premium for a combined product relative to stand-alone purchase by $4,355, or 3.1 percent.

Premiums for annuity and disability coverage, both under current underwriting practice and minimal underwriting, perhaps surprisingly, are about 13 percent below those at age 65. This relatively small differential is due to a trade-off between the life annuity premiums about 20 percent below those at age 65 and disability benefit premiums 50 to 60 percent higher.

At age 75, the cost of adverse selection in the life annuity with a ten-year guaranteed period is about 3 percent, and the cost of stand-alone long-term care insurance is about 3 percent higher for two-ADL benefits and about 6 percent higher for four- ADL benefits than the disability benefit premiums under minimal underwriting. There are some differences in the direct benefits for the risk groups relative to

Table 8.6
Results for purchase at age 75: Base policy[a] with no inflation protection

Risk group category	Number of persons	Combined premium: immediate annuity plus disability	Premium ratio: Relative to expanded purchase pool			
			Immediate annuity	2 + ADL Disability	4 + ADL Disability	Combined premium
All persons	1,516,000	$140,279	0.992	1.200	1.210	1.031
Prospective purchasers						
Current LTC underwriting	1,052,320	$140,450	1.030	1.034	1.061	1.032
Minimal underwriting only	1,432,844	$136,095	1.000	1.000	1.000	1.000
Nonpurchasers						
Current LTC underwriting	463,680	$141,911	0.922	1.576	1.550	1.043
ADL limitation	105,477	$179,331	0.896	3.049	3.750	1.318
Cognitive impairment	36,155	$216,717	0.885	4.919	3.653	1.592
Major illness	206,371	$123,141	0.914	0.874	0.805	0.905
Heart attack	68,649	$119,006	0.899	0.776	0.717	0.874
Stroke	118,335	$154,312	0.927	1.967	2.403	1.134
Lifestyle	80,431	$135,110	0.933	1.221	1.404	0.993
Minimal underwriting only	83,156	$216,288	0.886	4.644	4.836	1.589

Note: Base income annuity policy is $1,000 per month for life with a minimum ten-year benefit.
a. Immediate annuity benefit of $1,000 per month, two-ADL disability benefit of $2,000 per month, and four-ADL disability benefit of $1,000 per month.
Source: Authors' calculations

those at age 65. By age 75, in addition to those with ADL limitation and cognitive impairment, those with a history of stroke would have direct benefits exceeding premium under minimal underwriting. The indirect benefits from insurance value required to make purchase advantageous range from less than 1 percent for those with an unhealthy lifestyle to 13 percent for those with heart problems.

The Impact of Underestimating Benefits

Cash disability benefits have theoretical advantages over the service benefits most often provided by existing long-term care insurance. They allow the disabled person to select whatever goods or services provide the greatest benefit without imposing restrictions on the site of care or type of provider. They do not promote overuse of services because the amount of the benefit is not tied to the amount of service. However, cash benefits also are clearly of value to the nondisabled as well as the disabled. Thus, they may be even more subject than service benefits to moral hazard, the behavioral response in which losses are greater when benefits are available than when they are not. In the case of medical care or conventional long-term care insurance service benefits, moral hazard is overuse of services because insurance effectively reduces the price to the consumer. Needed services are more likely to be used, and services that otherwise would not be valued enough to purchase would be purchased at the lower insured price. This results not only in potential inefficiencies but also in higher expected claims costs to the insurer and higher premiums. A slightly different form of this response is sometimes called "ADL creep" in cases in which ADLs are used to determine eligibility for benefits, such as long-term care insurance or programs. ADL creep results from the incentive to overstate disability in order to become eligible for benefits at lower levels of disability or earlier in the course of disability. While this response would not have the same efficiency implications as overuse of services in the case of a service benefit, it would have similar impacts on costs and premiums. It also is distinct from a case in which those with no disability fraudulently claim benefits. Cash benefit policies are on the market, and we assume here that insurers can control outright fraud. Rather, "ADL creep" refers to a more subtle phenomenon in which the disabled and their medical providers respond to financial incentives to inflate disability levels.

Actual disability levels occurring in the population also might be higher than in our estimates because of underreporting of disability and disability duration in survey data (see the appendix). In that case, actual direct benefits also would be higher than we estimate, but not because of a behavioral response. To the extent that the impact of underreporting is greater (smaller) among groups with lower-than-average direct benefits, the percentage of premium attributable to direct benefits would be understated (overstated). Although the simulations are couched in terms of potential forms of ADL creep, they apply to the impact of underreporting to the extent that underreporting occurs in the stylized forms used.

We simulate three potential types of ADL creep (or underreporting) for the base policy at age 65 (table 8.7). Estimates in the top panel are from a simulation in which we assumed that "ADL inflation" occurred. Specifically, we assumed that persons with one ADL limitation would be willing and able to obtain certification that they had two ADL limitations to receive the first level of benefits earlier. Similarly, persons with three ADLs would obtain certification that they had four. The middle panel assumes that insured persons would be able to obtain certification immediately upon onset of two ADLs or four ADLs rather than have to meet the 90-day criterion for a chronic limitation. The final panel assumes that all persons entering a nursing home would immediately qualify for the first level of benefits. Because nursing home entry is not an explicit benefit criterion, this has the effect of providing benefits to some who used a nursing home but never met the two-ADL criterion and providing benefits earlier to some whose two-ADL disability occurred after nursing home entry. In all three panels, estimates are premiums for the disability benefits and for the combined product under the simulation, relative to base premiums.

The most serious impacts would be attributable to ADL inflation. Premiums for the two disability benefits would be 40 to 56 percent higher. It is clear why the expanded purchase pool's premium increase would be greater. All persons in the group excluded from long-term care purchase because they had one ADL limitation at age 65 would by definition meet the disability criterion soon after purchase. Even among those with no limitation at age 65, disability benefit premiums would be 40 percent higher. Nevertheless the impact on overall premiums for the combined product is modest—only 4 to 6 percent higher than with no ADL inflation. The small overall impact results in part from the fact that the monthly income annuity payment represents 90 percent of the combined premium because of the long period over which it is paid; this is despite the fact that the monthly income annuity

Table 8.7

Sensitivity analysis: Percentage premium increase due to "ADL creep," base policy at age 65

	$2,000 monthly 2 + ADL disability benefit	$1,000 monthly 4 + ADL disability benefit	Combined premium, immediate annuity plus disability benefits
ADL inflation[a]			
All persons	1.47	1.46	1.06
Prospective purchasers			
Current LTC underwriting	1.40	1.40	1.04
Minimal underwriting only	1.56	1.41	1.06
Nonpurchasers			
Current LTC underwriting	1.62	1.59	1.11
Minimal underwriting only	1.00	1.73	1.06
Earlier benefits[b]			
All persons	1.09	1.15	1.01
Prospective purchasers			
Current LTC underwriting	1.10	1.15	1.01
Minimal underwriting only	1.11	1.16	1.01
Nonpurchasers			
Current LTC underwriting	1.07	1.13	1.01
Minimal underwriting only	1.00	1.04	1.00
Nursing home users all meet criterion[c]			
All persons	1.28	1.00	1.03
Prospective purchasers			
Current LTC underwriting	1.32	1.00	1.03
Minimal underwriting only	1.31	0.99	1.03
Nonpurchasers			
Current LTC underwriting	1.18	1.00	1.03
Minimal underwriting only	0.99	0.97	0.99

a. Assumes that all those with one ADL would obtain certification for two ADLs, and those with three ADLs would obtain certification as having four ADLs if disability benefits were available.

b. Assumes that certification for chronic two-ADL and four-ADL disability, respectively, would be obtained three months earlier if disability benefits were available.

c. Assumes that all persons entering nursing homes would gain certification for chronic two-ADL disability on admission.

Source: Authors' calculations

payment is half the two-ADL disability benefit. Thus, even a substantial increase in the disability payment will have a relatively small impact on the overall premium. Interpreted in terms of underreporting, because there is a larger percentage increase (11 percent) in premiums for nonpurchasers under current underwriting than for purchasers under minimal underwriting (6 percent), the percentage of premium reflecting direct benefits for the excluded groups would increase slightly.

The impacts for the simulation of certification at onset in the middle panel are quite modest, and because they are proportional for the various groups, the impact on relative direct benefits is nil. This is not surprising since the simulation rolls back the benefit period only 90 days. The result is an increase of only 10 to 16 percent in disability benefit premiums and an overall impact on the premium for the combined product of only 1 percent. Clearly, the impact would be larger the earlier that certification occurred. In the extreme case, this simulation is bounded by the ADL inflation case, in which those with only one ADL limitation obtain certification for two-ADL benefits.

Finally, the impact of assuming that all nursing home users qualify for benefits on admission (bottom panel) is about a 30 percent increase in the two-ADL benefit premium. We did not model any change in the receipt of four-ADL benefits. The small drop in the four-ADL benefit for prospective purchasers under minimal underwriting occurs because 0.3 percent of persons are no longer eligible to purchase because they were already in nursing homes at age 65. (This can also be seen among the nonpurchasers. The newly excluded cases are expensive relative to purchasers, but inexpensive relative to the rest of nonpurchasers under minimal underwriting, resulting in a slight reduction in their expected benefits.) The net impact on the combined coverage premiums is again quite small—only a 3 percent increase—and proportional for purchaser and excluded groups. Thus, there is no impact on relative direct benefits.

Discussion

Our analysis has demonstrated our basic proposition that combining an income annuity with disability coverage has the potential to reduce the cost of both products as they now exist in the market and make them available to more potential purchasers. We showed that minimal underwriting, excluding only those who would be eligible for benefits at purchase, would increase the potential market to about 98 percent of 65-year-olds, compared with only 77 percent under current underwriting practice. After the 2 percent representing the worst risks for high disability payments were excluded, simulated premiums for both the income annuity and the disability benefits were lower than our simulated premiums for the current stand-alone markets.

In fact, in any mandatory purchase scheme for combined income and disability protection, such as a social insurance program, the estimates indicate that including those who are currently disabled would have little impact on costs because there are so few of these extremely high-cost cases and because their lower annuity costs partially offset their higher disability costs. The low direct income annuity benefits for all those with health problems, but particularly for this group, are due to their shorter average lifetimes. Whether the potential shown by our simulation is realized in the private market, in which purchase is voluntary, depends in large part on the direct benefits various would-be purchasers expect and the value they place on the indirect benefit of insurance protection. For the most part, direct benefits for those who would be newly able to purchase long-term care protection with minimal underwriting would be below the fair premium for the income annuity and above fair premium for the disability premium. This trade-off between lower survival and generally greater disability costs of the groups currently excluded from long-term care coverage purchase results in net direct benefits on average of 94 cents per premium dollar, with the worst case being those with heart problems, who would receive only about 78 cents on the dollar.

Several other factors would affect the direct benefits that would be received by the various groups. The first is inflation protection, which is more important the earlier in life that either an annuity or long-term care policy is purchased. Inflation protection increases the gap between benefits received and premium paid for the excluded groups because it increases benefits more for the longer-lived prospective purchasers under current underwriting. The second factor is specification of a ten-year minimum benefit in the income annuity. As noted earlier, this common feature in current annuity markets tends to favor those excluded under current underwriting because they are less likely to survive ten years. Removing the ten-year minimum benefit would reduce the price but also significantly reduce the value of the coverage to the groups excluded under current underwriting. Simulations that we did not report indicate that direct benefits for these groups would fall from 94 cents per premium dollar on average to 84 cents, before considering expense loadings, if there was no minimum benefit.

Finally, in addition to underwriting, insurers currently protect themselves against adverse selection in the long-term care market by imposing a waiting period before any benefits can be received. At least some of the new products combining an income annuity and disability benefits that have come onto the market since this research began have waiting periods of several years. A long waiting period is a substantial deterrent to purchase for those who have reason to expect near-term long-term care use because it makes the coverage less valuable to them. Because the combined benefit has to be attractive to a mix of high and low risks for both benefits in order for risk pooling to work in the way we demonstrate it can work, new approaches to product design are needed. A guaranteed ten-year minimum payout of the life annuity is one policy feature that makes a combined product more attractive to individuals who think they may have a shorter-than-average life expectancy. Allowing individuals to select a policy from a range of products that vary the ratio of the disability and life annuity payments is another option that should be considered. In any case, insurers need to be careful not to introduce significant "protections" against high-disability cases precisely because those who currently are underwritten out of the private long-term care insurance market or discouraged by long waiting periods are necessary for risk pooling in a combined product to result in lower premiums.

A final issue is how many retirees would find the combined benefits affordable, an issue that is beyond the scope of this study but that we intend to explore further in future work. Our estimated premium for a $1,000 monthly life annuity, with a $2,000 monthly base disability benefit and a $1,000 monthly increment for higher disability, is $156,000 at age 65 with no inflation protection and $219,000 with inflation protection. The products currently on the market are targeted in some, if not all, cases toward those with substantial retirement savings. The most obvious application is to those with tax-deferred retirement savings, such as 401(k) plans through an employer and/or individual retirement accounts, large enough to cover the initial investment. The trend away from annuitized pension benefits and toward lump-sum distribution options provides further currency for the idea of creating vehicles through which these distributions could be used to provide jointly for income security and disability protection. We have noted the inverse relationship between socioeconomic status, health, and mortality. This link suggests that affordability for a broad range of retirees is important not only for the size of the market but also for the ability to realize the benefits of risk pooling demonstrated here.

In future work, we will be examining more closely the implications of socioeconomic status, in particular, for the likely size of the market for a combined benefit and for the distribution of risks among likely purchasers. In addition, we will be developing new, more recent data that will allow us to examine the importance of gender and marital status for benefit design and premiums. Because women are more likely than men to be available to provide informal care to a disabled spouse and also more likely to be widowed and thus without a husband who could provide informal care, it is important to consider how potential informal care resources affect insurance decisions. These factors highlight the importance of analyzing the premium and risk implications of joint purchase by spouses. This likely purchase scenario could be used to offset the gender differences that make coverage more costly for women and that could promote adverse selection by gender in any voluntary system in which benefits are not priced by gender.

Appendix: Strengths and Weaknesses of the Data, Methods, and Assumptions

The National Mortality Followback Survey is a unique and highly valuable source of information on the lifetime health and disability history of a large, nationally representative cohort of decedents. By reweighting the survey, we can make projections of disability and the need for long-term care for current cohorts turning ages 65 and 75 that are useful for evaluating private and public policies. There are, however, limitations, as in any use of survey data.

First, proxy respondents may underreport health events, although carefully designed studies have found no evidence of a difference between proxy and self reports in other data (Moore, 1988; Mathiowetz and Groves, 1985). Long recall periods may also contribute to underreporting. Generally, research based on recall periods of a year or less suggests that long recall periods lead to underreporting (Marquis, 1978; Cannell, Marquis, and Laurent, 1977). A study of a longer recall period (two and a half years) found that, while there was underreporting overall, the major determinant of error was the importance of the event (Mathiowetz and Duncan, 1988). More than 80 percent of proxies in the NMFS are immediate family members (i.e., spouses, children, or siblings) who should be knowledgeable about changes in decedents' physical and cognitive functioning. Nevertheless, there could be some underreporting in our data, in particular, total length of time the decedent had an ADL limitation or cognitive impairment before death. Our analysis of ADL creep provides some indication of the magnitude of the potential impact on our results of substantial levels of underreporting.

Limitations in the survey data on disability also are a potential source of error. The survey does not capture information on an ADL limitation or cognitive impairment if it was not present at some point in the last year of life. Analyses of longitudinal data conducted by Manton, Corder, and Stallard (1993) suggest that some chronically disabled seniors experience improvement in their ability to perform IADLs [indicators of activities of daily living] and/or ADLs, although very few with significant levels of disability regained full independence in ADLs.

Our data also include information on only five ADLs (eating, toileting, dressing, bathing, and walking). Insurers typically include a sixth ADL, transferring from bed to chair, and, less often, incontinence. Inability to transfer has implications for whether an individual is independent in other activities such as toileting, dressing, and bathing, so that the impact on our estimates may not be large. On the other hand, we include walking, which is broader than the indoor mobility criteria more commonly used in benefit determinations. This would tend to overstate eligibility for benefits. Again, however, because of the financial incentive for persons to report higher levels of disability to obtain benefits, the impact on our cost estimates relative to what would happen in an operating program is not clear.

Finally, an assumption of the reweighting is that the past relationship among gender, age, and disability will continue in the future. Growing evidence shows that age-specific disability rates are declining (Waidmann and Manton, 1998; Manton, Corder, and Stallard, 1993; Freedman and Martin, 1998). On the other hand, the effect of the reweighting is to disproportionately increase the size of the weights of persons dying at old ages in 1986.

To assess the reasonableness of disability estimates from the reweighted NMFS, we compared the length of time persons were expected to be disabled after age 65 with published estimates of remaining lifetime disability. Although constructed from a decedent cohort, our estimates of remaining lifetime disability appear to be within the range of those from two other national surveys. Among those surviving to age 65, our estimate of the number of years of cognitive impairment or disability in two or more ADLs is 1.1 years for men and 1.9 years for women. For cognitive impairment or disability in one or more ADLs, our estimate is 1.6 years for men and 2.6 years for women. (These figures are slight underestimates of total duration because they exclude the first 120 days of disability, the effective length of time persons must be disabled in our analyses before receiving disability benefits.) Crimmins, Hayward, and Saito (1996) found lower remaining lifetime disability at age 70, using pooled data from all three rounds of the Longitudinal Study of Aging (LSOA). Their estimates of the average length of time between age 70 and death that individuals will be unable to perform "by oneself and without aids" one or more of five ADLs or will be residents of an institution are 0.8 years for men and 1.8 years for women. Manton, Stallard, and Liu (1993) use the National Long Term Care Survey (NLTCS) to estimate remaining years in each of various disability "profiles." Their estimates of the combined time between age 65 and death in four of the disability states (physical impairment, frail, high frail, and institutional), which together roughly approximate our two-ADL disability measure, are 1.1 years for men and 2.8 years for women. The different definitions of disability make the comparison of the NMFS estimates with others less than ideal, but our estimates appear to be within the range defined by the estimates from these two national surveys. Though well above LSOA estimates for both men and women, they are similar for men and low for women relative to the NLTCS estimates.

References

American Academy of Actuaries. 1999. *Long Term Care: Actuarial Issues in Designing Voluntary Federal-Private Long Term Care Insurance Programs*. Washington, DC: AAA.

Braden, Bradley R., Cathy A. Cowan, Helen C. Lazenby, Anne B. Martin, Patricia A. McDonnell, Arthur L. Sensenig, Jean M. Stiller, et al. 1998. National Health Expenditures. 1997. *Health Care Financing Review* 20 (Fall):83–126.

Cannell, C. F., K. H. Marquis, and A. Laurent. 1977. *A Summary of Studies of Interviewing Methodology*. Washington, DC: U.S. Government Printing Office.

Chen, Yung-Ping. 1994. A "Three-Legged Stool" for Financing Long-Term Care: Is It an Acceptable Approach? *Journal of Case Management* 3 (Fall):105–109.

Christopherson, David L. 1992. New IDEAs for Insuring Long-Term Care. *Journal of the American Society of CLU and ChFC* 46 (2):42–53.

Cohen, Marc. 1998. Emerging Trends in the Finance and Delivery of Long-Term Care: Public and Private Opportunities and Challenges. *Gerontologist* 38 (1):80–89.

Collett, Douglas A. 1999. Long-Term Care Insurance: A Rapidly Growing, Little Understood Product. *BestWeek Supplement—Special Report. October* 25:1–7.

Coronel, Susan. 1998. *Long-Term Care Insurance in 1996.* Washington, DC: Health Insurance Association of America.

Crimmins, Eileen M., Mark D. Hayward, and Yasuhiko Saito. 1996. Differentials in Active Life Expectancy in the Older Population of the United States. *Journal of Gerontology: Social Sciences* 51B (3):S111–S120.

Cutler, David. 1993. "Why Don't Markets Insure Long-term Risk?" unpublished paper.

Freedman, Vicki A., and Linda G. Martin. 1998. Understanding Trends in Functional Limitations among Older Americans. *American Journal of Public Health* 88 (10): 1457–1462.

Friedman, Benjamin, and Mark Warshawsky. 1988. Annuity Prices and Saving Behavior in the United States. In *Pensions in the US Economy,* ed. Z. Bodie, J. Shoven, and D. Wise, 53–77. Chicago: University of Chicago Press.

Friedman, Benjamin, and Mark Warshawsky. 1990. The Cost of Annuities: Implications for Saving Behavior and Bequests. *Quarterly Journal of Economics* 105 (1):135–154.

Gabrel, Celia S. 2000. *An Overview of Nursing Home Facilities: Data from the 1997 National Nursing Home Survey, Advance Data from Vital and Health Statistics.* Hyattsville, MD: National Center for Health Statistics. http://www.cdc.gov/nchs/data/ad311.pdf

Guralnik, Jack M., Suzanne G. Leveille, Rosemarie Hirsch, Luigi Ferrucci, and Linda P. Fried. 1997. The Impact of Disability in Older Women. *Journal of the American Medical Women's Association* 52 (Summer):113–120.

Kemper, Peter, and Christopher Murtaugh. 1991. Lifetime Use of Nursing Home Care. *New England Journal of Medicine* 324 (9):595–600.

Manton, Kenneth G. 1997. Demographic Trends for the Aging Female Population. *Journal of the American Medical Women's Association* 52 (Summer):99–105.

Manton, Kenneth G., Larry Corder, and Eric Stallard. 1993. Estimates of Change in Chronic Disability and Institutional Incidence and Prevalence Rates in the U.S. Elderly Population from the 1982, 1984, and 1989 National Long Term Care Survey. *Journal of Gerontology: Social Sciences* 48 (4):S153–S166.

Manton, Kenneth G., Eric Stallard, and Korbin Liu. 1993. Forecasts of Active Life Expectancy: Policy and Fiscal Implications. *Journal of Gerontology* 48 (Special Issue):11–26.

Marquis, K. H. 1978. *Record Check Validity of Survey Responses: A Reassessment of Bias in Reports of Hospitalizations.* Santa Monica, CA: Rand.

Mathiowetz, N. A., and G. Duncan. 1988. Out of Work, Out of Mind: Response Errors in Retrospective Reports of Unemployment. *Journal of Business & Economic Statistics* 6 (2):221–229.

Mathiowetz, N. A., and R. Groves. 1985. The Effects of Respondent Rules on Health Survey Reports. *American Journal of Public Health* 75:639–644.

Mitchell, Olivia, James Poterba, Mark Warshawsky, and Jeffrey Brown. 1999. New Evidence on the Money's Worth of Individual Annuities. *American Economic Review* 89 (5):1299–1318.

Moore, J. C. 1988. Self/Proxy Response Status and Survey Response Quality: A Review of the Literature. *Journal of Official Statistics* 4:155–172.

Murtaugh, Christopher, Peter Kemper, and Brenda Spillman. 1995. Risky Business: Long-Term Care Insurance Underwriting. *Inquiry* 32 (Fall):271–284.

Pappas, G., et al. 1993. The Increasing Disparity in Mortality between Socioeconomic Groups in the United States, 1960 and 1986. *New England Journal of Medicine* 329 (2): 103–109.

Pauly, Mark V. 1989. Optimal Public Subsidies of Nursing Home Insurance in the United States. *Geneva Papers on Risk and Insurance* 14 (50):3–10.

Pauly, Mark V. 1990. The Rational Nonpurchase of Long-Term-Care Insurance. *Journal of Political Economy* 98 (1):153–168.

Poterba, James, and Amy Finkelstein. 1999. Selection Effects in the Market for Individual Annuities: New Evidence from the United Kingdom. NBER working paper no. 7168.

Poterba, James, and Mark Warshawsky. 1999. The Costs of Annuitizing Retirement Payouts from Individual Accounts. NBER working paper no. 6918.

Rogers, Richard G. 1992. Living and Dying in the U.S.A.: Sociodemographic Determinants of Death among Blacks and Whites. *Demography* 29:287–304.

Seeman, I., G. S. Poe, and E. Powell-Griner. 1993. *Development, Methods, and Response Characteristics of the 1986 National Mortality Followback Survey*. Washington, DC: U.S. Government Printing Office.

Sloan, Frank A., and Edward C. Norton. 1997. Adverse Selection, Bequests, Crowding Out and Private Demand for Insurance: Evidence from the Long-Term Care Insurance Market. *Journal of Risk and Uncertainty* 15 (3):201–219.

Social Security Administration. 2000. *Income of the Population 55 or Older, 1998*. Washington, DC: Office of Policy, Office of Research, Evaluation, and Statistics, March. http://www.ssa.gov/policy/pubs/pages/IncomeoftheAged.htm

Spillman, Brenda C., and Liliana E. Pezzin. 2000. Potential and Active Family Caregivers: Changing Networks and the "Sandwich Generation.". *Milbank Quarterly* 78 (3):347–374.

Waidmann, Timothy A., and Kenneth G. Manton. 1998. International Evidence on Trends in Disability among the Elderly. Report for the Department of Health and Human Services Assistant Secretary for Planning and Evaluation, Office of Aging and Long-Term Care Policy. http://aspe.hhs.gov/daltcp/reports/trends.htm.

Warshawsky, Mark. 1988. Private Annuity Markets in the United States: 1919–1984. *Journal of Risk and Insurance* 55 (3):518–528.

Wiener, Joshua M., Jane Tilly, and Susan M. Goldenson. 2000. Federal and State Initiatives to Jump Start the Market for Private Long-Term Care Insurance. *Elder Law Journal* 8 (1):57–102.

9　Tax Issues and Life Care Annuities

with David Brazell and Jason Brown

Introduction

A life care annuity (LCA) is an integrated insurance product consisting of life annuity and long-term care insurance (LTCI) segments. It addresses inefficiencies in the separate private markets for its component parts—adverse selection, which increases the price of life annuities, and strict underwriting, which restricts the availability of LTCI. In this chapter, we argue that, by lowering prices and increasing availability, an LCA may be more attractive to retirees making critical choices in financing their lifetime retirement spending and insuring against the bankrupting contingency of severe disability. This attractiveness, in turn, may decrease pressures on government social insurance and welfare programs, such as Social Security and Medicaid, which are already underfinanced. This chapter first describes the product idea and its motivation in more detail and then explains the present and future tax treatment of the LCA, both as an after-tax product and in a qualified retirement plan.

Description of, and Motivation for, a Life Care Annuity

In return for the payment of one or more premium charges, an LCA product will pay a stream of fixed periodic income payments for the lifetime of the named annuitant and, for a higher premium charge, any named co-annuitant survivor. These payments may be fixed in nominal terms, increasing, or inflation-indexed. In addition, the LCA pays an

From John Ameriks and Olivia Mitchell, eds., *Recalibrating Retirement Spending and Saving* (New York and London: Oxford University Press for the Pension Research Council, 2008), pp. 295–317. By permission of Oxford University Press.

extra stream ("pop-up") of fixed payments if the annuitant (and/or the co-annuitant) has severe cognitive impairment or is unable to perform without substantial human assistance at least two of the six recognized activities of daily living (ADLs), such as walking or eating. These are the same triggers used in LTCI policies that may be qualified under current tax law.

Because this pop-up segment of the LCA is intended to function as comprehensive LTCI, it is important that the level of the additional layer of payments to the disabled annuitant be sufficient to cover the extra expenses incurred for home health care or nursing home care, perhaps increasing with the degree of disability and therefore the costs of providing care. Over time, such costs of care have risen rapidly, often in excess of the rate of general inflation, and therefore inflation-indexing or automatic increases of the level of disability payments would seem particularly advantageous for these segments. That being said, it is difficult to set a standard level of payment for the LTCI portion, given substantial geographic variation in costs of care, as well as different personal preferences and means of payment for care (e.g., private vs. shared room). Even more so, the appropriate or desired level of payments in the first or life-annuity segment of the LCA will vary considerably from household to household, reflecting preferences, means, and so on.

The premium (or premiums) charged for an LCA product would depend on many factors. Obviously, the number of insured, and whether there is a survivor benefit, would be influential. Risk factors such as the age(s) of the annuitant(s) at the start of the income payments also affect the price, but other observable risk factors may be prevented from being used by law or by marketing acceptance. Most significant, of course, the premium of the LCA will reflect the level of income and disability payments being guaranteed and whether inflation indexing is to be applied to either or both segments. The premiums charged on newly issued contracts will change over time, inversely with movements in interest rates available in the financial markets on fixed-income investments used to underpin the LCA, as well as with changes in expected trends in mortality and disability experience.

The integration of two already widely available products, life annuities and LTCI, is intended to address inefficiencies in the separate markets for those products. Research by Friedman and Warshawsky (1990) and by Mitchell et al. (1999) has shown that the costs of immediate life annuities increase by as much as 10 percent because of adverse selection by mortality risk classes in voluntary choice situations (i.e., individuals with lower life expectancies avoid life-annuity purchase). Using simulation analyses using a life-cycle framework and reasonable estimates of risk aversion, this work also showed that a large improvement in utility could be achieved by the annuitization of assets at fair actuarial value in retirement. But this improvement in welfare is, at least in part, blocked by market inefficiencies. Especially for couples, deviation from fair value (i.e., loads arising from adverse selection and marketing costs) dissuades annuity purchases (Brown and Poterba, 2000).

On the LTCI side, Murtaugh, Kemper, and Spillman (1995) show that insurance company underwriting practices prevent 25–33 percent of the retirement-age population (age 65–75) from purchasing individual LTCI policies because individuals in impaired health or unhealthy lifestyles cannot purchase LTCI. Brown and Finkelstein (2004a), using simulation analysis, predict a substantial willingness to pay for actuarially fair private LTCI coverage on top of Medicaid by individuals in most income groups. So, here too, market inefficiencies compromise otherwise large welfare gains available from insurance markets. Many of these research findings about annuities and LTCI are confirmed by observations from the insurance industry, including high rejection rates on LTCI policy applications at older ages and discussions among actuarial professionals of annuity pricing.

Nevertheless, enhancing the attractiveness of life-annuity and LTCI coverage is an important public policy issue. Employer's provision of retirement income support for workers has moved, for many, to the defined contribution (DC) plan form, where a life-annuity distribution is not required and indeed is not often even offered. Accordingly, the retiree must now search in the voluntary individual annuity market if he or she would like to purchase a life annuity at retirement. Even for workers covered by defined benefit (DB) pension plans, mandatory annuitization has become less common, and therefore the scope of adverse selection may have increased. Moreover, nearly all proposals for Social Security reform envision lower growth in scheduled retirement benefits, that is, life-annuity payments. Hence, the potential scope for the voluntary life-annuity market and the resulting need to improve its efficiency may be expected to get larger still.

In 2005, the U.S. Congress tightened eligibility for the long-term care benefits of Medicaid because it was concerned with apparent abuses of the spend-down eligibility requirements as well as by the runaway program costs. Indeed, research by Brown and Finkelstein (2004b) demonstrates the substantial crowd-out effect of Medicaid on the desire for private LTCI coverage, even without considering possible efforts to game the system. Hence, as Medicaid eligibility tightens, private LTCI coverage will become increasingly important for the lower ranges of the income and wealth distribution, and general concern about market inefficiencies will increase. Moreover, the conventionally proposed solutions by the insurance industry given the obvious problems of tight underwriting—sales of individual LTCI policies at young ages or employer provision of the benefit, where underwriting is a less significant factor—have not found wide favor in the marketplace. In addition, there is a natural focal point for the LCA in household life-cycle planning, namely, when that household is approaching or has just begun retirement and is considering the rest of its financial future in a serious way.

The idea of the LCA as a product that results in a more efficient market and better insurance product is an application of the economic insights of Rothschild and Stiglitz (1976). Specifically, it is a practical attempt to produce a self-sustaining pooling equilibrium that is superior to the separating equilibria currently in existence where insurance coverage is restricted and/or highly priced. The LCA works so as to blend the low-mortality risks of annuity buyers who would like cheaper life annuities with the high-disability (and high-mortality) risks of those desiring, but currently denied access to, LTCI coverage, combining these population pools of risk classes. To the extent that there is a positive correlation between impaired health and mortality probability, an integrated insurance product that combines the life annuity and LTCI can draw disparate risk groups together in such a way that there is less adverse selection and less need for strict underwriting.

In their prior work, Murtaugh, Spillman, and Warshawsky (2001) proposed three hypotheses about the LCA:

1. The life expectancy of voluntary purchasers of an integrated product will be less than that of voluntary purchasers of life annuities.

2. With minimal medical underwriting, less severe than current underwriting for LTCI, the cost of the integrated product will be less than the sum of the cost of the two products sold separately (here minimal underwriting means that only those who would go immediately into claim status for LTCI benefits, e.g., nursing home residents would be rejected for the LCA or, alternatively, face coverage delays of, say, two to three years).

3. The subpopulation eligible for, and likely to be attracted to, the integrated product will be larger than that eligible for, and attracted to, the two products issued separately.

The authors' empirical analysis suggested that only about 2 percent of the age 65+ population would be rejected by the lower underwriting standards, as opposed to 23 percent rejected by current underwriting criteria. The mean expected remaining life of the purchasers of the LCA at age 65 is 18 years, compared to 19.5 for current annuity purchasers. Hence, Murtaugh, Spillman, and Warshawsky (2001) provided support for their first and third hypotheses. They also calculated the premium at age 65 for a unisex individual for the simplest integrated product described above, and the authors reported that it would cost about 4 percent less than the two products sold separately. Finally, they also gave evidence for the assertion that a self-sustaining pooling equilibrium is likely. In particular, they showed that those who are rejected by current LTCI underwriting, but who would be eligible for the LCA, are made better off in simple value terms. That is, the ratio of actuarially fair premiums for the relevant risk groups (major illness, stroke, poor lifestyle) relative to those for the expanded purchase pool is above one for the LTCI coverage. The pooling property of this positive effect on value should be enhanced when the expected utility ("insurance") value of LTCI coverage is considered, to say nothing of the insurance value of having a life annuity.[1]

Possible Venues for the Life Care Annuity

Next, we explore two main forms of the LCA: an individual after-tax fixed annuity product, and a before-tax qualified retirement plan/individual retirement annuity. Home equity extraction through reverse LCA mortgages should also be considered eventually, as well as variable and gift annuities and other existing vehicles for distributing resources in retirement. The LCA might be a good distribution choice for personal retirement accounts in a reformed Social Security system.

LCAs as After-Tax Annuity Products

An LCA could be thought of as an individual immediate fixed annuity product; if purchased with after-tax income, this would be the most direct and straightforward application of their findings. As we explain below in more detail, the LCA could be offered as an immediate life annuity, with LTCI structured either as a single- or level-premium rider or as a contingent annuity. On the other hand, the market for immediate annuities is quite small at present. The after-tax deferred fixed annuity product, which represents a much larger market, could also be used as a venue for the LCA. In practice, the life-annuity distribution option under deferred annuity contracts is seldom used at present. Nonetheless, marketed deferred annuities contain the valuable right for the insured to get a life annuity at the better of the terms specified in the policy contract or as an immediate annuity available in the marketplace, and this right may be used increasingly in the future.[2] Moreover, inclusion of a deferred annuity product in the broad LCA concept framework could also result in the desirable outcome that LTCI coverage is provided even before any life-annuity distributions are made.

Of late, a few insurance companies have tentatively introduced product offerings that contain certain elements of the proposed product as either deferred or immediate annuities with LTCI riders. Reportedly, the relevant state insurance departments were mostly satisfied with the products, but federal tax issues with the combination product led to difficulties and ultimately caused these companies to stop issuance. Nevertheless, as is detailed below, an after-tax LCA will be more tax favored, beginning in 2010, owing to the passage of the PPA of 2006 (P.L. 109–280).

LCAs in Connection with Qualified Retirement Plans

An LCA could take various forms in a qualified retirement plan. One option would define it as the normal accruing benefit of a DB pension plan, with the LTCI segment denominated as some proportion of the final benefit. Thus for an average-wage full-career employee, the plan could be designed such that the level of disability-contingent benefits accrued would be sufficient to cover nearly all expected LTC needs. Another option would have the LCA added as an alternative choice to the DB pension plan's distribution options, just like various joint-and-survivor payout options are currently available at cost. In particular, if the plan sponsor would like to respond positively to a demand from participants for lump-sum distributions or already has a lump-sum distribution choice, but is concerned about the impact of adverse mortality selection on the cost of its annuity offering, providing the LCA could be an effective and responsible response. Moreover, provision through a retirement plan may be a more popular way for employers to offer LTCI coverage to workers than through group LTCI plans.

Similarly, if the sponsor of a DC plan offered a life-annuity distribution option, the LCA could be added to the menu of payout choices. Life annuity options are currently somewhat rare in the DC context, but a few employers are offering their workers a service of rolling over DC account balances to pre-negotiated individual retirement annuities from one or a few insurance companies. Others offer their workers the option of rolling over DC account balances to the DB plans that, of course, pay out benefits as life annuities. And, indeed, insurers are increasingly viewing retirement plans, especially 401(k) plans, as fertile ground for new annuity products. More broadly, it is important to consider individual retirement accounts (IRAs) as a home for the LCA, which would open a very large market. Yet as is explained below, various regulations may pose significant hurdles to the LCA in qualified retirement plans, and its tax treatment under current law is unknown or unclear, and perhaps adverse.

Table 9.1 shows total assets in various types of retirement plans and annuities to give a sense of the relative magnitudes where the LCA could reside. It would be even more relevant here to report accrued DB plan liabilities rather than assets, but these are not readily available on a consistent basis for state and local government plans. For private DB plans currently, assets are just about equal to or slightly exceed accrued liabilities, according to estimates based on financial accounting

Table 9.1
Total assets in annuities and pension and retirement plans (as of 12/31/06)

	Assets (billion $)
Private DB plans[a]	2,308.0
Private DC plans[a]	4,060.0
IRA accounts[a]	4,232.0
Annuities[a]	1,624.0
Federal government DB plans[b]	918.8
Federal government DC plans[b]	223.5
State and local government DB plans[c]	2,776.0
State and local government DC plans[c]	240.0
Total assets	16,382.3

[a]Investment Company Institute (2007). [b]Investment Company Institute (2007) and Thrift Savings Plan (2006) as of 12/31/2006. [c]Investment Company Institute (2007), Public Fund Survey (2007), and Watson Wyatt estimates.

information; for government plans, there are reports that liabilities are significantly higher than assets, especially if these pension liabilities were to be marked to the market.

Current Tax Treatment of Life Annuities and LTCI When Issued as Separate Contracts

Next, we turn to a discussion of tax treatment of different products underlying the LCA construct.

After-Tax Individual Life Annuity

Annuity payments from individual life annuities are treated partially as taxable income and partially as an untaxed return of the policy-holder's cost, or "investment in the contract." In general, an annuity's investment in the contract is recovered in equal increments over the annuitant's expected remaining life, although the details differ for "nonqualified" and "qualified" annuities. Nonqualified annuities are those not paid from a qualified employer plan or other qualified savings plan, such as an individual retirement account (Brown et al. 1999). The investment in the contract as of the annuity start date is used to determine the annual annuity exclusion amount.[3] It equals the sum of premiums or other consideration paid for the contract before the annuity start date, less any refunded premiums, dividends, or other amounts that were received before that date but were not included in gross income. Premiums paid for additional coverages (say, disability or double indemnity coverages) are excluded from investment in the contract.

Under the general rule for taxing nonqualified annuities, one must compute the contract's "expected return," or the total amount that annuitants can expect to receive under the contract. For life annuities, it is obtained by multiplying the annuity's initial periodic (annualized) payment by the annuitant's life expectancy in years. The latter is determined using published unisex tables from the Internal Revenue Service (IRS).[4] Published tables are also available for determining the expected return for temporary life annuities (where the number of total payments is limited), for joint-and-survivor annuities (where a periodic income is paid until the death of one annuitant, and an equal or different amount is paid until the death of a second annuitant), and for joint life annuities (where payments are made only if both named annuitants remain alive). For cases not covered by the published tables, taxpayers must request a ruling from the IRS to determine the contract's expected return. Dividing investment in the contract by the contract's expected return yields the contract's "exclusion percentage." This percentage is multiplied by the first regular periodic payment, and the result is the tax-free-exclusion amount of each annuity payment. This exclusion amount remains the same for all years, even if the annual annuity payment changes.

Once investment in the contract is recovered through annual exclusion amounts, then the annuity payments are fully included in gross income. Any unrecovered investment in the contract remaining at the death of the last annuitant is allowed as a miscellaneous itemized deduction on the last return of the final decedent. This deduction is not subject to the usual floor on miscellaneous deductions, equal to 2 percent of adjusted gross income (AGI), but it is allowed only for those (deceased) taxpayers who itemize their deductions on their final return.

For variable annuities, investment in the contract is simply divided by the number of expected payments to yield the tax-free-exclusion amount for each payment.[5] If the annual tax-free amount is more than the payments received for the year, then the excess may be divided by the expected number of remaining payments, and the result added to the previously determined exclusion amount. Contract distributions that are not periodic annuity payments (including policy loan proceeds) are generally taxed in full if received after the annuity start date. If received before the annuity start date, distributions are generally taxable, but only to the extent that the contract's cash value (determined immediately before the amount is received) exceeds investment in the contract at that time (i.e., such distributions are taxed on an "income-first" basis). Under certain circumstances, taxable distributions not received as an annuity payment are subject to an additional 10 percent tax.

Qualified Long-Term Care Insurance Policy: Premiums and Benefits
A qualified LTCI policy enjoys certain tax benefits under current U.S. law. To be qualified, the contract must meet certain conditions. Among these is the requirement that the only insurance protection provided under the contract is coverage of qualified long-term care services.[6] An exception to this restriction exists under current law for LTCI provided as a rider or as part of a life-insurance contract and, after 2009, for LTCI provided as a rider or as part of an annuity policy. In addition, the

contract cannot provide a cash surrender value that can be borrowed, paid, assigned, or pledged as collateral for a loan. Premium refunds and policyholder dividends must be applied as a reduction in future premiums or as an increase in future benefits, except when paid as a refund on the death of the insured or upon complete surrender or cancellation of the contract. Any refund cannot exceed the aggregate premiums paid under the contract. A qualified long-term care contract must also meet certain consumer protection requirements specified in law.

A qualified LTCI policy may pay benefits on a per diem or other periodic basis without regard to the actual long-term care expenses incurred. However, such payments are subject to a per diem limitation. This limitation is set at $260 in 2007, and it is also indexed to the medical-care component of the Consumer Price Index (CPI). The aggregate of such LTCI benefits must be added to any periodic "accelerated death" payments received (tax free) by a chronically ill insured from life-insurance policies. Any excess of the aggregate payment over the per diem limit, calculated for the period of coverage, is treated as taxable income.

A qualified LTCI policy is treated as a health or accident insurance contract, and benefit payments are treated as amounts received for personal injuries and sickness, implying that such benefits are generally excludable from taxable income. Amounts received from qualified policies are treated as reimbursement for expenses actually incurred for medical care. Employer-provided coverage under a qualified LTCI contract is treated as an accident and health plan, so that employer-paid premiums are excludable from employee income. Nevertheless, LTCI cannot be offered as part of an employer cafeteria plan.

Qualified status also bestows tax benefits as regards premiums. Premiums paid on individual qualified policies, up to specified age-based, inflation-indexed limits, are treated as medical insurance premiums, and thus as potentially deductible medical-care expenses. The excess of medical-care expenses over 7.5 percent of an individual's AGI is deductible as a "below the-line" itemized deduction. Finally, premiums on qualified LTCI contracts may be paid from a health savings account (HSA) established in connection with a high-deductible health-insurance policy. Because HSA amounts are pretax amounts, such a use of HSA funds effectively allows a full exclusion of amounts used to pay qualified LTCI premiums.

Life Annuity and Long-term Care Insurance in a Qualified Retirement Plan

The life annuity is currently the required default form of distribution in qualified pension plans (i.e., DB and money purchase DC plans). There are various regulatory requirements that must be met for distributions in this form. Moreover, if a DC plan offers a life annuity as a distribution option, these requirements must also be met when a life annuity is chosen. A few of the requirements even extend to IRAs. Interpreted strictly, some of the requirements would likely prevent, or at least impair, the offering of an LCA in a qualified retirement plan or as an individual retirement annuity, and therefore legislative and/or regulatory adjustments may be needed to facilitate LCAs within such plans.

Minimum Distribution Requirements

Minimum distribution requirements have been established under section 401(a)(9) of the Internal Revenue Code (IRC) to ensure that retirement plans and IRAs serve their intended purpose to support income security in retirement, and not as tax avoidance schemes to accumulate assets on a favorable tax basis for wealth transfer to another generation. In general, taxable distributions from the plan or IRA must start at retirement or age 70 1/2, whichever is later, and be no less than a specified percentage of the account balance. If the distributions are in the form of a life annuity, then, according to the regulations, all annuity payments must be nonincreasing or increase only in accordance with one of six specifically allowed exceptions. For example, payments may increase in accordance with annual increases in the CPI, or they may increase to pay higher benefits resulting from a plan amendment. These regulations do not contemplate distributions through an LCA, and hence that form or product would likely be disallowed under a strict reading of the regulation. That being said, the LCA does not appear to fall under the concerns that originally prompted the rules—the entire corpus of the account balance or accrued benefit is paid out over the lifetimes of the participant and spouse under the LCA, with nothing held back beyond any guaranteed periods chosen otherwise allowable under the regulation. Hence, it is possible that the LCA could be included as an allowable distribution form through an administrative process mentioned explicitly in the minimum distribution regulation. Under that process, the IRS commissioner could provide more guidance on additional benefits that may be disregarded for individual accounts, or for other methods of increasing distributions from a pension plan. In the alternative, the regulation itself could be amended to make the necessary allowances.[7]

Sex-Neutral Pricing of Life Annuities

As a result of Supreme Court decisions prohibiting the use of sex-specific mortality tables for group retirement benefits, pension plans and insurance companies issuing annuities to participants through employer-sponsored retirement plans must price life annuities using unisex mortality tables and determine benefits accordingly. This is in contrast to the general practice of insurance companies in the individual commercial market where life annuities (both on an after-tax basis and in IRAs) are priced on a sex-distinct basis. It should be noted, however, that current commercial practice in the individual market for LTCI is to make no distinction by sex in pricing, despite ample evidence that women, as a class, have a significantly higher incidence of longer LTCI claims (Murtaugh, Spillman, and Warshawsky, 2001; Brown and Finkelstein, 2004a). When offered as an employee benefit, LTCI clearly has to be priced on a unisex basis, by force of law, as would the LCA.

This legal requirement for unisex pricing could vitiate some of the reduction in adverse selection that is one of the goals of the LCA, as a unisex-priced product is more attractive to women than to men. That being said, the effect may be small, as most workers approaching retirement are married, and another legal requirement, explained immediately below, encourages the selection of joint-and-survivor annuities. Of course, the individual nonemployer market is not subject to the unisex rulings of the Supreme Court, and therefore is affected only indirectly, if at all, by those rulings.

Joint-and-Survivor Requirement

All tax-qualified pension plans provide that retirement benefits payable as a life annuity to an employee married to his or her current spouse for at least one year will be automatically paid in the form of a qualified joint-and-survivor annuity, unless the participant elects otherwise with the consent of the spouse. There are multiple provisions in law and regulation to ensure that surviving spouses receive more than a token stream of income from the annuity. DC plans must also follow these rules if they offer an annuity as a distribution option and the participant elects it. The rules do not apply, however, to IRAs and individual retirement annuities.

Again, these rules do not envision an LCA as a distribution option, and hence it is unclear if and how these requirements would be applied to the LCA. It is possible, but uncertain, that a regulatory interpretation would arise having the joint-and-survivor requirements applied just to the life annuity segment of the integrated form, thereby leaving the plan participant in control of the choice whether the LTCI segment, as an ancillary benefit, was to just the participant or also for the spouse.[8] Alternatively, rules could be written to reflect a public policy desire so that a joint-and-survivor requirement similar to current law should apply to the LTCI segment as well.

Incidental Benefits
In recognition of their tax-advantaged status and to focus their design and activities on certain desired public policy goals, Treasury and the IRS, even before the passage of ERISA in 1974, limited employer-sponsored retirement plans to certain types of benefits. In general, medical benefits may only be provided if they are subordinate to the plan's retirement benefits and are paid from a separate account established for such benefits. Without language in existing laws and regulations specifically referring to LCAs, it is not immediately clear how the IRS would view the LCA as part of a qualified retirement plan. It is possible that it would regard the LTCI segment of the LCA as akin to disability benefits and therefore allowed as a customary pension benefit. Yet such benefits are usually considered for workers who retire because of a disability, not people who encounter a disability subsequent to retiring. Alternatively, the IRS might take the view that the LTCI segment is a type of retiree health insurance, and hence, as long as it is "incidental" to the retirement benefits, it would be permitted. In a pension plan, the LTCI segment would be allowed under the specific requirements of section 401(h) (e.g., a separate account, specified benefits), or in a profit-sharing plan (most section 401(k) plans are profit-sharing plans), it would apparently be more generically allowed. Also asset transfers under section 420 from an overfunded pension plan might be allowed to pay for the premiums for the LTCI segment of the LCA. A requirement for section 401(h) treatment of the LTCI segment of an annuity distribution form in a pension plan, however, would be inconsistent with an optional distribution mechanism—the most likely design to be embraced by plan sponsors.

The IRS could alternatively take the position that the LCA as part of a retirement plan was not envisioned by these regulations and hence it would need a more formal and well-defined clearance by a change in the incidental benefit regulation or legislation.

"Current Law" Taxation of the LCA in a Qualified Retirement Plan

On the bold assumption that the various regulatory challenges mentioned above (some of which are themselves related closely to tax treatment) facing the inclusion of the LCA in a qualified retirement plan or IRA were surmounted, what would be the likely current law tax treatment of the LCA premium and the life-annuity payments and LTCI benefits in that venue? To the extent that employer and employee contributions to the retirement plan or IRA were made on a pretax basis, then obviously all the payments from the life-annuity segment would be included in taxable income. What about the benefits from the LTCI segment? It is possible that the benefits could be treated exactly as an incidental disability benefit ("contingent annuity") from the plan and therefore included in taxable income, but not triggering a taxable distribution from the plan for the payment of a premium charge. Or benefits could be treated as a separate stand-alone qualified LTCI policy, where benefits are not included in taxable income, without triggering a distribution from the plan.

The allowance of "health insurance" tax treatment outside of section 401(h) would require a bold interpretation by the IRS that, in the absence of a clear statement of law, the LTCI segment of the LCA in a retirement plan should receive "all-in" tax treatment more favorable than that of a stand-alone qualified LTCI policy. It may be unlikely that the IRS, on its own, would allow a situation where the LTCI segment premiums would be essentially deductible (a full "above-the-line" deduction) and benefits not included in taxable income. This would require the IRS to grant tax treatment superior to a qualified LTCI policy, under which premiums are rarely deductible, and then only subject to specified limits. The IRS would also note the provision in the PPA, mentioned below, that the favorable tax treatment of the LCA issued in an after-tax individual annuity is not available in employer plans and IRAs. On the other hand, employer payments for LTCI premiums in a group insurance plans or through HSAs and health reimbursement arrangements are not included in employee income and the IRS could find some comfort for favorable treatment there.

A different outcome would be one where the premiums for the LTCI segment would be considered to represent taxable distributions from the plan. In this case, the LTCI premiums might or might not be deductible from income (depending on the individual's income and tax situation and whether the LTCI policy was considered qualified) and benefits, as insurance would not be included in income.

The treatment of benefits is also unclear if the LTCI segment does not represent a qualified LTCI policy. The tax code is silent as to the treatment of benefits received from nonqualified LTCI contracts. It is possible that, as payments to retirees, they could be treated simply as taxable distributions from the plan. In this case, however, the amount of unreimbursed medical care expenses would be higher, and the probability of deducting that larger amount would be fairly high for most people. For certain taxpayers, however, the loss of the standard deduction, a need to itemize deductions on their tax return, and the lack of a deduction equal to 7.5 percent of AGI are significant considerations. In addition, for some taxpayers, an increase in their gross income will increase the amount of Social Security benefits that are included in taxable income, and this distinction would become important, as we show below. In addition, if payments from the LTCI segment take the form of per diem or other periodic payments that are higher than the costs of qualified long-term services, then the question of the contract being qualified or not may be important; the excess payment amounts might be taxed if the policy were nonqualified, tax exempt if qualified and not too large.

As is illustrated below, this tax treatment would be inferior to the treatment provided under the PPA of 2006 to the LTCI segment of an after-tax, nonqualified, LCA issued after 2009. It is also inferior to an IRS position under which the LCA would be considered not as an insurance policy but as a contingent annuity. Finally, it would be inferior to the proposed policy that provided an "above-the-line" deduction of LTCI premiums from gross income. The PPA provides an income tax exclusion for pension distributions that are used to pay for qualified health insurance premiums up to a maximum of $3,000 annually. This exclusion is available only to retired or disabled public safety officers but may be used for health insurance or LTCI. This is equivalent to an above-the-line deductibility of LTCI premiums, and, it is, by far, the most generous tax treatment currently available. It remains to be seen whether this limited PPA treatment will serve as a model in future legislation for the tax treatment of LTCI, whether as part of a LCA, or, otherwise, for a more widely defined set of retirees.

Tax Treatment of Life Annuities and LTCI When Combined in an After-Tax Product

Next, we turn to a discussion of tax treatment of different LTCI and annuity products when they are combined in an after-tax vehicle.

Life Care Annuity (Treatment before 2010)

Under current U.S. law, combining an LTCI product with an annuity automatically causes the LTCI product to be nonqualified. It is clear that this denies an itemized medical-care deduction for any recognized LTCI premiums. However, a reasonable argument may be made for treating an LCA as a single (contingent) annuity contract. In this case, the cash premiums paid into the contract (whether funding the annuity portion or the LTCI portion) would constitute the annuity's investment in the contract, and thus would be excludable over the expected remaining life of the policyholder. In addition, under this single contract concept, there might not be any tax consequence associated with charges against annuity cash values for LTCI coverage. There is a question, however, as to whether the expected LTCI benefits should be taken into account in determining the contract's expected return. If added to the expected return, they would lower the annual exclusion amount, and recovery of investment in the contract could occur over a period of years in excess of the owner's expected remaining life. In the illustrations presented below, we have not included the contingent payments in the LCA's expected return.

A life-insurance contract combined with LTCI is treated as two separate policies under current law. This will also be true for a combined annuity- LTC contract after 2009 under the PPA. An inference might be made, therefore, that such treatment should apply to such combined policies under current law. In this case, it is possible that premiums, investment in the contract, and cash value of an LCA might have to be allocated between the annuity and long-term care portions.[9] Also, LTCI charges against the annuity's cash value would likely be viewed as taxable distributions from the contract.

It is unclear as to how benefits of a nonqualified LTCI contract are treated. While the tax code specifies that benefits from a qualified LTCI contract are to be treated "as amounts received for personal injuries and sickness and shall be treated as reimbursement for expenses actually incurred for medical care," the code is silent regarding the treatment of benefits from nonqualified long-term care contracts. Even less clear is the treatment of per diem payments from nonqualified LTCI. In the analysis below, we treat indemnity benefits generally as being bona fide insurance reimbursements for medical care, but are conspicuously silent regarding the legal status of per diem payments. Alternatively, we could have assumed that payments from nonqualified LTCI are treated simply as additions to gross income, potentially allowing greater itemized deductions for the costs of long-term care services. This view is adopted when analyzing the "contingent annuity" below.

Life Care Annuity (Treatment after 2009)

The PPA altered the treatment of LTCI when combined with an annuity. In particular, it explicitly allows LTCI (whether qualified or not) to be offered by rider or as part of either a life-insurance contract or an annuity contract. In this case, the portion of the contract providing long-term care coverage is treated as a separate contract, but the law is silent as to whether this separate treatment requires an allocation of contract premiums or cash values.[10] The relevant provisions of the act generally apply to contracts issued after 1996, but only with respect to taxable years beginning after 2009. Thus, although state regulators have the ultimate authority in approving insurance products, the PPA acknowledges that such a combined product can exist after 2009 without the LTCI portion losing its tax-qualified status. This treatment, however, has not been extended to employer plans and other tax-exempt trusts, to IRAs or annuities, or to contracts purchased by an employer for the benefit of the employee or his or her spouse. The PPA provides that any charges against the cash value of an annuity contract or life-insurance contract for coverage under a qualified LTCI contract will not be includable in taxable income. Such premium charges will not be treated as medical expenses for purposes of the itemized medical-care deduction, and the investment in the contract of the annuity or life-insurance policy will be reduced by the amount of the charge. The premium charge continues to be tax-exempt even if the investment in the contract is zero. Only under this circumstance will the provision provide an exclusion for the full amount of qualified long-term care premiums.

While clarifying the treatment of LTCI premiums that take the form of explicit charges against the cash value of the annuity or life-insurance contract, the PPA's language is less illuminating regarding the treatment of a policy that is not a rider with explicit charges, or of cases where the full cost of LTCI is not embedded in the specified rider charges. For LCAs, the more premium that one can allocate to the annuity's investment in the contract, the greater the tax savings will be.

Possible Structures of the Life Care Annuity and Illustrations of Tax Treatment

There are several different ways in which the LCA could be structured, and the particular format may influence its tax treatment.

LCA Structures

One can imagine at least three different ways of integrating the LTCI policy with an annuity. One way is to set up the LCA as a life annuity with a single-premium LTCI policy rider. As such, an annuity is purchased, from which an immediate charge against it is made for the purchase of an LTCI policy. Subsequently, no more charges are made against the annuity for LTCI premiums. Another way of structuring the LCA is as a life annuity with an LTCI policy rider with an annual premium. As with the single-premium LTCI rider, charges are made against the annuity cash value to finance LTCI premiums, but the charges are made over the life of the policyholder. That the premium is not paid fully up front would presumably allow greater flexibility for either the policyholder or the insurer should future circumstances change. A final way of structuring the policy is as a contingent annuity, in which payments rise in the event of disability, but there is no explicit purchase of an LTCI rider. Such a policy would require an initial premium roughly comparable to that of a life annuity with a single-premium LTCI rider.

Illustrations

How the LCA is structured could play a large role in determining how it would be taxed. Furthermore, individual characteristics, particularly Social Security benefits, other sources of income, and health-care expenditures, also play a key role in determining how taxable income varies. A couple of simple illustrations bear this out.

In this exercise, two individuals are considering the purchase of the LCA whose LTC portion is organized in one of the three ways described in the prior section. The first way is as a level-premium LTCI rider, the second way is as a single-premium LTCI rider, the third way is as a contingent annuity that is treated as an annuity contract by the IRS. The issue of premium savings arising from purchasing an LTCI policy in conjunction with a life annuity is ignored here, as all policies can be assumed to be part of an LCA. Thus, we assume that the LCA pays nothing beyond what is required to finance LTCI premiums or benefits.

All three LTCI arrangements are assumed to be purchased by a single individual at age 65. They pay out $140 per day, with 5 percent annual inflation compounding, in the event long-term care services are needed; these payouts are assumed to cover exactly the cost of qualified long-term care services. The expected present discounted value of the policy, in all cases, is $45,583. Thus, the single-premium LTCI policy and the LTCI portion of the contingent annuity will cost $45,583 up front, and the level-premium policy will cost $4,008 annually. In order to fund this level premium, the up-front cost of the LCA must be increased by $45,583, given the assumed mortality and morbidity assumptions.

Projected utilization is assumed to be a function of mortality. Each claim is expected to last for 760 days, spanning three years' time. Those who encounter disability are assumed to die at the end of the third year. Additionally, each individual is assumed to have $1,200 in unreimbursed medical expenses each year, not associated with qualified long-term care services. Each individual is assumed to purchase a life annuity at the same time that costs $136,300, which pays $12,000 annually. Other income is assumed constant over time, except for Social Security benefits, which are assumed to grow at 2 percent per year. Long-term care deductibility limits, which are $2,950 annually for 61- to 70-year-olds and $3,680 for 71-year-olds and older, are expected to increase at 4 percent per year. The discount rate is assumed to be 6 percent.

The first individual, characterized as having moderate income, is assumed to start with $12,000 in Social Security benefits and $7,000 in other taxable income. The second individual, characterized as being of high income, receives $75,000 annually in additional taxable income. For the high-income individual, the issue of taxable Social Security benefits is ignored, because this individual would be subject to the maximum tax rate for Social Security benefits in every year. As mentioned above, each individual also receives $12,000 (nonindexed) in individual annuity income. This exercise estimates taxable income for the two individuals under the three different structures of LCA in three different regimes: before the implementation of the PPA, after implementation of PPA, and if, instead, LTCI premiums were subject to an above-the-line deduction. Over the past several sessions of Congress, above-the-line deductions for LTCI premiums have been proposed. This would allow all individuals to deduct LTCI premiums up to the annual cap regardless of whether they itemized their deductions or of whether their medical expenses exceeded 7.5 percent of AGI.

The tax impact is calculated relative to that where an immediate life annuity policy and a qualified single-premium LTCI policy are purchased as separate contracts, under the (unrealistic) assumption that the aggregate pretax cost of the two separate policies equals the pretax cost of the LCA. Under this baseline, the moderate-income individual is able to deduct some medical expenses in the first year, because the sum of other medical expenses and tax-deductible LTCI premiums in the first year exceeds 7.5 percent of AGI. The high-income individual cannot deduct any LTCI premiums. Table 9.2 shows the tax impact of the different scenarios relative to the baseline, with the tax impact measured as the differences in the actuarial present value of each individual's tax liabilities for the expected remaining lifetime.[11]

Under current law (pre-PPA), purchasing the LCA with a level-premium LTCI rider will increase taxable income relative to purchasing separate single-premium contracts. The annuity generates a return that is taxable, subject to the exclusion over time of the initial LCA

Table 9.2
Net effect on taxable income of purchasing lifetime care annuity under different arrangements ($)

	Level-premium LTCI policy	Single-premium LTCI policy	Contingent annuity
Moderate income			
Before 2010	22,568	31,139	(17,657)
After 2009	(3,267)	(3,806)	(3,806)
With ATL deduction	(23,590)	28,189	(17,657)
High income			
Before 2010	15,878	15,878	(23,787)
After 2009	(8,571)	(8,286)	(8,286)
With ATL deduction	(25,137)	12,928	(23,787)

Note: "LTCI policy" refers to a long-term care insurance policy. "ATL deduction" refers to an above-the-line deduction.
Source: Authors' calculations.

premium, and the LTCI premiums are treated as a taxable distribution from the annuity, and thus includable as income.[12] For the moderate-income individual, the additional income paid out by the annuity increases the taxable Social Security benefits. The result is, in expectation, an increase in taxable income of $22,568 for the moderate-income individual and an increase of $15,878 for the high-income individual.

The PPA will allow the exclusion of the distributions from the annuity cash value used to pay for the level-premium LTCI, a considerable tax benefit relative to current law. The corresponding reduction in the investment in the contract accelerates the exhaustion of that investment in the contract. For the moderate-income individual, this translates to a slight increase in the expected taxable Social Security benefits and a slight reduction in other deductible medical expenses. Overall, the net impact is a reduction in taxable income of $3,267 for the moderate-income individual and a net reduction in taxable income of $8,571 for the high-income individual.

To model the effects of an above-the-line deduction for LTCI premiums, we imagine how above-the-line deductibility to LCAs before the implementation of PPA might have been granted. We posit that charges against annuities for the purposes of paying LTCI premiums would be fully taxable, but the premiums would be deductible above-the-line up to the annual cap on deductible LTCI premiums. The original investment in the annuity contract would be excluded over the expected remaining lifetime of the annuitant, but charges for LTCI premiums would not accelerate the exhaustion of that investment as under PPA. Consequently, an above-the-line deduction of LTCI premiums would further increase tax benefits conferred upon the level-premium LTCI policy. Deductibility of premiums above the line would reduce taxable income, increasing the amount of other deductible medical expenses for the moderate-income individual. And deductibility of premiums would not require an offsetting reduction in annuity basis, which would be excluded over the expected remaining lifetime of the individual. The net reduction in taxable income is substantial: for the moderate-income individual, it is $23,590, and for the high-income individual, it is $25,137.

Single-premium policies, both before and after implementation of the PPA, receive similar tax treatment as level-premium policies. Before 2010, charges against the annuity for the single LTCI premium are included in taxable income. Because the charge is so large, for the moderate-income individual, Social Security benefits are taxable in the first year. For the high-income individual, the net effect on taxable income is identical for the single-premium LTCI policy and the level-premium LTCI policy. As with the level-premium policy, after 2009, the charge against the annuity for the LTCI policy is not taxable. There are some minor differences between LCAs with level-premium LTCI riders and those with single-premium LTCI riders as regards the timing of the exhaustion of investment in the contract, which has minor ripple effects on deductibility of other medical expenses and taxable Social Security benefits. But the overall effect is to improve the tax treatment for the LCAs with single-premium LTCI riders relative to the baseline by roughly the same magnitude as LCAs with level-premium LTCI riders. However, extending an above-the-line deduction for LTCI premiums that supersede the relevant measures in the PPA causes the LCA to be treated much as it would under current law, with the exception of a one-year deduction of the capped limit on LTCI premium, currently $2,950 for a 65-year-old.

The contingent annuity, assuming it is viewed strictly as an annuity by the IRS, before 2010, would receive considerably more favorable tax treatment than the other two arrangements. Unlike with policies that require taxable charges to finance LTCI premiums, the entire premium is excludable as investment basis over the course of the remaining life of the annuitant. This exclusion lowers taxable Social Security benefits for the moderate-income individual in years without disability. If payouts are made, additional Social Security benefits become taxable for that individual. And the payouts raise taxable income considerably, but most of them are deductible because qualified medical expenses easily exceed 7.5 percent of AGI in those years. Projected taxable income falls by $17,657 for the moderate-income individual and $23,787 for the high-income individual. The PPA, however, uses broad language in defining insurance coverage as part of an annuity contract, raising the question of whether the IRS would allow a contingent annuity to be defined as strictly an annuity contract without an LTCI component. If the IRS requires this to be treated as two separate contracts, then the taxation of the product would likely be the same as for a life annuity with a single-premium LTCI rider, as shown in table 9.2. Because we model the effects of allowing an above-the-line deduction for LTC insurance before implementation of PPA, we show that the tax treatment of the contingent annuity under above-the-line deductibility of insurance premiums would revert back to the pre-2010 treatment, before the product was assumed to have an LTCI component.

It would seem that the contingent annuity would offer more favorable tax treatment for anyone before the implementation of the PPA. Yet in the absence of clear guidance from the IRS, insurers may be fearful that such a product would not be granted the tax advantages detailed here. After the implementation of PPA, however, LCAs with traditional LTCI policy riders are clearly granted considerably more tax advantages than are currently available. Above-the-line deductibility would increase the tax advantages further for LCAs with level-premium LTCI policy riders.

Conclusions

Combining LTCI with an immediate life annuity into a single policy, the LCA, will result in a lower total price for the combined product less adverse selection in the individual annuity market, and greater availability of long-term care to more retired households, when compared to offering the two products separately. This chapter discusses two principal venues in which this product might be marketed: a qualified retirement plan and an after-tax individual annuity. We explain both the tax and the regulatory treatment afforded to the product, highlighting the uncertainties that arise largely because of the different tax and regulatory treatments of standalone annuities and LTCI policies.

Looking ahead, we argue that the PPA will make the LCA a tax-preferred way of obtaining LTCI coverage, but that an above-the-line deduction of qualified LTCI premiums would provide an even greater tax preference. Such a preference was recently bestowed on distributions from qualified retirement plans of public safety officers used to purchase qualified LTCI.

Notes

1. Moreover, sensitivity analysis demonstrated that the likely "woodwork" effect on disability claims, as well as inflation indexing of the LTCI segment, increase value to those currently rejected by LTCI underwriting, and therefore further support the second maintained hypothesis that the integrated product will be cheaper and more desired in a self-sustaining pooling equilibrium.

2. The recently enacted PPA of 2006 expanded the tax-free exchange provisions contained in the IRC. After 2009, a policyholder will be able to exchange tax free both a deferred annuity and a deferred annuity–LTCI integrated product for an immediate annuity-LTCI integrated product (or a stand-alone LTCI contract). However, the policyholder will not be able to exchange tax free a stand-alone LTCI contract for an LCA.

3. The annuity start date is generally the first day of the first period for which one receives an annuity payment under the contract (which may be earlier than the date of the first payment).

4. In general, for contracts under which all contributions were made prior to June 30, 1986, the annuitant must use sex-based tables published by the IRS. However, for annuity payments received after that date, the annuitant can make a one-time election to use the unisex tables.

5. This is similar to the simplified method used for taxing payments from qualified annuities, although different tables are used to determine the number of expected payments.

6. Qualified long-term care services are necessary services (including personal care services) that are required by a chronically ill individual and are provided pursuant to a plan of care prescribed by a licensed health-care practitioner. A chronically ill individual is one who is generally unable to perform at least two out of six listed ADL for a period of at least 90 days due to a loss of functional capacity, or one that requires substantial supervision due to severe cognitive impairment. To qualify as an itemized medical-care deduction, a qualified long-term care service cannot be performed by a spouse or other relative (unless such person is a licensed professional with respect to the service).

7. The PPA of 2006 allows the combination of an annuity with an LTCI contract after 2009. It further states that the LTCI component will be treated as a separate contract, which seemingly would allow the minimum distribution rules to apply only to the life-annuity segment of a qualified plan LCA. However, the act also states that a qualified employer plan or individual retirement account is not to be treated as an annuity contract for the purpose of the above separate contract rule, so that the impact of the act on the issue at hand is somewhat unclear.

8. This treatment would be similar to how the required minimum distribution rules treat a plan that also offers a disability pension—the disability benefit is considered separate from the retirement benefit. But the analogy may be stretched too far, as the IRS has taken the position that disability benefits cease once the participant attains the normal retirement age stated in the plan.

9. Such allocations are not explicitly required under current law or the PPA. However, under an allocation regime, there would be an incentive to overstate the annuity's share of premiums, so as to maximize the amount of premiums that could be recovered through the annuity exclusion ratio.

10. As under current law with respect to life insurance combined products, "portion" is defined as "only the terms and benefits that are in addition to the terms and benefits under a life-insurance contract or annuity contract without regard to longterm care insurance coverage."

11. In these illustrations, the "Before 2010" entries are computed on the basis that the PPA was not enacted. That is, under the PPA, the tax treatment of a contract issued after 1996 will change in 2010; we assume that it will not.

12. We consider payouts for LTC services under the single-premium and level premium riders as reimbursement for qualified LTC services, and thus excludable from taxable income. If the IRS considered the LTCI riders in either the single premium or level-premium examples as components of an annuity, however, payouts from the LTC component would not be considered as reimbursements from an insurance policy, and the

amount would be fully taxable. Nonetheless, LTC expenses would be deductible to the extent qualified medical expenses exceeded 7.5 percent of AGI, so the net tax impact would only be slightly higher than the amounts shown in the table.

References

Brown, Jeffrey R., and Amy N. Finkelstein. 2004a. The Interaction of Public and Private Insurance: Medicaid and the Long-Term Care Insurance Market. NBER working paper no. 10989. Cambridge, MA: National Bureau of Economic Research.

Brown, Jeffrey R., and Amy R. Finkelstein. 2004b. Supply or Demand: Why Is the Market for Long-Term Care Insurance So Small? NBER working paper no. 10782. Cambridge, MA: National Bureau of Economic Research.

Brown, Jeffrey R., Olivia S. Mitchell, James Poterba, and Mark Warshawsky. 1999. Taxing Retirement Income: Nonqualified Annuities and Distributions from Qualified Accounts. *National Tax Journal* 52 (3): 563–591.

Brown, Jeffrey R., and James M. Poterba. 2000. Joint Life Annuities and Annuity Demand by Married Couples. *Journal of Risk and Insurance* 67 (4): 527–553.

Friedman, Benjamin, and Mark Warshawsky. 1990. The Cost of Annuities: Implications for Saving Behavior and Bequests. *Quarterly Journal of Economics* 105 (1): 135–154.

Investment Company Institute. 2007. Appendix: Additional Data on the U.S. Retirement Market, 2006. *Research Fundamentals* 16 (3A): 1–16.

Mitchell, Olivia S., James Poterba, Mark Warshawsky, and Jeffrey R. Brown. 1999. New Evidence on the Money's Worth of Individual Annuities. *American Economic Review* 89 (5): 1299–1318.

Murtaugh, Christopher, Peter Kemper, and Brenda Spillman. 1995. Risky Business: Long-term Care Insurance Underwriting. *Inquiry* 32 (3): 271–284.

Murtaugh, Christopher, Brenda Spillman, and Mark Warshawsky. 2001. In Sickness and in Health: An Annuity Approach to Financing Long-term Care and Retirement Income. *Journal of Risk and Insurance* 68 (2): 225–254.

Public Fund Survey. 2007. *Public Fund Survey*. National Association of State Retirement Administrators and the National Council on Teacher Retirement. www.publicfundsurvey.org/publicfundsurvey/index.htm.

Rothschild, Michael, and Joseph Stiglitz. 1976. Equilibrium in Competitive Insurance Markets: An Essay on the Economics of Imperfect Information. *Quarterly Journal of Economics* 90 (4): 630–649.

Thrift Savings Plan. 2006. The Official Thrift Savings Plan Homepage. Federal Retirement Thrift Investment Board. www.tsp.gov.

10 Recent and Proposed Legal and Regulatory Developments Affecting Retirement Plan Distributions, Especially Annuities

with Jeffrey R. Brown

Introduction

This chapter is composed of two main sets of sections. In the first set, recent legislative and regulatory requirement changes affecting plan distribution are reviewed. In particular, the section explains changing rules for lump-sum calculations for distributions from pension plans, joint-and-survivor annuities, fiduciary obligations on sponsors of plans with annuities, and minimum distribution requirements affecting life annuities. In the second set, various public policy ideas in this area are discussed, and their pros and cons are evaluated.

Lump-Sum Calculations

Employer-sponsored defined benefit plans that offer retiring workers a lump sum or an annuity option should offer a different pattern of loading than the commercial individual annuity markets do. Employers sponsoring a pension plan do not have the marketing and sales costs that commercial insurers incur in attracting individual annuity purchasers. One might also expect the mortality rates used to calculate a pension annuity to be different from those used in calculating individual annuities, presuming more adverse selection in the latter than

From pp. 289–293 in Dan McGill, Kyle Brown, John Haley, Syl Schieber, and Mark Warshawsky, *Fundamentals of Private Pensions*, Ninth Edition (Oxford University Press for the Pension Research Council of the Wharton School, 2010) plus a new section on other recent requirements and proposals, including joint-and-survivor, fiduciary obligations, minimum distribution, and trail income, and from "Longevity-Insured Retirement Distributions from Pension Plans: Market and Regulatory Issues," pp. 361–366, in William Gale, John Shoven, and Mark Warshawsky, eds., *Private Pensions and Public Policies* (Washington, D.C.: Brookings Institution Press, 2004). By permission of Oxford University Press. Reprinted with Permission of Brookings Institution Press.

in the former. Moreover, adverse selection might not exist at all in employer-sponsored pensions that provide annuities to all retirees (mandatory annuitization). Nonetheless, the life expectancy patterns of people covered by pensions might be different from those for the general population because of the broadly higher socioeconomic status of those covered by pensions. Moreover, the plan's actual experience notwithstanding, the lump-sum value of pension benefits, when made available from the plan, is generally determined by law using standard group mortality rates and interest rates.

The General Agreement on Tariff and Trade Act of 1994 amended the Internal Revenue Code to require the use of a specific mortality table and interest rate for determining minimum lump-sum cash-outs. Under the law, the mortality assumption must be based on the table used to determine insurance company reserves for group annuity contracts. The initial regulations in IRS Revenue Ruling 95–6 specified the 1983 Group Annuity Mortality table, often referred to as the GAM83 table. Because that table is gender based and pension plans must determine all benefits on a unisex basis, Revenue Ruling 95–6 provides for using a unisex table based on a fixed blend of male and female mortality rates from the GAM83 table.[1] The interest rate specified in the law for lump-sum calculations was the current yield on thirty-year Treasury bonds.

One interesting facet of the lump sum versus annuity equivalence is that when someone purchases an individual annuity, a lower interest rate means a smaller regular annuity payment. But when someone cashes out a pension annuity, a lower interest rate means a higher lump sum. Consequently, the decline in interest rates during the early 2000s might have changed some perceptions about the relative values of the benefit options. Of course, at the same time interest rates were falling, other aspects of the financial markets were also in turmoil, which could have had an offsetting effect on people choosing between receiving a lifetime annuity from their pension or going it alone with the cash value of their pension.

The Pension Protection Act of 2006 (PPA) mandated the eventual use of corporate bond yields rather than thirty-year Treasury yields to calculate minimum lump sums payable from defined benefit plans that define benefits in terms of annuities. Proponents of this change argued that with thirty-year Treasury bonds yields at historical lows compared with other rates, using the Treasury rates made the lump-sum equivalents unreasonably more valuable than the annuity benefits, especially given that the Treasury did not sell thirty-year bonds from 2001 through 2005. Congress, along with most pension experts, believed that encouraging workers to take their retirement benefits in a lump sum, rather than in an annuity payable over their lifetime, served neither the participants' nor the public's long-term retirement interests. Congress also adopted a mortality table that reflects today's longer life expectancies, thereby moderating slightly the depressing effect of using higher-yielding corporate bonds to determine lump-sum benefits.

The transition to the new lump-sum basis, during which corporate bond rates are blended with Treasury bond rates, began in 2008 and will be complete in 2012. The mortality change is fully effective in 2008. Participants' lump-sum benefits under the new basis are expected to decline gradually over the next five years [through 2012] compared with what the payouts would have been under the old basis.

The New Lump-Sum Basis

On October 9, 2007, the IRS issued guidance on the new corporate bond yield curve and segment rates used to determine minimum lump-sum values for participants with annuity starting dates on or after the beginning of the 2008 plan year. IRS Notice 2007–81 describes the methodology used to develop the corporate bond yield curve and provides the full yield curve and segment rates. The IRS publishes updated monthly yields monthly on its Web site and in print.

On November 6, 2007, the IRS released the mortality table to use in determining minimum lump-sum values for 2008 plan years. The applicable mortality table is a unisex table based on the tables prescribed for determining minimum funding contributions for plans with fewer than 500 participants. The IRS updates the table annually to reflect expected mortality improvements. For a participant aged 60 in 2007, the new table is expected to increase his or her lump-sum value by slightly more than 2 percent, all else being equal.

The Segment Rates

Under the PPA, funding requirements and lump-sum calculations are tied to three interest rates derived from a corporate bond yield curve, corresponding to three segments:

Segment 1   Payments expected to be due within five years

Segment 2   Payments expected to be due within five to twenty years

Segment 3   Payments expected to be due after twenty years

Beginning in plan year 2008, the interest rate basis used to determine minimum lump-sum values will be determined by phasing in the new three-segment rates and phasing out the old thirty-year Treasury basis evenly over five years.

Comparisons of Lump Sums Determined under Pre- and Post-PPA Rules

Towers Watson compared estimated lump sums under the new-law minimum assumptions with lump sums developed under pre-PPA law. Table 10.1 shows the relative comparison for hypothetical pension plan participants of various ages in 2007 and as they age over the five-year transition period. All lump sums are based on annuity values of $100 per month payable at age 65, continuation of the September 2007 segment rates, and the new mortality table, including estimated future mortality improvements after 2008.

Implications of New Lump-Sum Basis for Participants

The transition to the new basis gradually eliminates the purported subsidy reflected in the old-law lump-sum rates. In general, the relative decrease in lump sums will be more for younger participants. For employees in frozen plans in 2007, there might be several years in which their lump-sum values do not increase or possibly even decrease; again, this is more likely for younger participants:

• Participants might want to consider electing an annuity form of payment rather than a lump sum, especially after the transition is complete.

• For participants older than 55 who are still accruing benefits and who plan to retire in the next few years, when they retire should not make a big difference provided interest rates remain relatively constant. Additional accruals should more than offset the relatively modest decrease in lump-sum values (relative to the old basis) during the transition period.

• Even in a frozen plan, lump sums are expected to continue to increase from year to year for participants older than 55. For example, under the old basis, a 60-year-old participant in a frozen plan could expect the value of the lump-sum distribution to grow 31.5 percent over the next five years if interest rates remain unchanged. Under the new basis, she could expect the lump sum to grow 20.5 percent. However, if interest rates rise over the next five years, values could decline under both the old and the new basis.

Table 10.1
Comparisons of lump-sum benefits under old and new law basis for various ages of defined benefit plan participants

2007	2008		2009		2010		2011		2012	
Old law	Old law	New law	Old law	New law	Old law	New law	Old law	New law	Old law	New law
Age 60 in 2007 to age 65 in 2012										
$10,955	$11,549	$11,378	$12,187	$11,690	$12,871	$12,090	$13,610	$12,601	$14,408	$13,206
Age 55 in 2007 to age 60 in 2012										
$8,489	$8,924	$8,687	$9,386	$8,755	$9,876	$8,877	$10,398	$9,079	$10,955	$9,341
Age 45 in 2007 to age 50 in 2012										
$5,217	$5,474	$5,154	$5,744	$4,995	$6,027	$4,876	$6,326	$4,816	$6,640	$4,795
Age 35 in 2007 to age 40 in 2012										
$3,239	$3,397	$3,095	$3,562	$2,890	$3,735	$2,709	$3,917	$2,567	$4,108	$2,450

Note: For September 2007, the thirty-year Treasury rate was 4.79 percent, and the three segment rates were 5.28 percent, 6.12 percent, and 6.55 percent.
Source: Watson Wyatt.

• Participants younger than 50 in a frozen plan that bases the value of lump sums on the normal retirement benefit should expect the value of their lump sum to either remain unchanged or possibly decrease for at least five years. Of course, if the plan continues to provide additional benefits, the accruals might increase the lump-sum value. But depending on the relative value of the additional accruals and the participant's age, the lump-sum value might not increase for some period.

Implications for Plan Sponsors

For plans that calculate lump sums as the present value of an annuity, liabilities will be lower under the new rules than they would have been under the old rules. Because the expected reduction is greater for younger participants—whose associated liabilities are generally smaller—the overall relative decrease in liabilities for current employees may be "only" 10 to 15 percent. Such a decline is still significant enough that sponsors of frozen plans that are considering termination and settling their liabilities might find it worthwhile to wait until after the transition period.

The new basis will not affect the value of lump sums in plans that define benefits in terms of a lump sum, such as cash balance plans. These plans, however, will likely be required to convert defined lump-sum values into equivalent annuity amounts under the new minimum basis. This will make larger annuity payment amounts available to participants and, to the extent that more participants choose annuities, hybrid plan costs might be higher than they would have been under the old basis.

Joint-and-Survivor Requirements

Since the mid-1980s, pension law requires defined benefit pension plans to provide benefits in the form of a qualified joint-and-survivor annuity (QJSA) unless the participant and his or her spouse consent to another form of benefit. Note that the annuity paid to the retiring worker will seem smaller under the QJSA than if a single annuity had been the default annuity distribution, and this may tilt the playing field toward the choice of a lump sum. The QJSA is an annuity for the life of the participant, with a survivor annuity for the life of the spouse not less than, and usually equal to, 50 percent of the amount of the annuity payable during the joint lives of the participant and his or her spouse.

The purpose of this requirement was to reduce the poverty of widows whose husbands had taken a single life annuity benefit from his pension on retirement in order to maximize his income. In PPA, this general requirement was expanded to require the offering of an additional option: the qualified option survivor annuity (QOSA). The applicable percentage for the survivor annuity is 75 percent of the annuity payable during the joint life of the participant and the spouse. This expands the menu of annuity options available to DB plan participants, encouraging income provision for spouses.

Fiduciary Obligation on Choice of Annuity Provider by Plan Sponsor

PPA also responded to a complaint by defined contribution plan sponsors about the undue burden of choosing an annuity provider if that distribution option were in the plan. The Department of Labor had in the past, in response to some insurance company failures, imposed the rule that the plan sponsor had to essentially choose the "safest available" annuity, based on the providers' claims-paying ability and creditworthiness. PPA directed the department to issue a regulation dropping the safest available requirement for defined contribution plans, while otherwise maintaining all other fiduciary standards.

The final regulation implementing this provision was issued in October 2008. It stated that the selection of a provider of a distribution annuity would satisfy a safe harbor and was prudent if the fiduciary (1) engaged in an objective, thorough, and analytical search for a provider; (2) appropriately considered sufficient information to assess the financial ability of the provider to make future payments under the annuity contracts; (3) appropriately considered the cost in relation to benefits and services; (4) concluded at the time of selection that the provider was financially able to make all future payments under the contract and that the cost was reasonable; and (5) consulted with an appropriate expert to comply with the safe harbor conditions. This review must be done periodically if the selection of the annuity provider is done for a class of participants and beneficiaries at future dates. An earlier attempt to set up a checklist of factors that a fiduciary should consider when evaluating an annuity provider was eliminated in the final requirement, as was the requirement for a "qualified independent expert" as opposed to the more generic "appropriate expert, when needed." Reportedly, many plan sponsors are dissatisfied with this regulation and provision and still view the diffuse and uncertain

fiduciary obligations as a burden outweighing any potential participant interest or need for annuities.

Regulation That Allows Defined Contribution Plans to Eliminate Optional Forms of Distribution

In 2000, the IRS issued a regulation allowing sponsors of defined contribution plans to amend their plans to eliminate an optional form of
benefit without violating the code section 411(d)(6) anticutback rules
as long as a lump-sum distribution form is available. These optional
forms of benefits include annuity and installment options. Although
originally, the IRS would have required 90-day advance notice to
participants of the elimination of options, subsequent legislation
removed this requirement; it only now need be mentioned in an
amended summary plan description or other communication 210 days
after the close of the plan year in which the modification is adopted.

This regulatory change apparently arose because many defined contribution plan sponsors felt that the small demand for annuities from
participants did not warrant the administrative cost and liability
burden of keeping the option in the plan.

Rules under Minimum Distribution Requirements Governing Annuity Distribution from Retirement Plans or Accounts

Code section 401(a)(9) has a requirement that plan participants (as well
as IRA holders) get their entire account or interest in a plan distributed,
beginning not later than a certain date, over the life or life expectancy
of the participant and a designated beneficiary. The required beginning
date is the later of the year after the participant turns 70 1/2 or, if in a
qualified plan, retires. The purpose of these rules is to ensure that
retirement plans not be used as tax-avoidance vehicles, particularly
across generations. Annuities from retirement plans and accounts are
also subject to these rules on the theory that it is possible to structure
them to delay payments until late in life or to leave estates to young
nonspouse beneficiaries. The IRS issued final regulations in 2004 on
annuity distributions from defined benefit plans and annuity contracts
purchased with an employee's account balance under a defined
contribution plan.

In general, the regulation requires that distribution of an employee's
entire interest (account or accrued benefit) must be paid in the form of

a periodic annuity for the employee's life or joint lives of employee and beneficiary. The payments must, in general, be nonincreasing or increase only in certain circumstances. The permitted increases include an annual or cumulative adjustment to reflect increases in the cost of living, using an official price index, or in rate instances, compensation for the position held before retirement, or for variable and increasing payments for an annuity contract purchased from an insurance company as long as the total expected future payments (disregarding any payment increases) as of the annuity start date exceed the premium being annuitized. Acceleration of payment is allowed for these annuity contracts. For defined benefit plans paying annuities from the pension trust, variable payments are allowed, solely reflecting better-than-assumed investment performance but only if the assumed interest rate calculating initial payments is at least 3 percent. Fixed-rate increases may be provided but only if the rate of increase is less than 5 percent. Other permitted increases include any increase in benefits as a result of a plan amendment; a pop-up in payments in the event of the death of the beneficiary or the divorce of the employee and spouse; return of employee contributions on an employee's death; or a payment at death to the extent that the payments after annuitization are less than the present value of the employee's accrued benefit as of the annuity starting date calculated using the standard-law interest rate and mortality rates.

The employee's entire interest must be distributed. The regulations declare that this value includes the actuarial value of any additional benefits (such as survivor benefits in excess of the account balance) provided under the annuity contract. These additional benefits may be disregarded, however, in the form of a guaranteed return of premiums on death or when there is a pro-rata reduction in the additional benefits for any withdrawal, provided actuarial present value of the additional benefits is not more than 20 percent of the account balance.

Legislative and Think-Tank Proposals to Encourage Annuitization

In December 2009, Senators Jeff Bingaman, Johnny Isakson, and Herb Kohl introduced the Lifetime Income Disclosure Act. This would require at least one pension benefit statement each year to disclose the annuity equivalent of a participant's or beneficiary's total account balance. In general, the act would require that the statement disclose the monthly payments the participant or beneficiary would receive at the plan's normal retirement age if the individual's total accrued benefits or current account balance were used to purchase an annuity commencing at normal retirement age. The act directs the Department of Labor to develop a model disclosure explaining the hypothetical or illustrative nature of the annuity disclosure, as well as to prescribe to plan administrators the assumptions used in calculating the annuity equivalents. The act would absolve from liability any disclosures following the regulations.

Policy analysts at the Retirement Security Project at the Brookings Institution have proposed a policy that would increase the role of lifetime income products in retirement plans.[2] In particular, they propose that a substantial portion of an individual worker's 401(k) and other similar plan accounts be automatically directed (defaulted) into a two-year trial income product when retiring and taking distributions unless she affirmatively chooses not to participate. Retirees would receive twenty-four consecutive monthly payments from the plan. At the end of the trial period, retirees could elect an alternative distribution option, such as a lump-sum or minimum distribution, or, if they do nothing, be defaulted into a permanent income distribution plan. The permanent distribution plan could be a life annuity with various death benefits or a recalculated withdrawal program, as chosen by the plan sponsor. Note that a recalculated withdrawal program is similar to the minimum distribution requirements, that is, an annual recalculation of account divided by life expectancy.

Most recently, in spring 2010, the Departments of Labor and Treasury asked for responses to thirty-nine questions in a request for information (RFI) about lifetime income options for participants and beneficiaries in retirement plans. In addition to background data and information, the RFI sought input into whether and how to promote the use of lifetime income arrangements in employer retirement plans and IRAs. Nearly eight hundred responses from citizens and interested parties were sent to the Department of Labor.

Evaluation of Options to Encourage Annuitization

In this section, we evaluate a range of policy options related to the annuitization of account balances in defined contribution plans. These options extend from mandating minimum levels of annuitization, to tax incentives, to the establishment of a government-sponsored program or organization where plan participants can purchase

annuities. It is assumed that the laws and regulations currently apply-
ing to annuities from pension plans, such as joint-and-survivor requirements, will be extended to defined contribution plan annuities. We do
not discuss other policy proposals that have been made to improve
the functioning of pension annuities, such as inflation indexing or the
enhancement of joint-and-survivor rules.

The evaluation of policy options will clearly differ depending on
what one believes is the underlying reason for why individuals do not
choose to annuitize more of their wealth. There are many possible
reasons that individuals may not annuitize, and it is highly unlikely
that any one reason is sufficient to explain the lack of annuitization. It
could be that rational actors are making an optimal decision based on
their expectations about future health expenditure needs and preferences toward risk and bequests. If so, then the lack of annuitization
may not be viewed as a major problem for policymakers, and it should
be left to the private market to design products accommodating individuals' needs and preferences. Alternatively, it may be that rational
actors would like to annuitize but simply do not have access to fairly
priced annuities because their defined contribution plan does not offer
them and the private market for individual annuities suffers from
adverse selection. In this case, policymakers may wish to require that
defined contribution plan sponsors offer an annuity option. They might
even consider mandating annuities to overcome the adverse selection
problem; otherwise, many individuals would be at risk of relying on
government assistance if they live longer than expected and exhaust
their resources.

If, however, individuals are not behaving rationally at all, but rather
are failing to purchase welfare-enhancing annuities due to myopia or
a lack of understanding of the benefits of annuitization, then paternal-
istic policymakers might wish to simply mandate annuitization. Unfortunately, existing evidence does not allow us to specify what fraction
of the population falls in each category. Therefore, we will explore a
range of policy alternatives and discuss under what assumptions each
policy does or does not make economic sense.

Mandate a Minimum Level of Annuitization

An obvious and highly controversial way to increase annuitization
levels would be to mandate that every tax-qualified employer-
sponsored retirement plan provide that any benefits payable to a
participant below a certain dollar level be paid entirely in life annuity

form. Such a mandate could apply to all types of plans, including pension, profit-sharing, and stock bonus plans. For example, one might select the dollar level so that the (joint-and-survivor) lifelong annuity income produced at the normal retirement age would be sufficient, when combined with Social Security benefits, to keep retirees above some minimum income level. If the account balance or plan benefit fell below this (age-adjusted) level, the entire account would have to be annuitized; if it were above this level, discretion for the disposition of the remaining account balance would be left to the plan participant.[3]

An annuity mandate would greatly increase annuitization rates in tax-qualified, especially defined contribution, plans. Therefore, the mandate would improve the retirement income security of many plan participants and reduce the adverse selection problem affecting the life annuity market (thereby enhancing annuity payout rates).

However, an annuity mandate has several important negative effects as well. Annuitization may be inappropriate and even harmful for many plan participants, such as those in poor health or those who wish to leave a large estate. In addition, a mandate has the potential to be administratively burdensome. It is also likely to be politically very unpopular in the United States because it severely restricts individual choice.

Some recent policy discussions in the United Kingdom are relevant to these proposals. Current pension law in the United Kingdom requires that those with personal or occupational pension plan assets must buy a life annuity by the age of 75.[4] The main aim of the law is to cure the moral hazard problem, that is, the possibility that pensioners will spend their assets quickly and fall back on state welfare provisions. Recent declines in annuity rates owing to falling interest rates, as well as chafing at the (perceived and real) inflexibility and illiquidity inherent in life annuities, have led to demands that these requirements be softened. The semiofficial Retirement Income Working Party recently issued a report recommending that the obligation for total annuitization should be changed to a requirement that when an individual retires, he or she purchase an inflation-indexed annuity to meet a minimum retirement income.[5] The minimum income would be set at a level related to eligibility for state welfare support. Formulas would be established to determine that individuals had pension entitlements, from both state and private sources, sufficient to deliver the minimum retirement income on an inflation-adjusted basis going forward.[6]

Make Annuitization the Default Option for Defined Contribution Plan Distributions

A less drastic proposal is to mandate that employers make annuitization the default distribution option in defined contribution plans. Plan distributions other than in annuity form would require the active and affirmative choice of the plan participant. This is the recommendation of the Department of Labor Advisory Council Working Group: "Require that all defined contribution plans offer annuities as the primary form of benefit for all distributions in excess of $5,000 and comply with the joint and survivor rules, unless the participant elects otherwise in conformance with the joint and survivor rules, including spousal consent."[7] To reduce the administrative burden on plan sponsors and providers, defined contribution plans that are not primary plans might also be exempted from the default option mandate.

This proposal has several advantages and disadvantages compared with the proposals for mandatory annuitization and current practice. Clearly, the element of compulsion is missing, and therefore freedom of choice and flexibility are preserved. Yet annuitization is encouraged, and this presumably would lead to some improvement in the functioning of annuity markets. Still, an additional administrative burden would be imposed on hundreds of thousands of plans that heretofore have avoided offering the annuity payment form.

There is empirical evidence that creating a default option has a powerful effect on plan participant behavior. Madrian and Shea examined the impact of a shift in one large 401(k) plan from affirmative election of participation to automatic enrollment with the right to decline.[8] No other economic feature of the plan changed, and therefore it might be thought that behavior would not change. They found, however, that participation is significantly higher under automatic enrollment: the overall participation rate increased by 25 percentage points, and the variation in participation rates with respect to demographic characteristics was reduced considerably. Similarly, the default contribution rate and fund allocation chosen by the plan sponsor had a significant influence on the behavior of plan participants. Madrian and Shea make reference to psychological factors such as procrastination, framing, and anchoring in explaining these results. This evidence implies that mandating an annuitization default option would probably substantially increase the selection of life annuities by plan participants.

Mandate or Encourage Primary Defined Contribution Plans to Offer Life Annuities

A less stringent requirement than mandating plans to provide annuitization as the default option is to require that primary defined contribution plans simply offer annuities as one of many distribution options. Alternatively, tax credit incentives could be given to plan sponsors to offer annuities through their plans. Such tax credits have been proposed for small employers to cover the administrative costs of sponsoring a new retirement plan.

It is unclear whether the mere fact that the retirement plan offers an annuity option would be sufficient to increase annuitization rates. Hence, it is uncertain whether this proposal would result in substantial public welfare gains. Furthermore, the requirement to offer annuities presumably would result in some increase in administrative burden for plan sponsors, at least initially. Clearly, however, it is the least intrusive on participant choice; indeed, it effectively expands the choice set available to most retirement plan participants.[9]

Although any annuity from a retirement plan is currently subject to the joint-and-survivor rules, unless the annuity is the default distribution option, other distributions from the retirement plan are not subject to the joint-and-survivor requirements. This exemption could be viewed as either an advantage or disadvantage. It is an advantage in that it results in a smaller administrative burden on the plan sponsor or provider; it is a disadvantage in that it exposes spouses to unexpected impoverishment in retirement.

Encourage Plan Participants to Choose Life Annuities for Asset Distribution

Under this proposal, distributions from retirement plans would receive favored tax treatment if they occurred through life annuities. For example, capital gains rates could be applied to the entire annuity payment or to the percentage of the distribution attributable to investment gains. Alternatively, a flat dollar amount or a percentage of annuity payments could be exempted from income taxation, similar to the current treatment of Social Security retirement annuity payments.

Although this alternative approach would presumably encourage annuitization, it would not be a mandate on either plan sponsors or a constraint on participant choice and therefore might be more attractive than some of the proposals mentioned above. The demand from plan participants for annuities, as well as the current legal requirement that retirement plans be run in the interests of their participants, would presumably be sufficient cause for many defined contribution plans to offer life annuities. Of course, there would be a revenue loss of unknown magnitude to the federal government from the change.[10] Furthermore, placing a tax wedge between alternative distribution options could lead to pure efficiency losses if it distorts the decisions of individuals who would otherwise rationally choose not to annuitize.

Create a Government-Sponsored Agency to Provide Life Annuities to Plan Participants

The last proposal we examine, which could operate either independently or in conjunction with the proposals listed above, would be to create an agency or organization sponsored by the federal government to offer life annuities to retirement plan participants. An analogy might be the TSP or the Federal Employee Group Life Insurance program for federal government workers. Theoretically this organization could lower transaction and search costs and could underwrite product research and innovation to encourage annuitization, which in turn would lead to reduced adverse selection. There would be no increased burden on plan sponsors. A government-sponsored organization might be viewed as unfair competition to tax-paying and regulated commercial insurance companies, particularly those efficiently run and already providing safe and low-cost annuities to retirement plan participants. Warshawsky (1997), writing in the context of Social Security reform, discussed the possibility of creating a federal board of overseers of annuity providers as well as a national clearinghouse for commercially sold annuities. This mechanism would be analogous to the health plan for federal government workers; annuities from competing insurers could be offered in a clear and rational platform.

Notes

1. See Bureau of National Affairs (1995).

2. See Gale et al. (2008).

3. Nondiscrimination requirements presumably would have to be amended to allow the differential treatment of participants by size of account.

4. Under present rules, however, 25 percent of the pension account can be taken as a tax-free lump-sum distribution. Prior to age 75, the plan participant can choose to substitute income drawdown for the purchase of an annuity. In income drawdown, the capital sum remains invested and individuals are allowed to draw an income from the

account, as long as the income drawdown level stays within strict guidelines set forth by the government regulator.

5. See Retirement Income Working Party (2000).

6. The enforcement mechanism for the current and proposed requirements, however, is left unclear in the report.

7. See U.S. Department of Labor (1998).

8. See Madrian and Shea (2001).

9. Of course, a plan participant can currently roll over 401(k) assets to an individual retirement annuity; this economically equivalent action, however, requires significant effort, particularly in search costs. A plan sponsor, who has already conducted a search for the best plan provider and investment manager, presumably is better capable of doing the search and negotiating the best deal possible.

10. Another approach that would increase government revenues and still encourage annuitization would be to penalize, say by the imposition of an excise tax, retirement plan distributions, both pre- and postretirement, not in the form of life annuities.

References

Bureau of National Affairs. 1995. *BNA Pension and Benefits Reporter,* January 9, 114–115.

Gale, William G. J. Mark Iwry, David C. John, and Lina Walker. 2008. Increasing Annuitization in 401(k) Plans with Automatic Trial Income. Retirement Security project no. 2008-2.

Madrian, Brigitte C., and Dennis F. Shea. 2001. The Power of Suggestion: Inertia in 401(k) Participation and Savings Behavior. *Quarterly Journal of Economics* 116 (4): 1149–1187.

Retirement Income Working Party. United Kingdom. 2000. Choices—An Independent Report to Encourage the Debate on Retirement Income. www.bbk.ac.uk/res/pi/reports.

U.S. Department of Labor, Advisory Council on Employee Welfare and Pension Benefits. 1998. Are We Cashing Out Our Future? Report of the Working Group on Retirement Plan Leakage, November 13. www.dol.gov/dol/pwba/public/adcoun/leaknew1.htm.

Warshawsky, Mark J. 1997. The Market for Individual Annuities and the Reform of Social Security. *Benefits Quarterly* Third Quarter: 66–76.

Index